GLASGOW
ATLAS

The greatest care and attention is taken when we produce these atlases but, if you find any errors, we would be grateful to hear from you.

If you wish to send us information relating to this product, please contact:-

The Chief Cartographer,
Geographia,
105/107 Bath Road,
Cheltenham,
Glos. GL53 7LE

© Geographia 1989

Based upon Ordance Survey maps with the sanction of the Controller of her Majesty's Stationery Office. Crown Copyright reserved.

Sixth edition 1990

Printed by Bartholomew in Edinburgh, Scotland
UND

Contents

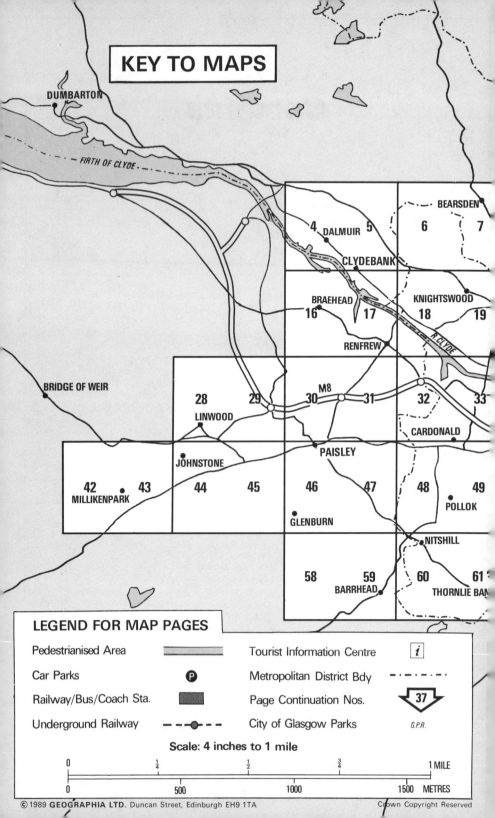

KEY TO MAPS

DUMBARTON

FIRTH OF CLYDE

BEARSDEN

4 DALMUIR 5 6 7

CLYDEBANK

BRAEHEAD KNIGHTSWOOD

16 17 18 19

R. CLYDE

RENFREW

BRIDGE OF WEIR

28 29 M8 30 31 32 33

LINWOOD CARDONALD

PAISLEY

JOHNSTONE

44 45 46 47 48 49

42 43 POLLOK

MILLIKENPARK GLENBURN

NITSHILL

58 59 60 61

BARRHEAD THORNLIE BAN

LEGEND FOR MAP PAGES

Pedestrianised Area		Tourist Information Centre	i
Car Parks	P	Metropolitan District Bdy	—·—·—
Railway/Bus/Coach Sta.		Page Continuation Nos.	37
Underground Railway	—●—	City of Glasgow Parks	G.P.R.

Scale: 4 inches to 1 mile

0	¼	½	¾	1 MILE
0	500	1000	1500	METRES

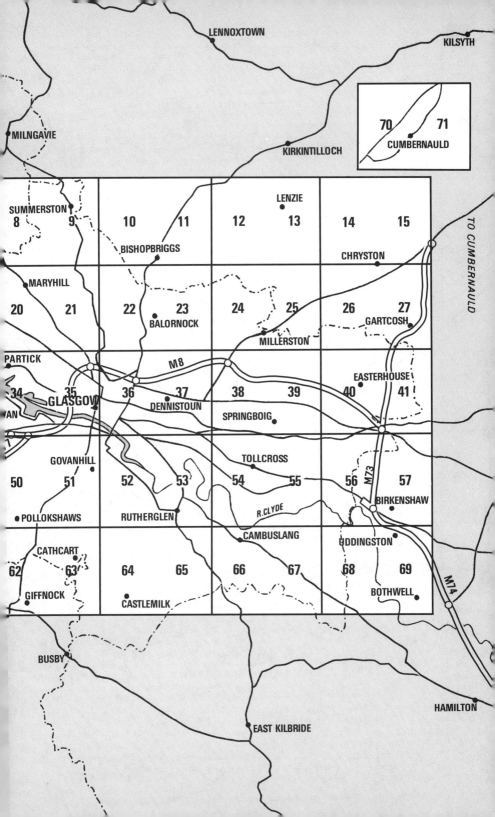

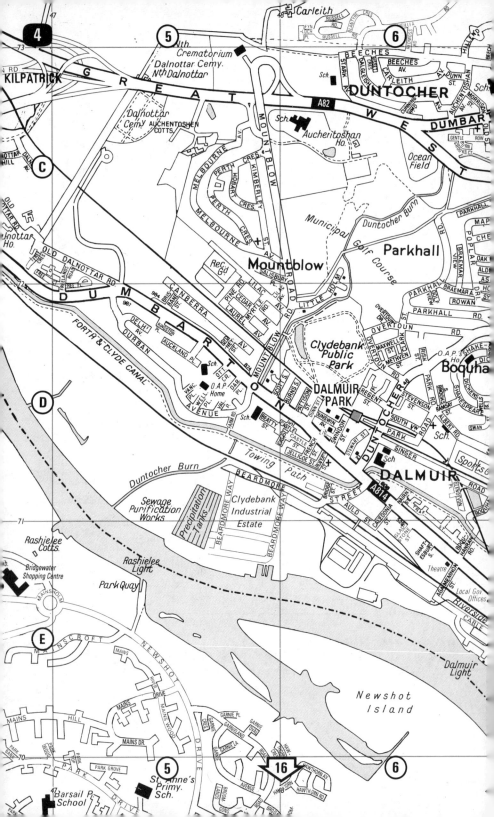

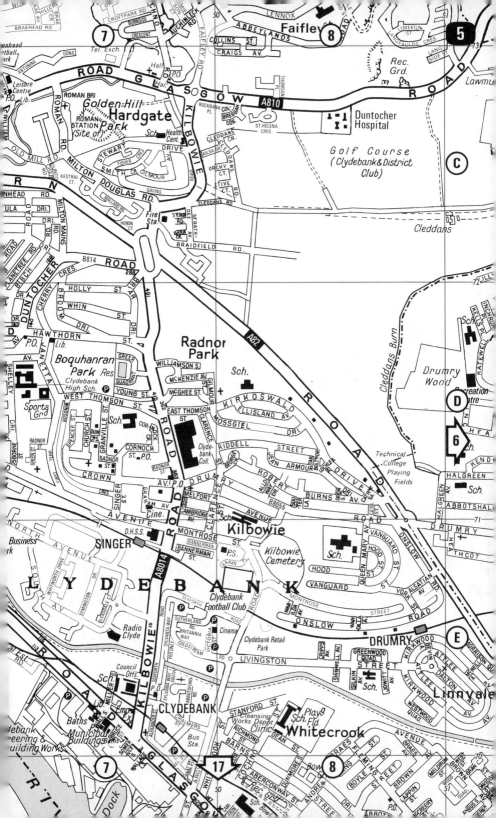

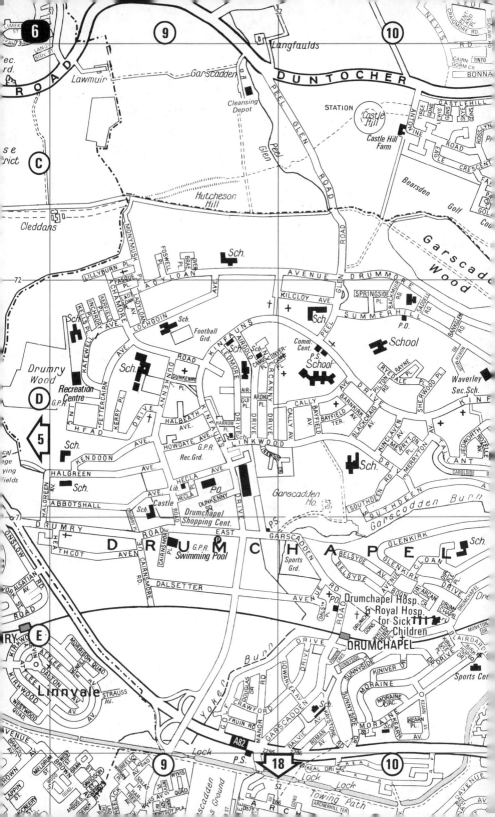

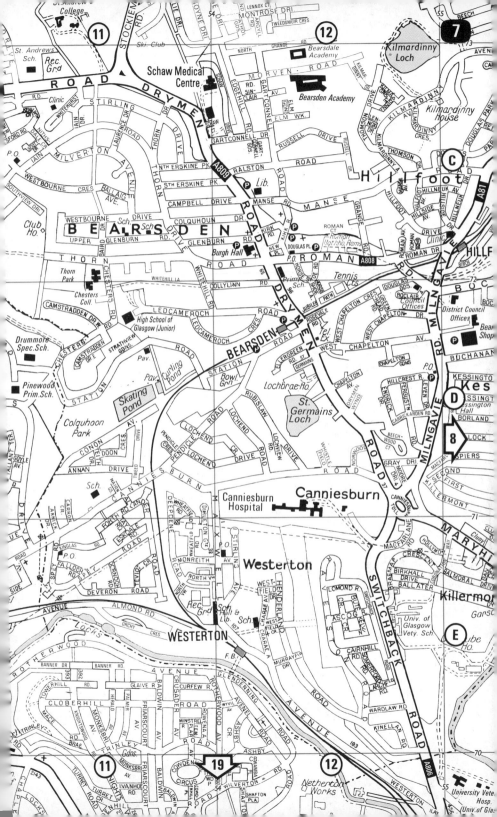

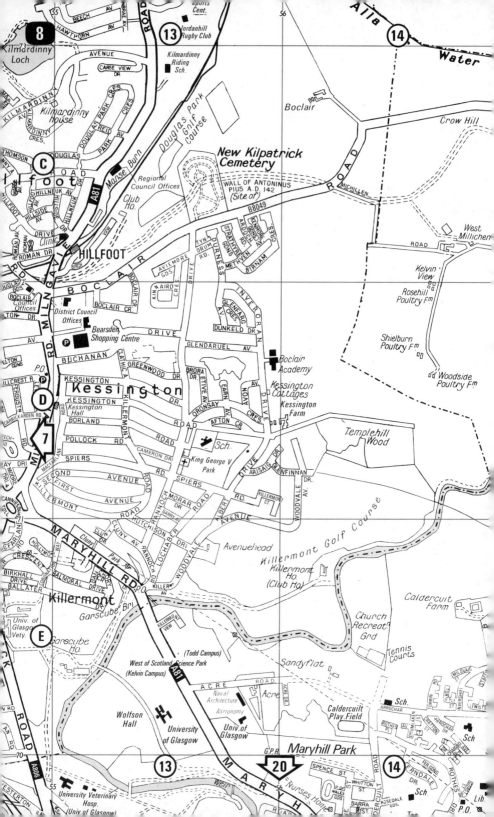

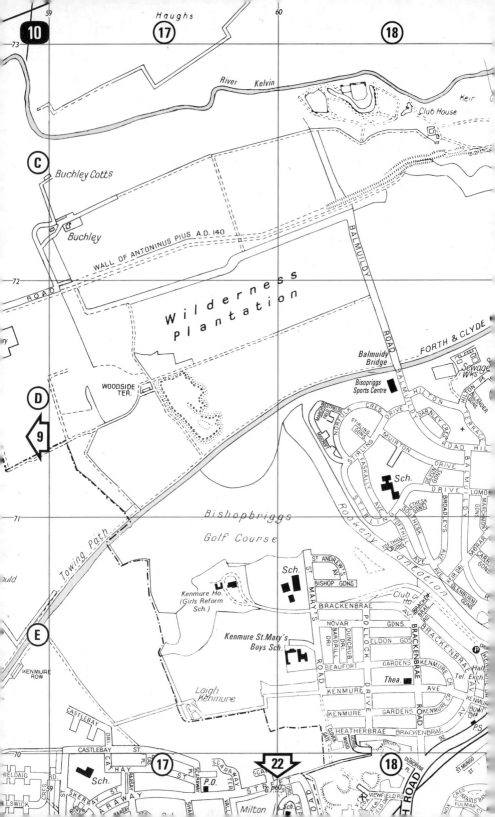

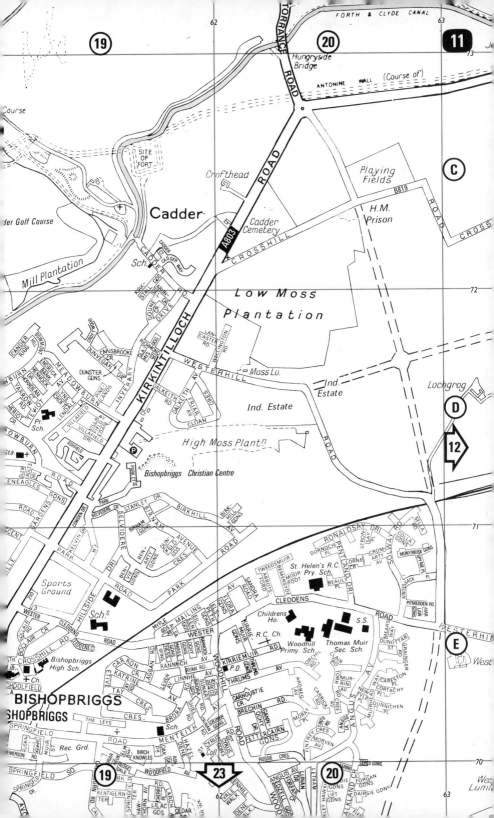

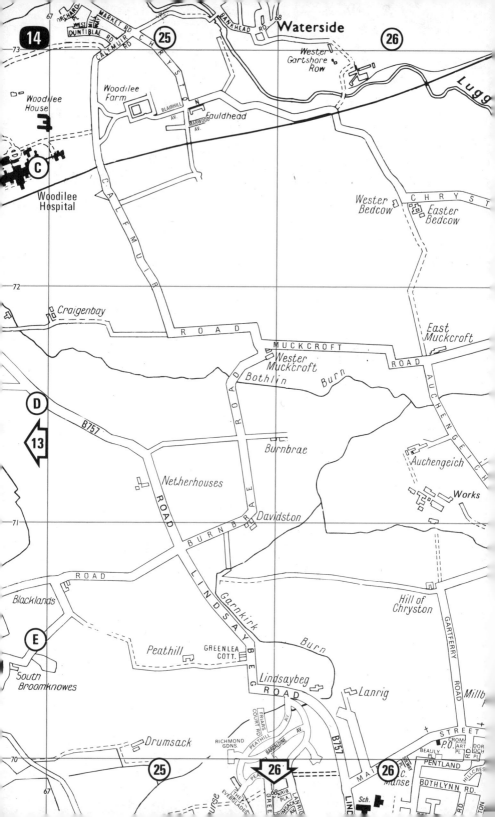

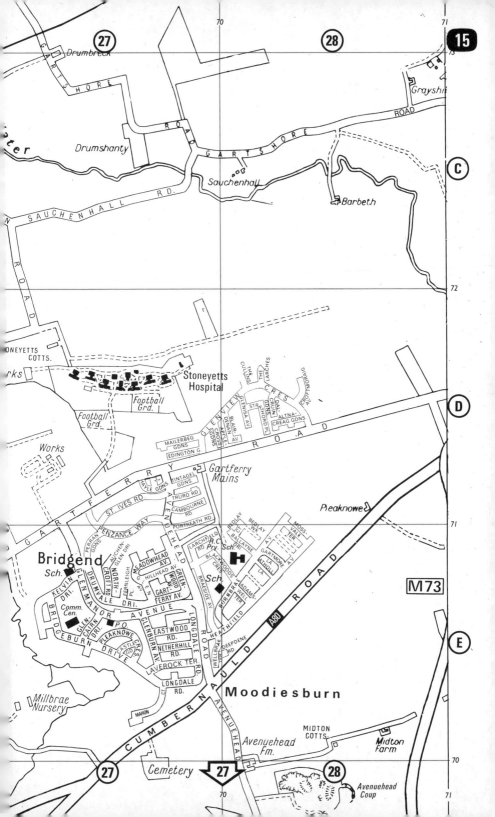

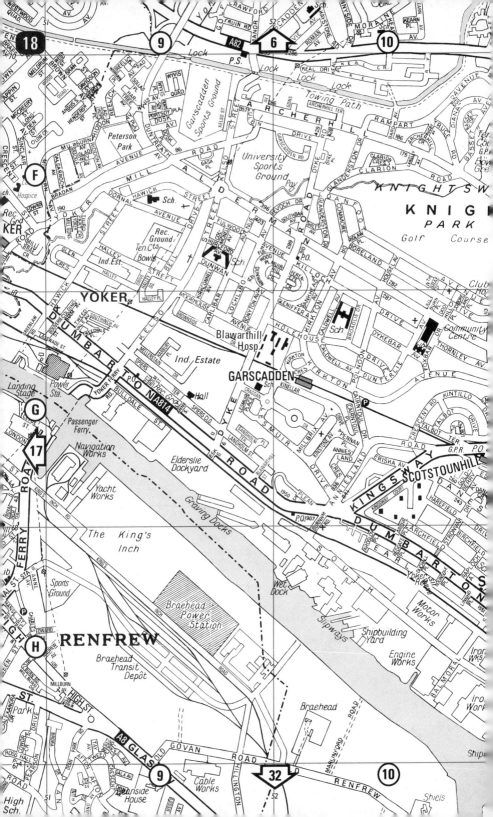

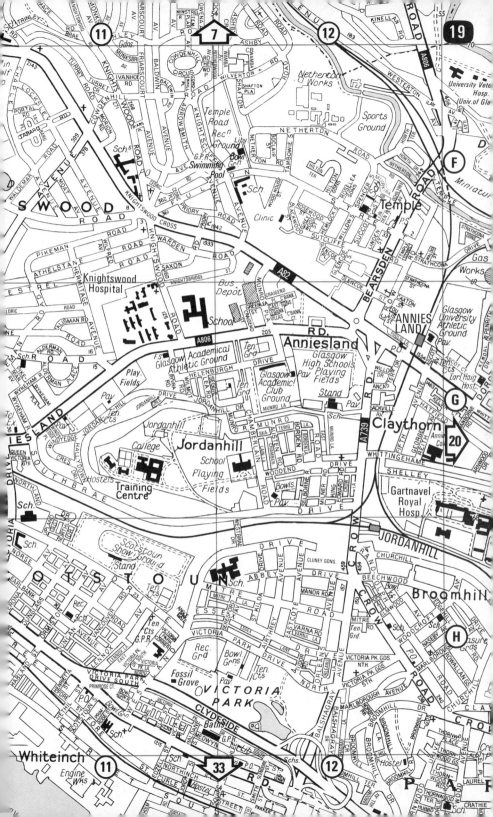

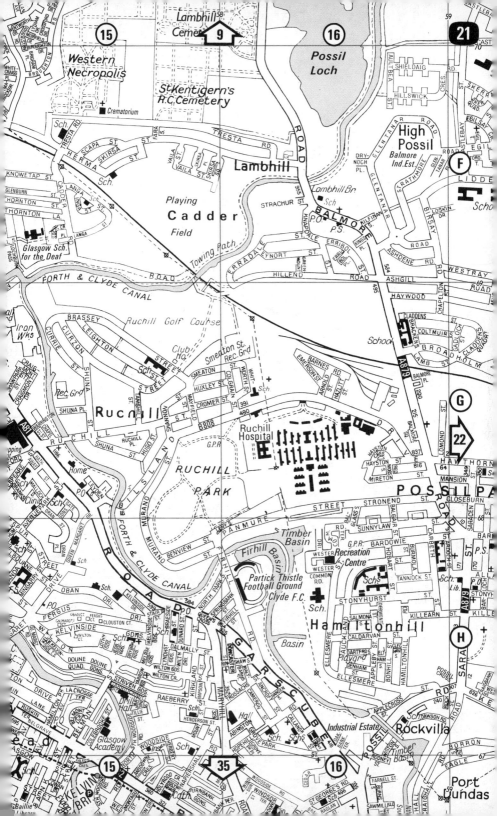

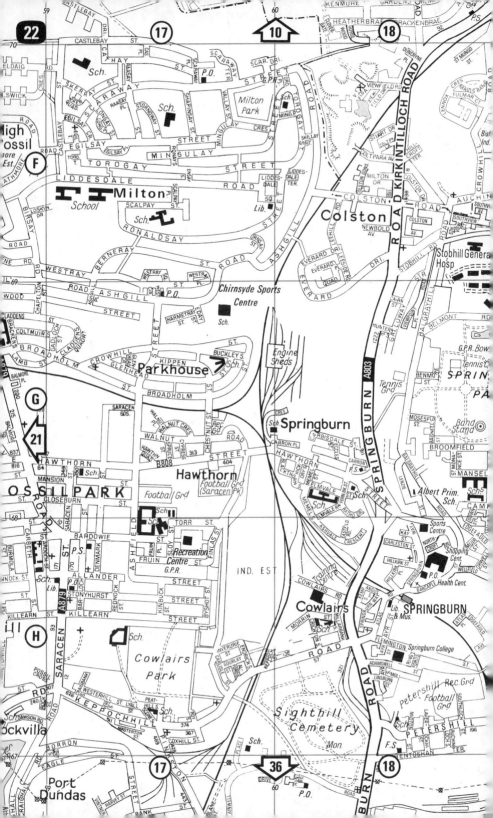

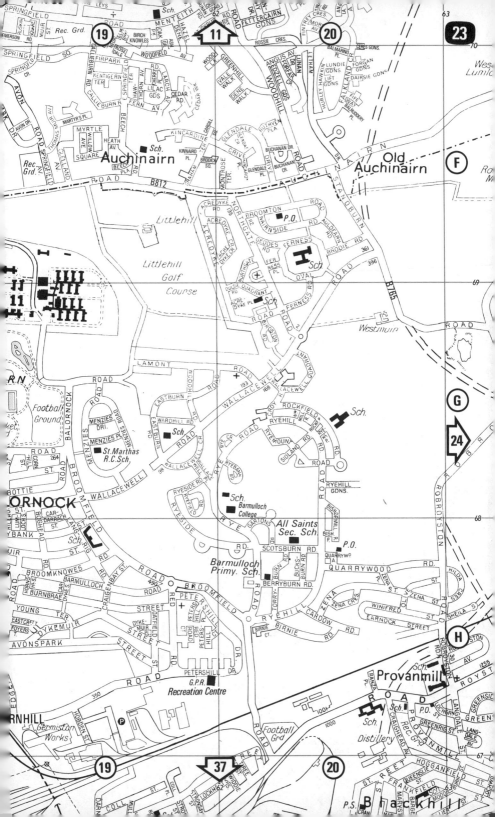

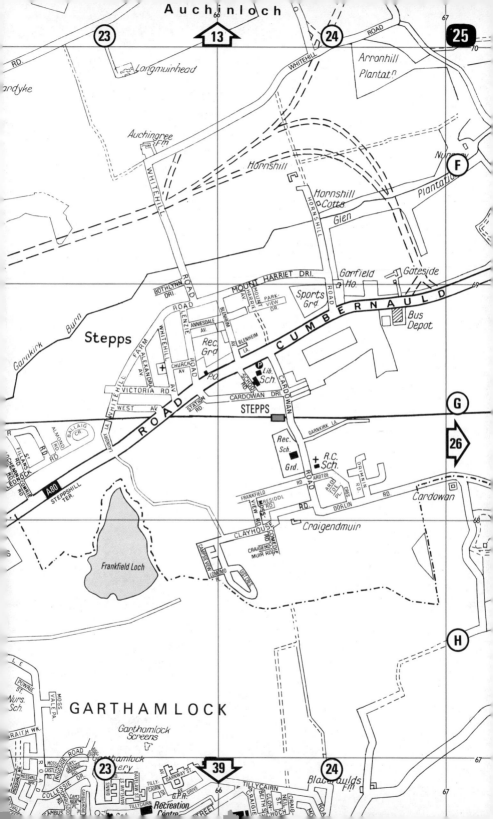

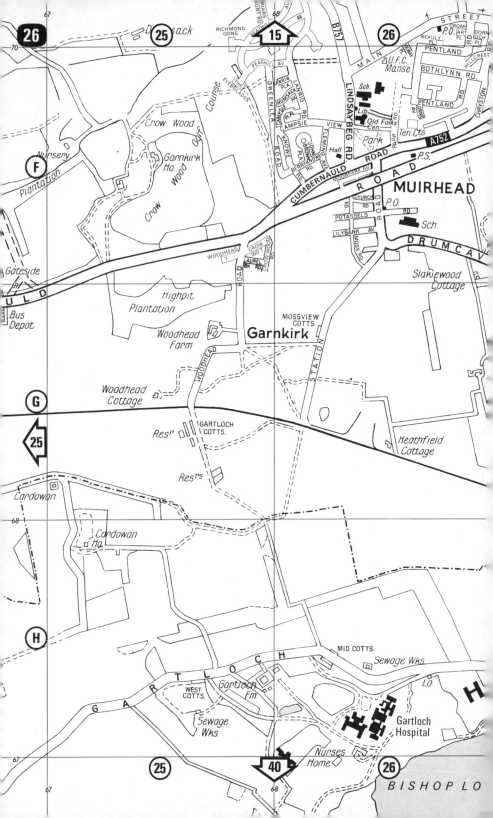

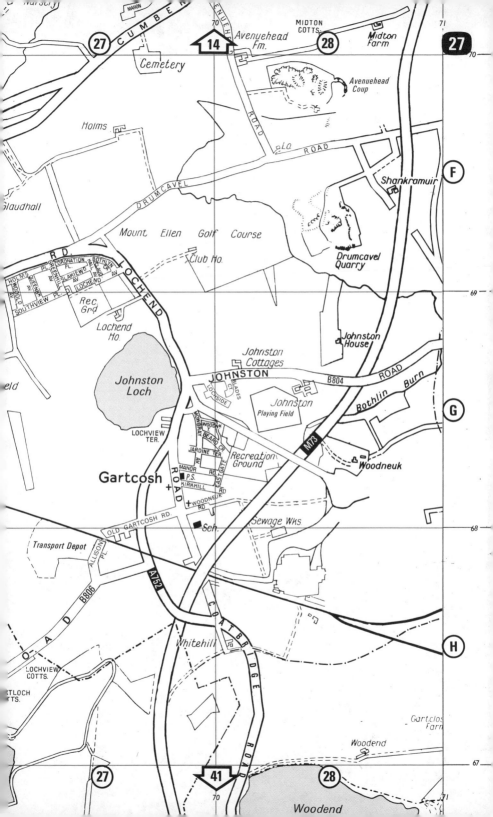

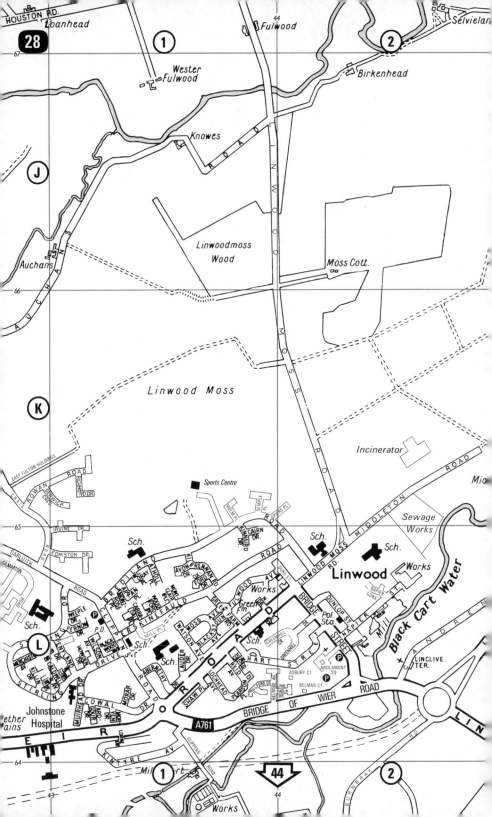

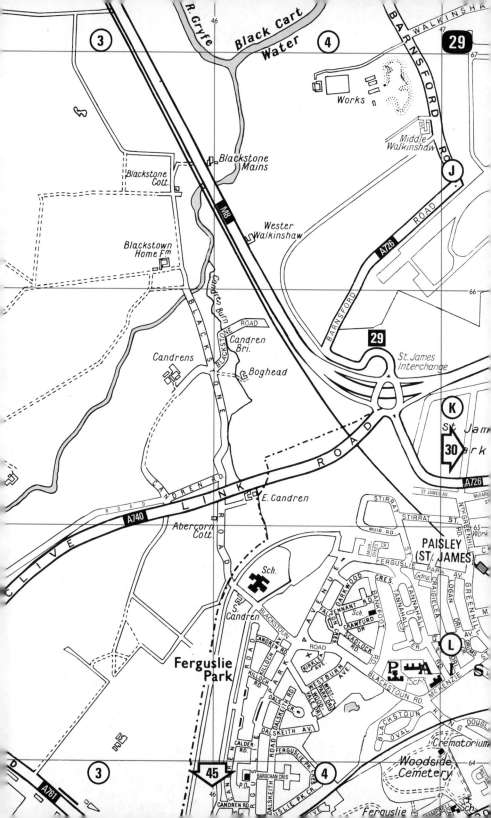

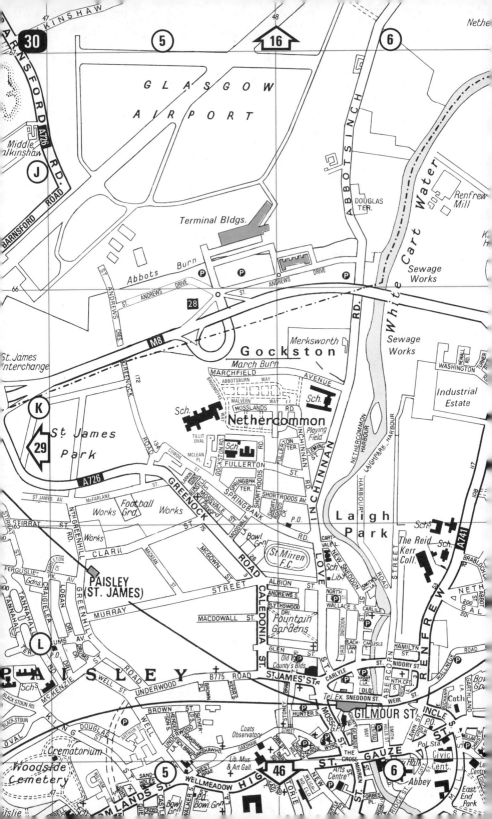

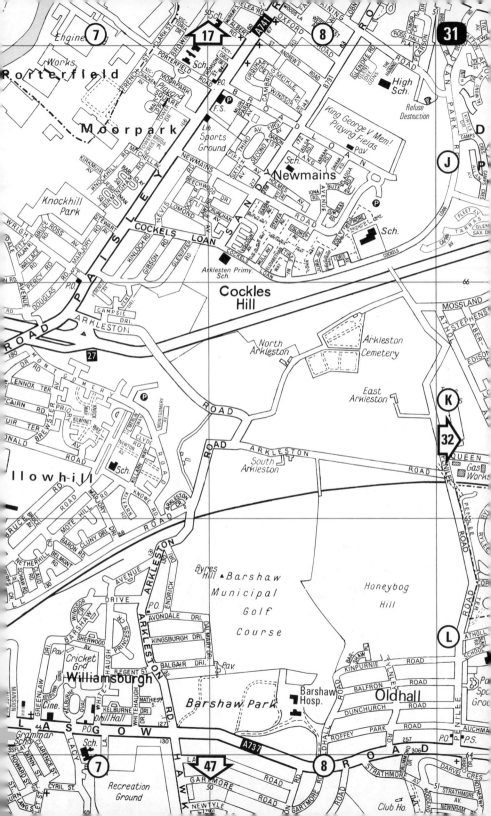

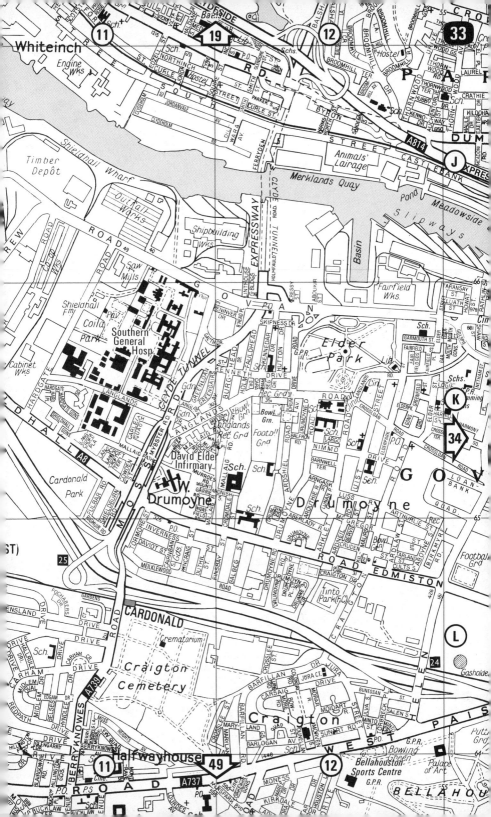

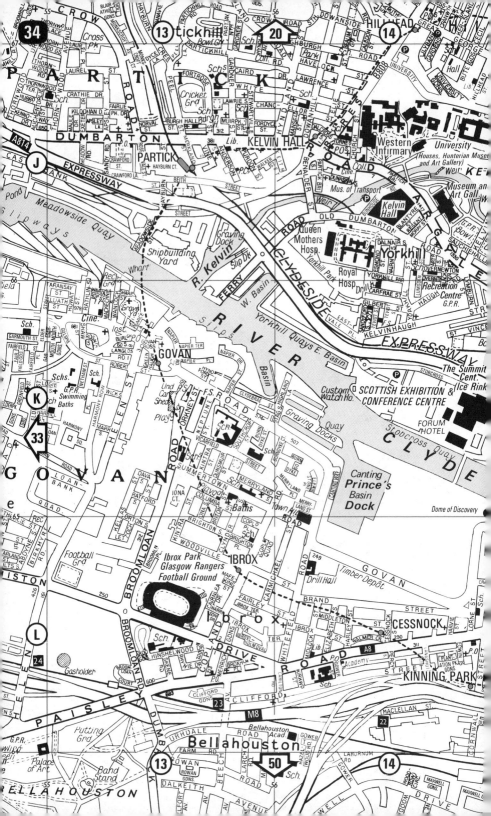

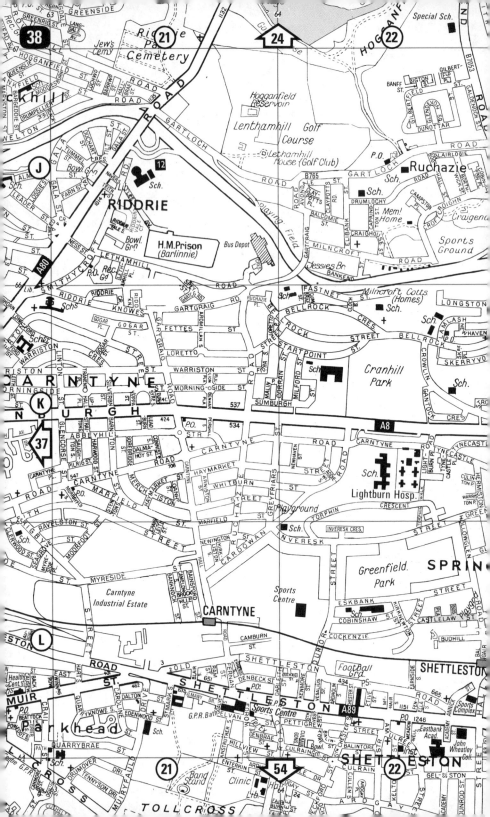

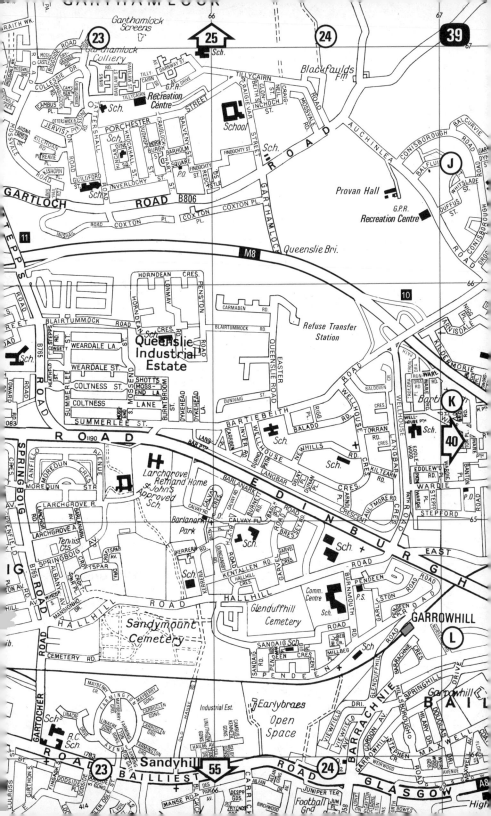

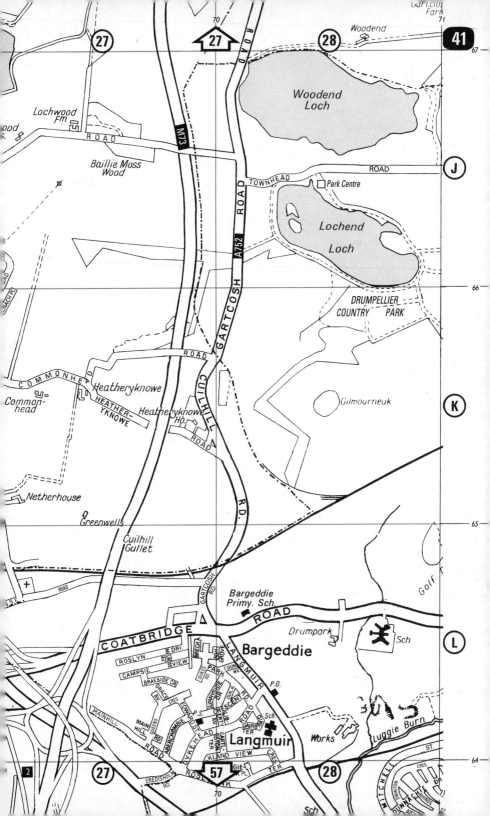

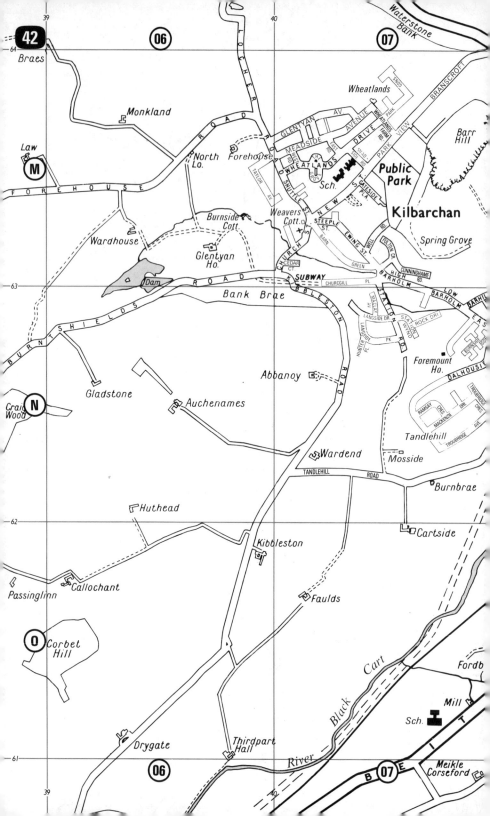

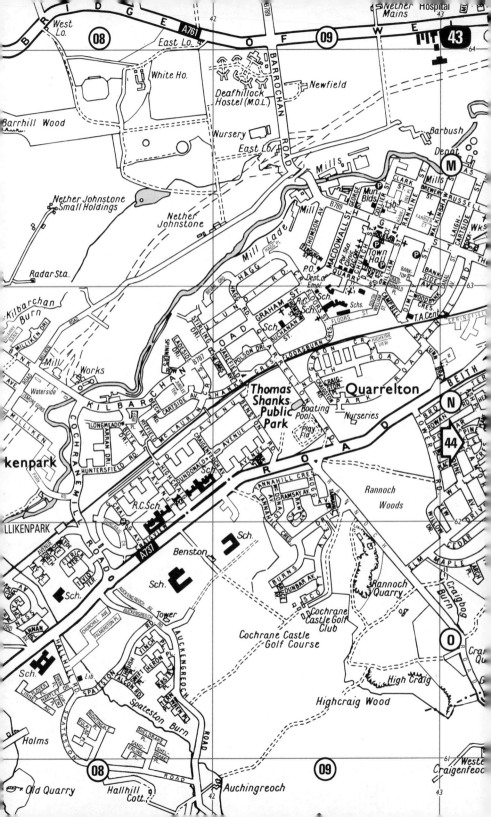

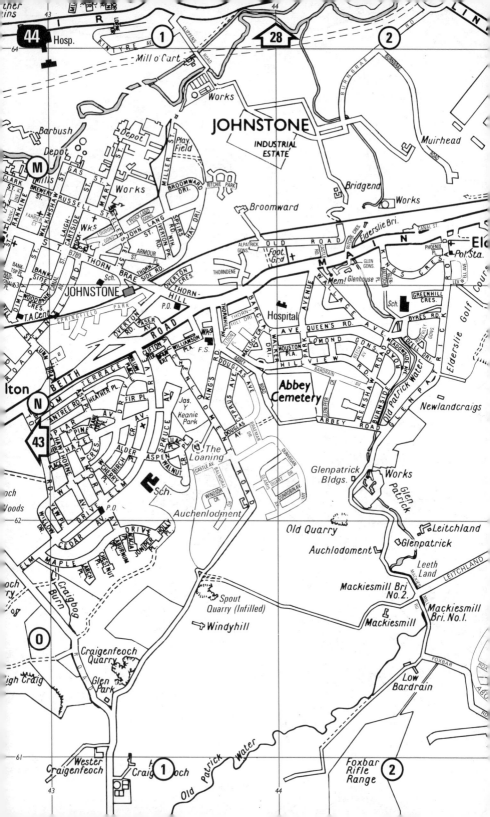

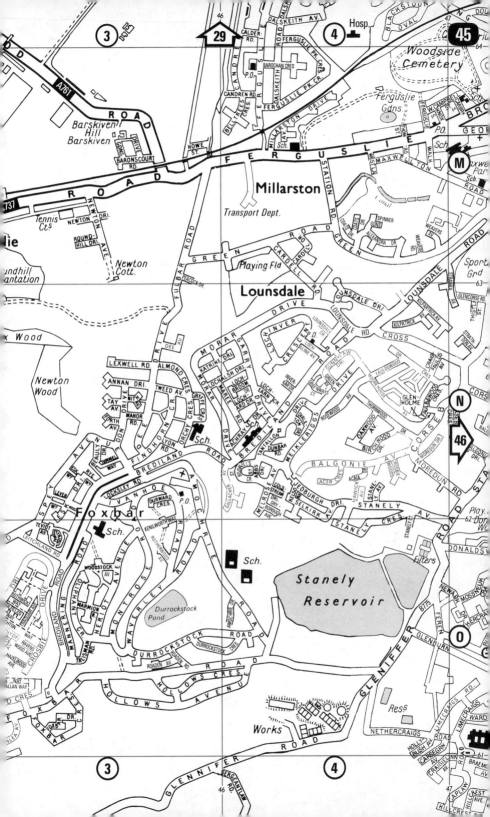

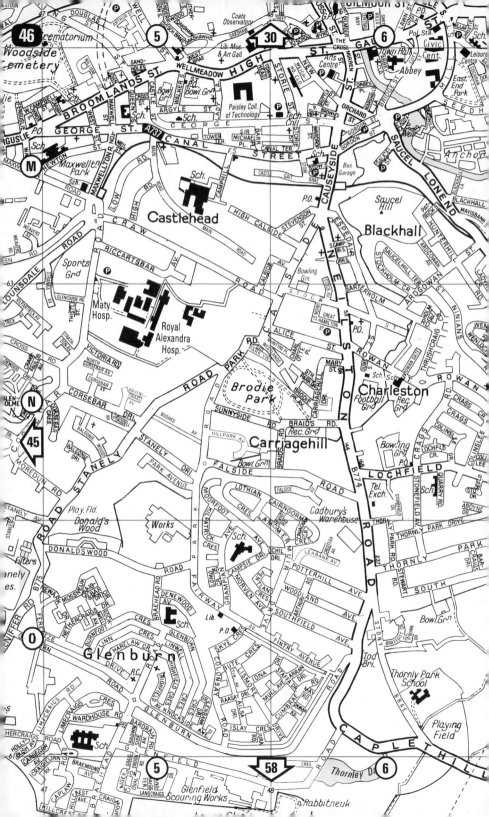

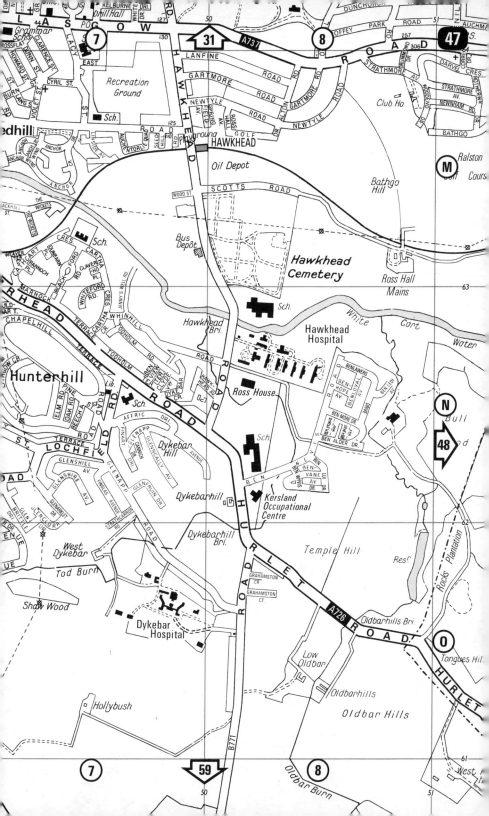

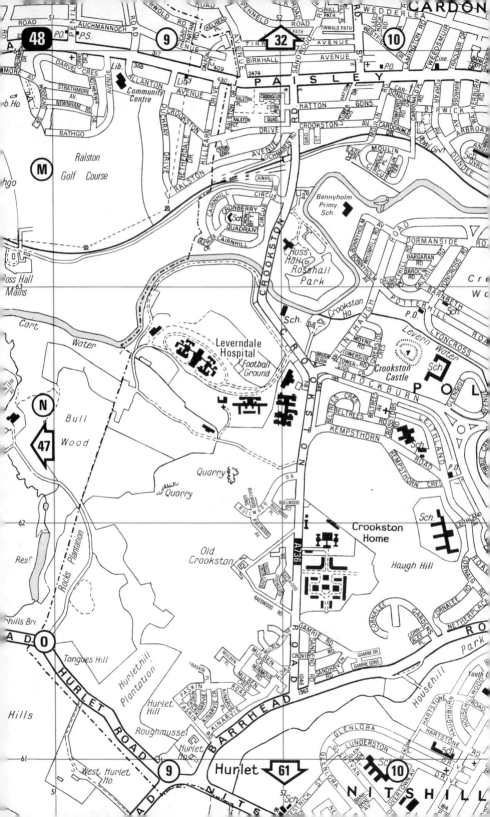

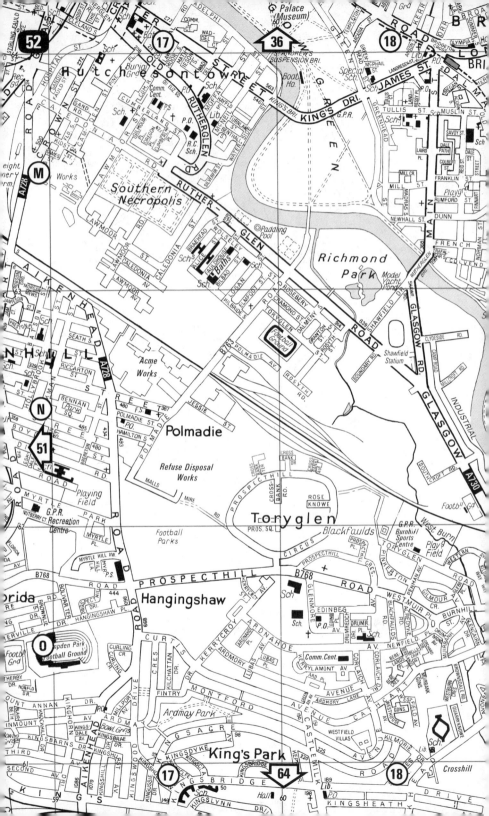

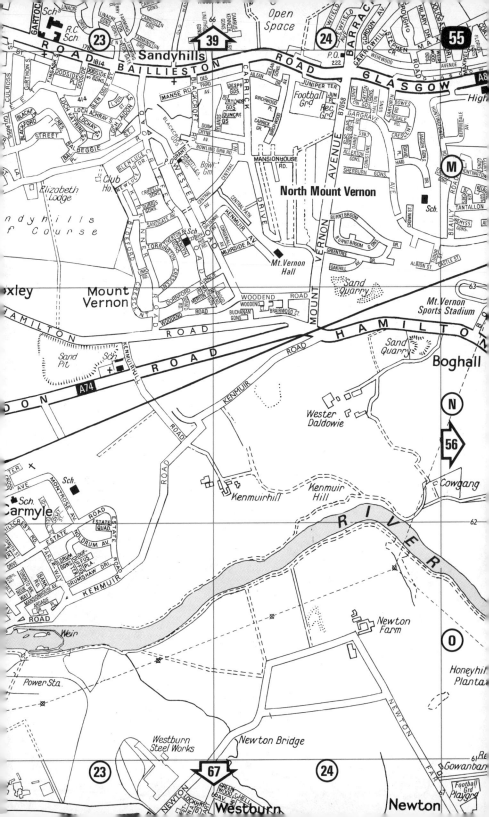

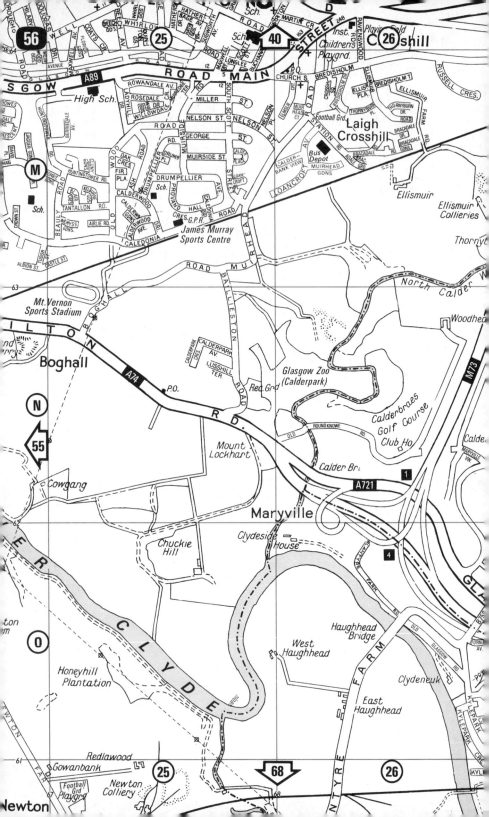

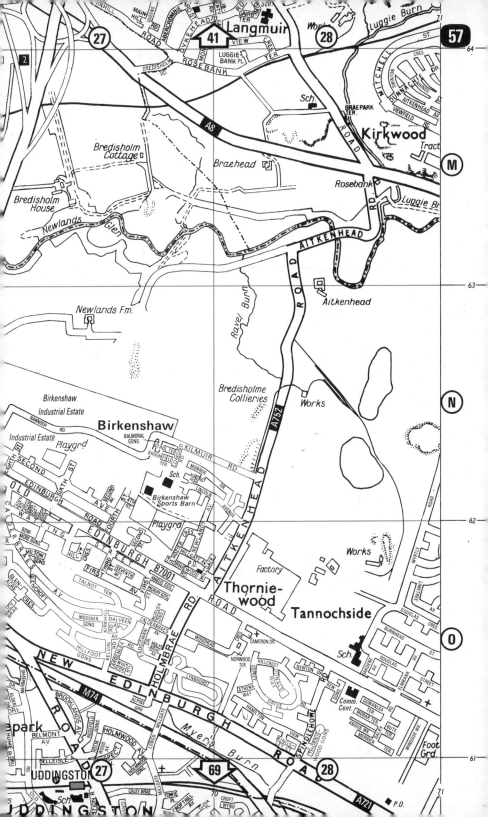

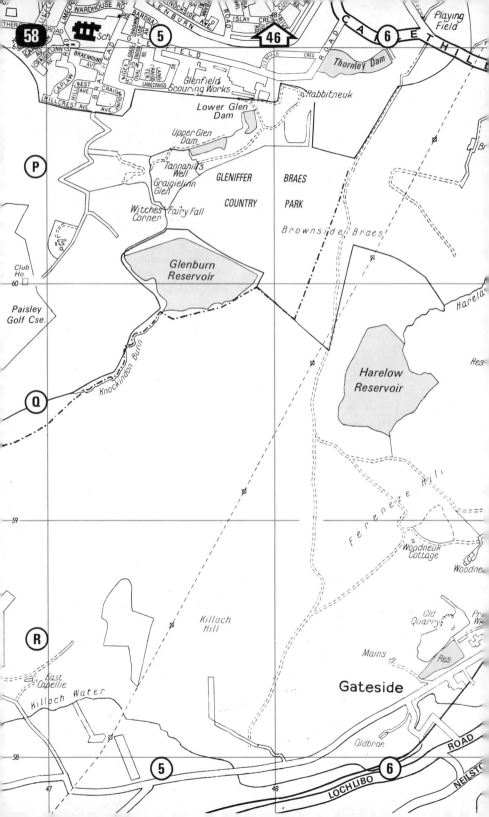

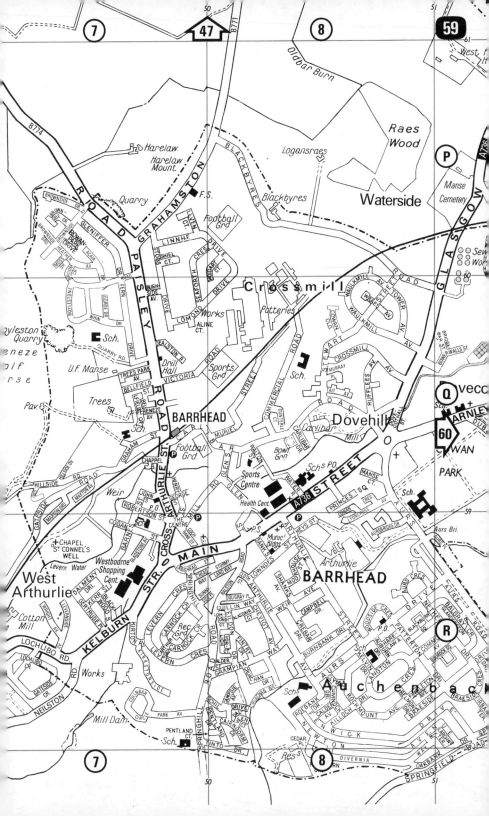

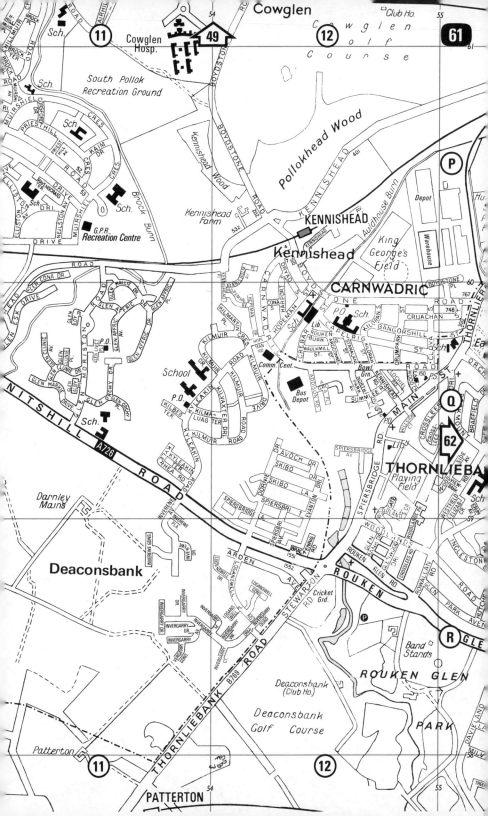

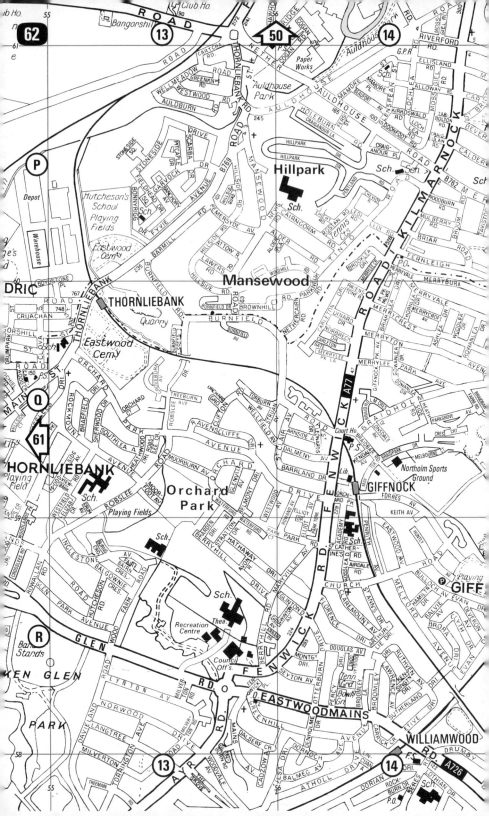

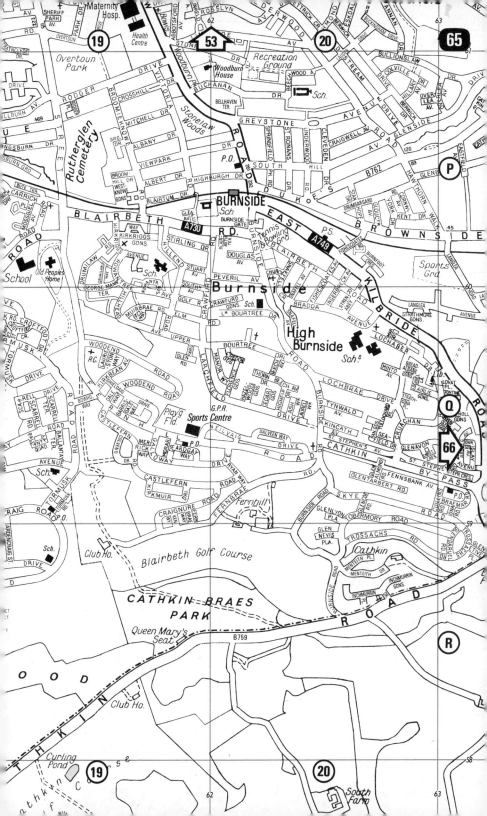

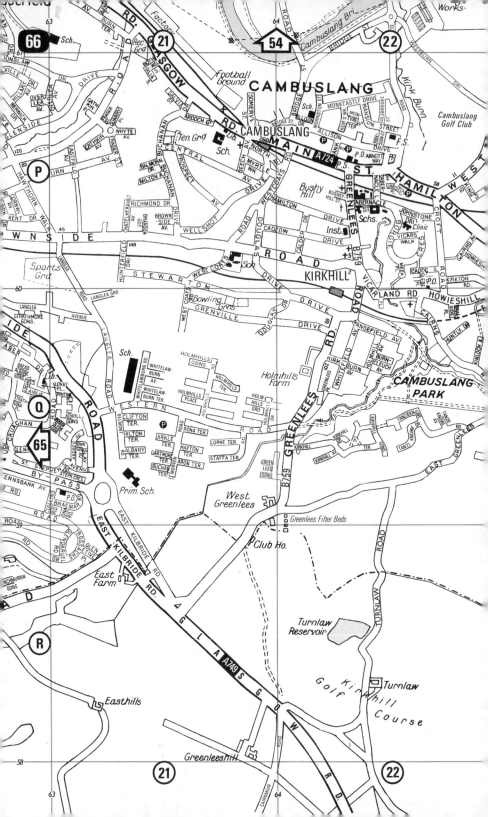

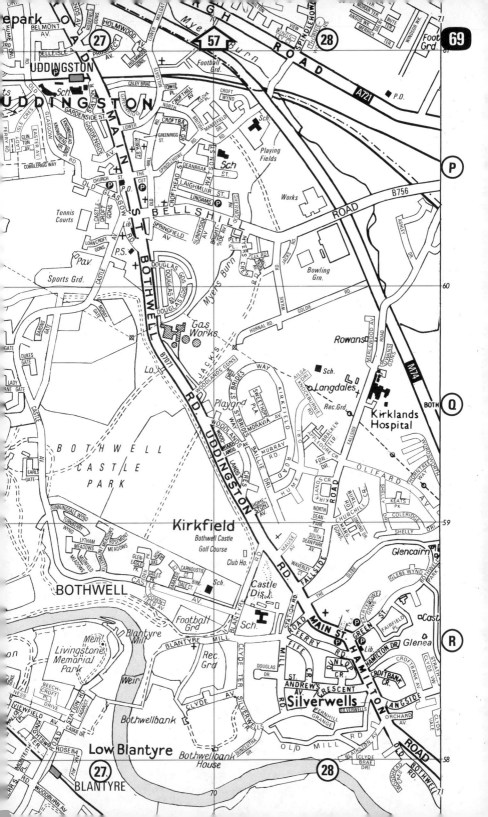

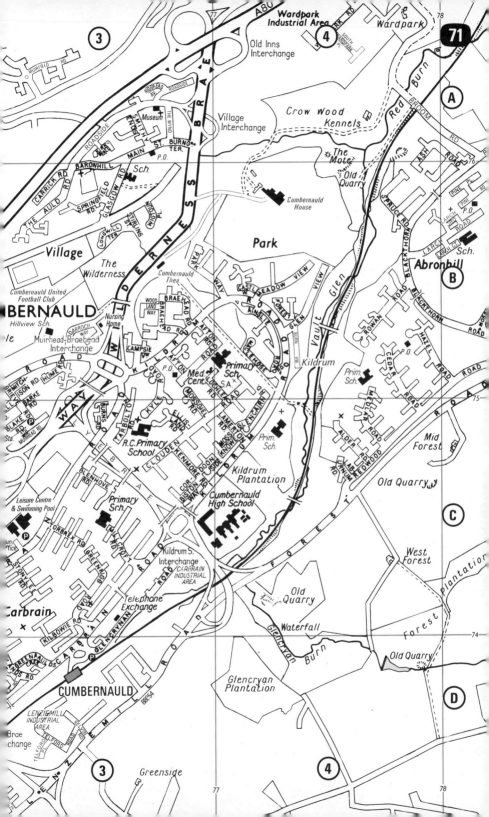

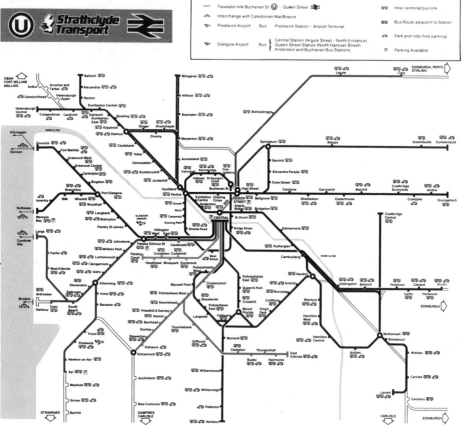

Personal Information

Name	Address	Tel. No.	Notes
	Post Code		
	Post Code		
	Post Code		
	Post Code		
	Post Code		
	Post Code		
	Post Code		
	Post Code		
	Post Code		
	Post Code		

Personal Information

Name	Address	Tel. No.	Notes
	Post Code		
	Post Code		
	Post Code		
	Post Code		
	Post Code		
	Post Code		
	Post Code		
	Post Code		
	Post Code		
	Post Code		

Personal Information

Name	Address	Tel. No.	Notes
	Post Code		
	Post Code		
	Post Code		
	Post Code		
	Post Code		
	Post Code		
	Post Code		
	Post Code		
	Post Code		
	Post Code		

Personal Information

Name	Address	Tel. No.	Notes
	Post Code		
	Post Code		
	Post Code		
	Post Code		
	Post Code		
	Post Code		
	Post Code		
	Post Code		
	Post Code		
	Post Code		

Personal Information

Name	Address	Tel. No.	Notes
	Post Code		
	Post Code		
	Post Code		
	Post Code		
	Post Code		
	Post Code		
	Post Code		
	Post Code		
	Post Code		
	Post Code		

Personal Information

Name	Address	Tel. No.	Notes
	Post Code		
	Post Code		
	Post Code		
	Post Code		
	Post Code		
	Post Code		
	Post Code		
	Post Code		
	Post Code		
	Post Code		

Glasgow

Local Information Guide

Contents

City of Glasgow Local Information Guide

Useful information

Area of City 79 sq. miles (approx)

Population (Glasgow City)
(1989 estimate) 696,577

Early Closing Days
Tuesday with alternative of Saturday.
Most of the shops in the central area
operate six-day trading.

Electricity 240 volts A.C.

Emergency Services
Police, Fire and Ambulance. Dial 999
on any telephone.

Licensing Hours
Public Houses
Daily (except Sundays) 11 a.m. to
2.30 p.m. and 5 to 11 p.m. (many
open continuously 11 a.m. to
11 p.m.)
Sundays, 12.30 to 2.30 p.m. and 6.30
to 10.30 p.m.
Restaurants, Hotels and Public
Houses with catering facilities, same
as above but can be extended for
drinks with meals.

Information Bureau
Tourist Information Centres:
35–39 St. Vincent Place
Glasgow. 041-227 4880

Town Hall, Abbey Close
Paisley. 041-889 0711

Glasgow Airport 041-848 4440

Strathclyde Transport Travel Centre
St. Enoch Square
Open Monday–Saturday 9.30 a.m.
to 5.30 p.m. 041-226 4826 (Monday
to Saturday 7 a.m. to 9 p.m.,
Sunday 9 a.m.to 7-30 p.m.) for City
services, ferry services, local airlines,
train and express services. Free
timetables are available.

Help & Advice
British Broadcasting Corporation
Queen Margaret Drive, G12.
041-339 8844

British Council
6 Belmont Crescent, G12 8ES
041-339 8651

British Telecom Scotland

Glasgow Area
Westergate Chambers, 11 Hope Street,
Glasgow G2 6AB
All Enquires 041-220 1234 or dial
100 and ask for FREEFONE BT
GLASGOW

Chamber of Commerce
30 George Square, G2.
041-204 2121

Citizens Advice Bureau
212 Bath Street, Glasgow G2 4HW.
041-331 2345/6/7/8
119 Main Street, Glasgow G40 1HA.
041-554 0336

27 Dougrie Drive, Castlemilk,
Glasgow G45 9AD 041-634 0338
139 Main Street (Town Hall)
Rutherglen G73 4HG 041-647 5100
216 Main Streeet, Barrhead
041-881 2032
Civic Centre, East Kilbride
East Kilbride 21295
1143 Maryhill Road, Glasgow G20
041-946 6373/4
46 Township Centre, Easterhouse,
Glasgow G34 9DS 041-771 2328

Consumer Advice Centre
St. Enoch House, 1 St. Enoch Square
Glasgow G1 4BH. 041-204 0262

Customs and Excise
21 India Street, G2 4PZ
041-221 3828

H.M. Immigration Office
Admin Block D, Argyll Avenue
Glasgow Airport
Tel. 041-887 4115

Housing Aid and Advice
Shelter, 53 St. Vincent Crescent
Glasgow G3 8NQ. 041-221 8995/6

Legal Aid and Advice
Castlemilk Advice & Law Centre
27 Dougrie Drive, Glasgow G45.
041-634 0338

Law Centre
30 Dougrie Drive
041-634 0313

Lost Property
Strathclyde Passenger Transport
Executive
St. Enoch Underground Station
Tel. 041-248 6950 (City Buses)
12 West George Street G32
041-332 6811. (Underground)
Other Buses–Office of Bus Company.
Trains–Station of arrival.
Elsewhere in City–Strathclyde Police
Lost Property Department,
173 Pitt Street, G2
041-204 2626

Passport Office
Northgate 96 Milton Street
Glasgow G4. Tel. 041-332 0271

**Registrar of Births, Deaths and
Marriages**
1 Martha Street, G1. 041-227 6343
Hours – Monday to Friday 9.15 a.m.
to 4.00 p.m.

Births must be registered within
twenty-one days, deaths within eight
days, and marriages within three
days. The Registrar should be
consulted at least one month before
intended date of marriage.

**Royal Scottish Society for the
Prevention of Cruelty to Children**
15 Annfield Place, G31.
041-556 1156

**RNID–
Royal National Institute for the
Deaf**
9   Clairmont Gardens, Glasgow
G3 7LW. 041-332 0343

Samaritans
218 West Regent Street, Glasgow
G2 4DQ. 041-248 4488

**Scottish Society for the Mentally
Handicapped**
13 Elmbank Street, Glasgow G2.
041-226 4541

Scottish Television
Cowcaddens. G2. 041-332 9999

**Society for the Prevention of
Cruelty to Animals**
15 Royal Terrace, G3.
(Business Hours)   041-332 0716

Newspapers

Morning Daily
Daily Record
Anderston Quay, G3.   041-248 7000

Glasgow Herald
195 Albion Street, G1. 041-552 6255

Scottish Daily Express
Park Circus Place, G3. 041-332 9600

The Scotsman
181-195 West George St., G2 2LB
                         041-221 6485
Evening Daily
Evening Times
195 Albion Street, G1. 041-552 6255

Weekly
Scottish Sunday Express
Park Circus Place, G3. 041-552 3550

Sunday Mail
Anderston Quay, G3.   041-248 7000

Sunday Post
144 Port Dundas Road, G4.
041-332 9933

Parking

Car parking in the central area of Glasgow is controlled. Parking meters are used extensively and signs indicating restrictions are displayed at kerbsides and on entry to the central area. Traffic Wardens are on duty.

British Rail Car Parks
(Open 24 hours)
Central Station
Queen Street Station

Multi-Storey Car Parks
(Open 24 hours)
Anderston Cross: Cambridge Street: George Street: Mitchell Street: Port Dundas Road: Waterloo Street.

(Limited Opening)
Charing Cross
Sauchiehall Street Centre

Surface Car Parks
Carrick Street: Holland Street: Ingram Street: McAlpine Street: North Frederick Street: Albion Street: Oswald Street: Shuttle Street.

Post Offices
Head Post Office
George Square, G2   041-248 2882
Open Monday to Thursday 9 a.m. to 5.30 p.m. Fridays 9.30 a.m. to 5.30 p.m. Saturdays 9.a.m. to 12.30 p.m. Closed Sunday.
Branch Offices
85–91 Bothwell Street, G2.
4 Dixon Street, G1.

216 Hope Street, G2.
533 Sauchiehall Street, G3.

Taxis

Glasgow has over 1400 traditional London type taxis, all licensed by the Glasgow District Council and all fitted with meters sealed and approved by the Council. A fare card stating the current tariff is displayed in a prominent position within each taxi. At the time of publishing a three mile journey costs £2.40 and waiting time is charged at 10p per minute the total price of each journey is shown on the meter. Fares are normally revued annually by the council. Each taxi can carry a maximum of five passengers.

The major taxi companies in the city offer City tours at fixed prices, listing the places of interest to be visited, leaflets are available at all major hotel reception areas. Tours vary from 2 to 3 hours and in price between £17 and £24.

Any passenger wishing to travel to a destination outside the Glasgow District Boundary should ascertain from the driver the fare to be charged or the method of calculating the fare PRIOR to making the journey.

Complaints

Any complaints regarding the conduct of a taxi driver should be addressed to the Senior Enforcement Officer, Town Clerk's Office, City Chambers, Glasgow. Tel: 041-227-4535.

Local Government
Strathclyde Regional Council
Strathclyde House, 20 India Street
Glasgow G2 4PF
041-204 2900

District Councils:
Argyll & Bute
District Council Headquarters
Kilmory, Lochgilphead PA31 8RT
0546 2127

Bearsden & Milngavie
Municipal Building, Boclair
Bearsden G61 2TQ
041-942 2262

Clydebank
Council Offices, Rosebery Place
Clydebank G81 1TG
041-941 1331

Clydesdale
Clydesdale District Offices
Lanark ML11 7JT
0555 61331

Cumbernauld & Kilsyth
Council Offices, Bron Way
Cumbernauld G67 1DZ
02367 22131

Cummock & Doon Valley
Council Offices, Lugar
Cumnock KA18 3JQ
0290 22111

Cunninghame
Cunninghame House
Irvine KA12 8EE
0294 74166

Dumbarton
Crosslet House
Dumbarton G82 3NS
0389 65100

East Kilbride
Civic Centre
East Kilbride G74 1AB
035-52 28777

Eastwood
Council Offices
Eastwood Park, Rouken Glen Road
Rouken Glen, Giffnock
Glasgow G46 6UG
041-638 6511
041-638 1101

Glasgow City
City Chambers
Glasgow G2 1DU
041-221 9600

Hamilton
Town House
102 Cadzow Street
Hamilton ML3 6HH
0698 282323

Inverclyde
Municipal Buildings
Greenock PA15 1LY
0475 24400

Kilmarnock & Loudoun
Civic Centre
Kilmarnock KA1 1BY
0563 21140

Kyle & Carrick
Burns House
Burns Statue Square
Ayr KA7 1UT
0292 281511

Monklands
Municipal Buildings
Dunbeth Road
Coatbridge ML5 3LF
0236 41200

Motherwell
PO Box 14
Civic Centre
Motherwell ML1 1TW
0698 66166

Renfrew
Municipal Buildings
Cotton Street
Paisley PA1 1BU
041-889 5400

Strathkelvin
Tom Johnston House
Civic Way
Kirkintilloch
Glasgow G66 4TJ
041-776 7171

SEE MORE OF SCOTLAND WITH BARTHOLOMEW

TOURING MAP SCOTLAND

Ideal for use when visiting Scotland or for planning a day out. This excellent map gives an index to places of interest while showing them on the map using clear red and yellow symbols. Also included a full list of tourist information centres, and a listing of tourist attractions.

CLEAR FULLY INDEXED COLOUR MAP

GEOGRAPHIA

A BARTHOLOMEW MAP & GUIDE

WALK LOCH LOMOND & THE TROSSACHS
INCLUDING STIRLING & THE OCHILS

35 WALKS SELECTED & DESCRIBED BY GILBERT SUMMERS
* EASY TO FOLLOW COLOUR MAPS
* HISTORY * WILDLIFE * CAR PARKS * VIEWPOINTS
* DETAILED ROUTE DESCRIPTIONS

BARTHOLOMEW WALK GUIDES

Each of these handy guide books gives details of at least 30 walks giving a full description of all routes and including notes on local history, geography and wildlife. Special maps are provided as well as details where to park. All walks are graded for distance and difficulty.

WALK SOUTH WEST SCOTLAND

WALK LOCH LOMOND & THE TROSSACHS

WALK OBAN MULL & LOCHABER

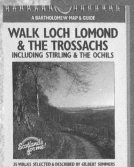

A BARTHOLOMEW MAP & GUIDE

WALK OBAN MULL & LOCHABER
INCLUDING FORT WILLIAM & THE LANDS OF LORN

40 WALKS SELECTED & DESCRIBED BY RICHARD HALLEWELL
* EASY TO FOLLOW MAPS * CAR PARKS
* PICNIC SITES * PUBLIC TRANSPORT * HISTORY * GEOLOGY
* ECOLOGY * PANORAMIC ILLUSTRATIONS

A BARTHOLOMEW MAP & GUIDE

WALK SOUTH WEST SCOTLAND
INCLUDING ARRAN AND THE CLYDE

DESCRIBED BY RICHARD HALLEWELL
* CAREFULLY SELECTED WALKS * VIEWPOINTS
* EASY-TO-FOLLOW MAPS * HISTORY * WILDLIFE
* CAR PARKS * DETAILED ROUTE DESCRIPTIONS

For a full list of maps, atlases and walk guides please write to Gillian Thom, Bartholomew, 12 Duncan Street, Edinburgh EH9 1TA.

The City of Glasgow began life as a makeshift hamlet of huts huddled round a 6thC church, built by St Mungo on the banks of a little salmon river — the Clyde. It was called Gleschow, meaning 'beloved green place' in Celtic. The cathedral was founded in 1136; the university, the second oldest in Scotland, was established in the 15thC; and in 1454 the flourishing mediaeval city wedged between the cathedral and the river was made a Royal burgh. The city's commercial prosperity dates from the 17thC when the lucrative tobacco, sugar and cotton trade with the New World flourished. The River Clyde, Glasgow's gateway to the Americas, was dredged, deepened and widened in the 18thC to make it navigable to the city's heart.

By the 19thC, Glasgow was the greatest shipbuilding centre in the world. From the 1820s onwards, it grew in leaps and bounds westwards along a steep ridge of land running parallel with the river. The hillside became encased in an undulating grid of streets and squares. Gradually the individualism, expressed in one-off set pieces characteristic of the 18thC and early 19thC, gave way to a remarkable coherent series of terraced squares and crescents of epic proportions — making Glasgow one of the finest of Victorian cities. But the price paid for such rapid industrialisation, the tremendous social problems manifest in the squalor of some of the worst of 19thC slums, was high. Today the city is still the commercial and industrial capital of the West of Scotland. The most notorious of the slums have been cleared but the new buildings lack that sparkling clench-fisted Glaswegian character of the 19thC. Ironically, this character was partially destroyed when the slums were cleared for it wasn't the architecture that had failed, only the bureaucrats, who designated such areas as working class ghettos.

Districts

Little remains of mediaeval Glasgow, which stood on the wedge of land squeezed between the cathedral and the River Clyde. Its business centre was The Cross, a space formed by the junction of several streets — the tall, square Tolbooth Steeple, 1626, in the middle. Opposite is Trongate, an arch astride a footpath, complete with tower and steeple salvaged from 17thC St Mary's Church — destroyed by fire in 1793. The centre of 20thC Glasgow is George Square, a tree-lined piazza planned in 1781 and pinned down by more than a dozen statues including an 80-foot-high Doric column built in 1837 to carry a statue of Sir Walter Scott. Buildings of interest: the monumental neo-Baroque City Chambers 1883-88 which take up the east side and the Merchants' House 1874, on the west. To the south of the square, in a huddle of narrow streets, is the old Merchant City. Of interest here is the elegant Trades House, 85 Glassford Street, built by Robert Adam in 1794. An elegant Ionic portico stands on a rusticated ground storey flanked by domed towers. Hutcheson's Hospital, 158 Ingram Street, is a handsome Italianate building designed by David Hamilton in 1805. Nearby is Stirling's Library, originally an 18thC private residence, it became the Royal Exchange in 1827 when the Corinthian portico was added. To the north west is Kelvingrove, Victorian Glasgow at its best. Built around a steep saddle of land, landscaped by Paxton in 1850 and lined along its edge with handsome terraces.

Last but not least are the banks of the River Clyde. From Clyde Walkway on the north bank you can see: the Suspension Bridge of 1871 with its pylons in the form of triumphal arches; the old clipper ship, C. V. Carrick, a contemporary of the Cutty Sark, moored by Victoria bridge; 17thC Merchants' Steeple; the Gothic Revival St Andrew's R.C. Cathedral of 1816; the church, built 1739, in nearby St Andrew's Square is a typical copy of London's St Martin-in-the-Fields.

Interesting buildings

Victorian Glasgow was extremely eclectic architecturally. Good examples of the Greek Revival style are Royal College of Physicians 1845, by W. H. Playfair and the Custom House 1840, by G. L. Taylor. The Queen's Room 1857, by Charles Wilson, is a handsome temple used now as a Christian Science church. The Gothic style is seen at its most exotic in the Stock Exchange 1877, by J. Burnet. The new Victorian materials and techniques with glass, wrought and cast iron were also ably demonstrated in the buildings of the time. Typical are: Gardener's Stores 1856, by J. Baird; the Buck's Head, Argyle Street, an amalgam of glass and cast iron; and the Egyptian Halls of 1873, in Union Street, which has a masonry framework. Both are by Alexander Thomson. The Templeton Carpet Factory 1889, Glasgow Green, by William Leiper, is a Venetian Gothic building complete with battlemented parapet.

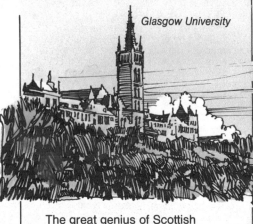

Glasgow University

The great genius of Scottish architecture is Charles Rennie Mackintosh whose major buildings are in Glasgow. In the Scotland Street School 1904-6, he punctuated a 3-storey central block with flanking staircase towers in projecting glazed bays. His most famous building — Glasgow School of Art 1897-9 — is a magnificent Art Nouveau building of taut stone and glass; the handsome library, with its gabled facade, was added later in 1907-9.

Stirling's Library

Galleries & museums

Scotland's largest tourist attraction, The Burrell Collection, is situated in Pollok Country Park, Haggs Road and has more than 8,000 objects, housed in an award-winning gallery. The Art Gallery and Museum, Kelvingrove Park, Argyle Street, a palatial sandstone building with glazed central court, has one of the best municipal collections in Britain; superb Flemish, Dutch and French paintings, drawings, prints, also ceramics, silver, costumes and armour, as well as a natural history section. Provand's Lordship c1471, in Castle Street, is Glasgow's oldest house and now a museum of 17th-18thC furniture and household articles. Pollok House, Pollok Country Park, a handsome house designed by William Adam in 1752, has paintings by William Blake and a notable collection of Spanish paintings, including works by El Greco. The Museum of Transport, housed in Kelvin Hall, Bunhouse Road, has a magnificent collection of trams, cars, ships models, bicycles, horse-drawn carriages and 7 steam locos. The People's Palace, The Green, built 1898 with a huge glazed Winter Garden, has a lively illustrated history of the city. But the oldest museum in Glasgow is the Hunterian Museum, University of Glasgow, University Avenue, opened in 1807, it has a fascinating collection of manuscripts, early printed books, as well as some fine archaeological and geological exhibits. 400-year-old Haggs Castle, St Andrew's Drive, is now a children's museum with practical demonstrations and exhibits showing how everyday life has changed over the centuries.

Streets & shopping

The Oxford Street of Glasgow is Sauchiehall (meaning 'willow meadow') Street. This with Buchanan Street and Argyle Street is the main shopping centre. Here you will find the department stores, boutiques and general shops. All three streets are

Sheriff Court

partly pedestrianised, but the most exhilarating is undoubtedly Buchanan Street. Of particular interest is the spatially elegant Argyll Arcade 1828, the Venetian Gothic-style Stock Exchange 1877, and the picturesque Dutch gabled Buchanan Street Bank building 1896. In Glasgow Green is The Barrows, the city's famous street market, formed by the junction of London Road and Kent Street. The Market is *open weekends*. Some parts of the city have *EC Tue*.

Art Gallery & Museum Kelvingrove

Cathedrals & Churches

Glasgow Cathedral is a perfect example of pre-Reformation Gothic architecture. Begun in 1238, it has a magnificent choir and handsome nave with shallow projecting transepts. On a windy hill to the east is the Necropolis, a cemetery with a spiky skyline of Victoriana consisting of pillars, temples and obelisks, dominated by an 1825 Doric column carrying the statue of John Knox. Other churches of interest: Lansdowne Church built by J. Honeyman in 1863; St George's Tron Church by William Stark 1807; Caledonian Road Church, a temple and tower atop a storey-high base, designed by Alexander Thomson in 1857; a similar design is to be found at the United Presbyterian Church, St Vincent Street, 1858, but on a more highly articulated ground storey; Queen's Cross Church 1897 is an amalgam of Art Nouveau and Gothic Revival by the brilliant Charles Rennie Mackintosh.

Churches within the central area of Glasgow are:

Church of Scotland
Glasgow Cathedral
Castle Street
Renfield St. Stephen's Church
262 Bath Street
St. George's Tron Church
165 Buchanan Street
St. Columba Church (Gaelic)
300 St. Vincent Street

Baptist
Adelaide Place Church
209 Bath Street

Congregational
Hillhead Centre
1 University Avenue

Episcopal Church of Scotland
Cathedral Church of St. Mary
300 Great Western Road, G4.

First Church of Christ Scientist
1 la Bell Place, Clifton Street, G3.
(off Sauchiehall Street)

Free Church of Scotland
265 St. Vincent Street

German Speaking Congregation
Services held at 7 Hughenden
Terrace, G12.

Greek Orthodox Cathedral
St. Luke's, 27 Dundonald Road, G12.

Jewish Orthodox Synagogue
Garnethill, 29 Garnet Street

Methodist
Woodlands Church
229 Woodlands Road

Roman Catholic
St. Andrew's Cathedral
190 Clyde Street
St. Aloysius' Church
25 Rose Street

Unitarian Church
72 Berkeley Street

United Free
Wynd Church,
427 Crown Street, G5.

Glasgow Cathedral

Entertainment

As Scotland's commercial and industrial capital, Glasgow offers a good choice of leisure activities. The city now has 6 theatres where productions ranging from serious drama to pantomime, pop and musicals are performed. The Theatre Royal, Hope Street, is Scotland's only opera house and has been completely restored to its full Victorian splendour. The Scottish National Orchestra gives concerts at the City Hall, Candleriggs, every *Sat night in winter,* while the Kelvin Hall is the venue for the proms in *Jun.* Cinemas are still thriving in Glasgow, as are the many public houses, some of which provide meals and live entertainment. In the city centre and Byres Road, West End, there is a fair number of restaurants where traditional home cooking, as well as international cuisines, can be sampled. More night life can be found at the city's discos and dance halls — Tiffany's, Sauchiehall Street and the Plaza, Eglinton Toll. Outdoors, apart from the many parks and nature trails, there is Calderpark Zoological Gardens, situated 6 miles from the centre between Mount Vernon and Uddingston. Here you may see white rhinos, black panthers and iguanas among many species. Departing from Stobcross Quay, you can also cruise down the Clyde in 'P.S. Waverley' – the last sea-going paddle-steamer in the world.

Cinemas

Cannon Cinema, 380 Clarkston Rd, G44.
041-637 2641
Cannon Film Centre–
326 Sauchiehall St, G2.   041-332 9513
(Admin Dept), 326 Sauchiehall St, G2
041-332 1592
326 Sauchiehall St, G2.   041-332 1593
Caledonian Associated Cinemas Ltd–
Regent House, 72 Renfield St, G2
041-332 0606
Cannon Grand–
18 Jamaica St, G1.   041-248 4620
Glasgow Film Theatre–
12 Rose St, G3. (Box Off)   041-332 6535

Grosvenor Cinema–
Ashton Lane, G12.   041-339 4298
Kelburne Cinema–
(Manager), Glasgow Rd, Paisley
041-889 3612
Odeon Film Centre, 56 Renfield St, G2.
041-332 8701
Salon Cinema, Vinicombe St, G12.
041-339 4256

Halls

City Hall, Candleriggs, G1.
Couper Institute
86 Clarkston Road, G44.
Dixon Halls, 650 Cathcart Road, G42.
Govan Hall, Summertown Road, G51.
Kelvin Hall, Argyle Street, G3.
Langside Hall, 5 Langside Avenue, G41.
Partick Hall, 9 Burgh Hall Street, G11.
Pollokshaws Hall
2025 Pollokshaws Road, G43.
Woodside Hall, Glenfarg Street, G20.

(More information about the above G.D.C. halls and others from the Director, Halls and Theatres Department, Candleriggs, G1. 041-552 1201).

Theatres

Citizens' Theatre
Gorbals Street.   041-429 0022
King's Theatre, Bath Street.
Mitchell Theatre and Moir Hall
Granville Street.
Pavilion Theatre
Renfield Street.   041-332 1846
Theatre Royal
Hope Street.   041-331 1234
Tron Theatre
38 Parnie Street.   041-552 3748
The Ticket Centre
Glasgow's Central Box Office for King's Theatre, Mitchell Theatre, Kelvin Hall, Citizen's Theatre, Theatre Royal and City Hall at Candleriggs, G1.
Open Monday to Saturday 10.30 a.m. to 6.30 p.m.
041-227 5511

Glasgow *(Abbotsinch)* Airport

Glasgow Airport is located eight miles West of Glasgow alongside the M8 motorway at Junction 28. It is linked by a bus service to Anderston Cross Bus Station, the journey time is 25 minutes and buses leave at 30 minute intervals. There is a frequent coach service linking the Airport with

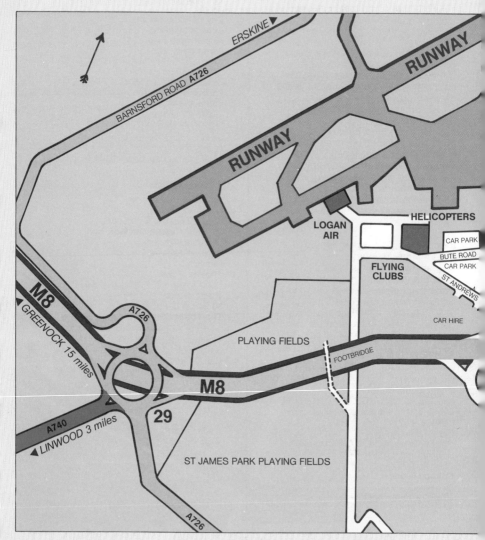

all major bus and rail terminals in the City and a Coach/Air link to and from Prestwick Airport.

The Airport Terminal has a restaurant, grill, buffet, three bars, lounges, shop, post office and banking facilities.

Car parking is available with a graduated scale of charges.

The Airport telephone no is 041-887 1111.

Airlines

(Domestic Routes)
British Airways
66 Gordon Street
Glasgow G1
Reservations Tel: 041-332 9666
British Caledonian Airways
(contact British Airways)
British Midland
Merlin House, Mossland Road,
Hillington, Glasgow
Reservations Tel: 041-204 2436
Loganair Ltd.
Glasgow Airport (administration)
Tel: 041-889 3181.
Trident House, Renfrew Road, Paisley

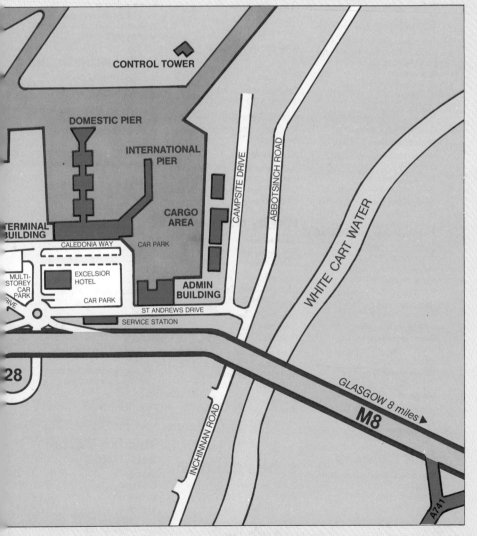

Sport & Recreation

For both spectator and participant, football is Glasgow's favourite sport. Both Celtic and Rangers, Scotland's most famous rival teams, have their grounds within the City. Glasgow houses Scotland's national football stadium at Hampden Park.

Badminton

Scottish Badminton Union's
Cockburn Centre, Bogmoor
Place, G51 4TQ.
041-445 1218

Bowling Greens

There are greens in all the main Parks. Information about clubs from the Scottish Bowling Association:
50 Wellington Street, G2.
041-221 8999.

Cricket Grounds

Cartha Haggs Road, G41.
Clydesdale Beaton Road, G41.
Huntershill Crowhill Road, Bishopbriggs.
Poloc 'Shawholm'
2060 Pollokshaws Road, G43.
West of Scotland Peel Street, G11.

Football Grounds

Celtic Park (Celtic F.C.)
95 Kerrydale St. G40
Firhill Park (Partick Thistle F.C. & Clyde F.C.)
Firhill Rd. G20
Hampden Park (Queen's Park F.C.)
Somerville Dr., G42
Ibrox Park (Rangers F.C.)
Edmiston Dr., G51
Kilbowie Park (Clydebank F.C.)
Argyll Rd., Clydebank
Mertland
Kirkintilloch
St. Mirren Park (St. Mirren F.C.)
Love St., Paisley

Golf Courses

Glasgow District Council
9 holes
Alexandra Park
King's Park.
Knightswood, Lincoln Avenue, G13.
Ruchill, Brassey Street, G20.

18 holes
Lethamhill, Cumbernauld Road, Littlehill, Auchinairn Road, G64.
Linn Park.

(Charges displayed)
Dougalston Golf Course
Strathblane Road, Milngavie.
(Five miles from Glasgow).
Open to the public daily.
041-956 5750 for charges.

Putting Greens

There are putting greens in all main Parks.

Pitch & Putt

Courses at Alexandra Park, Bellahouston Park, Dawsholm, Queen's Park, Rouken Glen and several others.

Rugby Grounds

Garscadden (Glasgow University)
Garscadden Road South, G15.

Hughenden (Hillhead High School)
Hughenden Road, G12.

New Anniesland (Glasgow Acad.)
Helensburgh Drive, G13.

Old Anniesland (Glasgow High School F.P. & Kelvinside Academicals)
Crow Road, G11

Westerlands (Glasgow University)
Ascot Avenue, G12

Sports Centres

Bellahouston
Bellahouston Drive, G52.
041-427 5454.

Burnhill
Toryglen Road, Rutherglen.
041-643 0327.

James Murray
Caledonia Road, Baillieston.
041-773 0881

Springburn
Springburn Way, Springburn.
041-558 7358.

Helenvale Park
Outdoor Sports Complex
Helenvale Street, G31.
041-554 4109.

Swimming Baths

Glasgow District Council
Castlemilk, 137 Castlemilk Drive, G45.
Drumchapel, 199 Drumry Road East.
Easterhouse, Bogbain Road, G34.
Govan, Harhill Street, G51.
Govanhill, 99 Calder Street, G42.
North Woodside, Braid Square.
Pollokshaws (Dry-Land/Water Sports Complex) Ashtree Road, G43.
Rutherglen, 44 Greenhill Road, G73.
Shettleston, Elvan Street, G32.
Temple, Knightscliffe Avenue, G13.
Whitehill, Onslow Drive, G31.
Whiteinch, Medwyn Street, G14.

Hours
Monday to Friday 9 a.m. to 9 p.m.
Saturday 9 a.m. to 1 p.m.
*Sunday 9 a.m. to 1 p.m.

Charges
Admission charges are minimal.
OAPs free at certain times.

Turkish Baths/ Sun Beds

available at:
Govanhill   041-423 0233
Pollokshaws   041-632 2200
Shettleston   041-778 1346

and Whiteinch, 041-959 2465

Men and women on separate days. Telephone direct to baths for more information.

Hours
(All the year round).
Monday to Friday 9 a.m. to 9 p.m.
Saturday 9 a.m. to 1 p.m.

SAUNA at:

Castlemilk,	041-634 8254
Drumchapel,	041-944 5812
Rutherglen,	041-647 4530
and Whitehill,	041-551 9969

Tennis

There are courts in all the main parks. Information about clubs from the Secretary of the West of Scotland Lawn Tennis Association:
Mr. N. Floyd, 1 Boclair Road
Bearsden   041-942 0162

Weather

The City of Glasgow is on the same latitude as the City of Moscow, but because of its close proximity to the warm Atlantic Shores, and the prevailing westerly winds, it enjoys a more moderate climate. Summers are generally cool and winters mostly mild, this gives Glasgow fairly consistent summer and winter temperatures. Despite considerable cloud the City is sheltered by hills to the south-west and north and the average rainfall for Glasgow is usually less than 40 inches per year.

The following table shows the approximate average figures for sunshine, rainfall and temperatures to be expected in Glasgow throughout the year:

Weather Forecasts
For the Glasgow Area including Loch Lomond and the Clyde Coast:
Weatherline
0898 500421 (Recording)
The Glasgow Weather Centre
(Meteorological Office)
33 Bothwell Street, G2
041-248 3451

Month	Hours of Sunshine	Inches of Rainfall	Temperature °C		
			Ave. Max.	Ave. Min.	High/Low
Jan	36	3.8	5.5	0.8	−18
Feb	62	2.8	6.3	0.8	−15
Mar	94	2.4	8.8	2.2	21
Apr	147	2.4	11.9	3.9	22
May	185	2.7	15.1	6.2	26
June	181	2.4	17.9	9.3	30
July	159	2.9	18.6	10.8	29
Aug	143	3.5	18.5	10.6	31
Sept	106	4.1	16.3	9.1	−4
Oct	76	4.1	13.0	6.8	−8
Nov	47	3.7	8.7	3.3	−11
Dec	30	4.2	6.5	1.9	−12

Renfrew District

A selection of leisure, recreational and cultural attractions in Renfrew District:

Barrhead Sports' Centre

The Centre contains swimming-pools, sports halls, activity rooms and sauna suite. Bar and restaurant facilities add to the wide range of sporting and leisure activities available.

Barshaw Park, Glasgow Road, Paisley

The park is extensive with formal and informal areas. It adjoins the public golf course and incorporates a boating-pond, playgrounds, model "ride-on" railway and a nature corner.

Castle Semple Country Park, Lochwinnoch

Castle Semple Loch is a popular feature for sailing and fishing. Canoes, rowing boats and sailing boards for hire. Fishing permits available. Tel: Lochwinnoch 842882.

Coats Observatory

The Observatory has traditionally recorded astronomical and meteorological information since 1882. Now installed with a satellite picture receiver, it is one of the best equipped Observatories in the country. Monday, Tuesday, Thursday 2 p.m.-8 p.m., Wednesday, Friday, Saturday 10 a.m.-5 p.m, October to end March 7-15 p.m.-9.45 p.m. Tel: 041 889 3151

Erskine Bridge

The bridge is an impressive high level structure opened by HRH Princess Anne in 1971 and provides a direct link from Renfrew District to Loch Lomond and the Trossachs. The bridge replaced the Erskine Ferry and affords extensive views up and down river to pedestrian users.

Finlayston Estate

Off the A8 at Langbank. The Estate is now a garden centre with woodland walks. The house has connections with John Knox and Robert Burns and is open April to August on Sundays from 2.30–4.30pm. At other times groups by appointment. Tel: Langbank 285.

Formakin Estate, By Bishopton

A group of buildings and landscaped grounds designed in the Arts and Crafts style at the turn of the century. Currently being restored, the estate has a visitor centre, tea room and guided tours. Open Saturday and Sunday 11 a.m.-6 p.m. Tel: 0505 863400

Gleniffer Braes Country Park, Glenfield Road, Paisley

1,000 breathtaking acres including Glen Park nature trail, picnic and children's play areas. Open dawn till dusk, the park affords extensive walks and spectacular views from this elevated moorland area, and contains an area reserved for model aero flying. Tel: 041-884 3794

Houston Village

Houston was developed in the 18th century as an estate village. The traditional smiddy building, village pubs and terraced houses combine to create a quiet, sleepy atmosphere which has successfully survived the development of extensive modern housing on its periphery.

Inchinnan Bridges

Early 19th century stone bridges over the White Cart and Black Cart rivers close to St Conval's stone, and the site of the Inchinnan Church which houses the graves of the Knights Templar, whose order was introduced to Scotland in 1153 by King David I.

Johnstone Castle

The remnants of a 1700 building formerly a much larger structure but largely demolished in the 1950's. The castle has significant historical links with the Cochrane and Houston families, major landowners who were instrumental in the development of the Burgh of Johnstone.

Kilbarchan Village

A good example of an 18 Century weaving village with many original buildings still fronting the narrow streets. A focal point is the steeple building in the square, orginally a school and meal market and now used as public meeting rooms. A cycle route/footpath system links it to Glasgow and the Clyde Coast.

Laigh Kirk, Paisley

Originally built in 1738, the Laigh Kirk has been converted to an Arts Centre, with a theatre, workshop, bistro and bar open daily 10 a.m.-11 p.m. For further information telephone 041-887 1010

Linwood Sports Centre

A wide range of indoor and outdoor sporting activities include football and Rugby pitches, games hall, squash courts, BMX track, fitness trail, tennis courts and conditioning suite.

Lochwinnoch Village

An attractive rural village close to the Castle Semple Water Park, Muirshiel Country Park and the R.S.P.B. nature reserve, Lochwinnoch contains a small local museum with displays reflecting agricultural, social and industrial aspects of village life. Museum open Monday, Wednesday and Friday 10am–1pm, 2–5pm and 6–8pm. Tuesday and Saturday 10am–1pm and 2–5pm. Open most days throughout the year, visitors should telephone Lochwinnoch 842615.

Muirshiel Country Park

Four miles north of Lochwinnoch, the park features trails of varying length radiating from the Information Centre. open daily 9 a.m.-4-30 p.m. (Winter), 9 a.m.-7-30 p.m. (Summer). Tel: Lochwinnoch 842803

Paisley Town Trail

An easy-to-follow route taking in the town's historic and architecturally significant buildings. Visitors can spend an hour or two walking round the trail and referring to a printed guide and wall plaques on the main buildings.

Paisley, Lagoon Leisure Centre

Ultra-modern complex with extensive "fun" pool featuring artificial wave machine and water slides. Also has cafe/bar facilities. Unique within the area, the complex is easily reached by public trasport and has ample parking. Monday-Friday 10 a.m.-10 p.m., Saturday and Sunday 10 a.m.-5.00 p.m. Tel: 041-889 4000.

Paisley Abbey

Birthplace of the Stewart Dynasty, the Abbey dates, in part, to the 12th century and features regimental flags, relics, the Barochan Cross and beautiful stained glass windows. Monday-Saturday 10.00 a.m.-12.00 p.m., 1.00-3.00p.m. Tel: 041-889 3630.

Paisley Town Hall

A Renaissance style building by the River Cart in the heart of Paisley, it features a slim clock tower and houses a Tourist Information Centre. It accommodates many exhibitions during the year and is also available for conferences and functions. Monday–Saturday 9am–5pm. Tel: 041-887 1007.

Paisley Museum and Art Gallery, High Street, Paisley

In addition to the world famous collection of Paisley shawls, the Museum traces the history of the Paisley pattern, the development of weaving techniques and houses collections of local and natural history, ceramics and paintings. Monday-Saturday 10 a.m.-5 p.m. Tel: 041-889 3151.

Renfrew Town Hall

The Town Hall has a ''fairy-tale'' style to its 105 feet high spire and was the administrative centre of the Royal Burgh of Renfrew. Originally the principal town in the area, Renfrew was strategically placed on the River Clyde, and a passenger ferry continues to operate daily.

Robert Tannahill, Weaver Poet

The works of Tannahill ranks with those of Burns. Born 1774 he took his own life in 1810 and is buried in a nearby graveyard. Visitors can visit his early home, site of his death, and his grave, and read his works in Paisley Library.

Royal Society for Protection of Birds, Lochwinnoch

An interesting visitor centre with observation tower, hides, displays and gift shop. Thursday, Friday, Saturday and Sunday 10 a.m.-5.15 p.m. Shop open 7 days. Tel: Lochwinnoch 842663

Sma' Shot Cottages, Paisley

Fully restored and furnished artisan's house of the Victorian era; exhibition room displaying photographs plus artefacts of local interest. 18th century weaver's loomshop with combined living quarters. Open May-September 1-5 p.m. Group visits arranged by appointment. Tel: 041-812 2513 or 041-889 0530.

The Clyde Estuary

Visitors travelling along the rural route of the Old Greenock Road above Langbank village at the western end of the District are able to take advantage of extensive views of the upper and lower Clyde Estuary, the Gareloch and the mountains beyond.

Thomas Coats Memorial Church

Open Monday-Friday 9 a.m.-12 noon. Visitors should check in advance. Another gift from the Coats family to Paisley, the church was built in 1894 and constructed of red sandstone, is one of the finest Bapist Churches in the country. Tel: 041 889 9980.

Wallace Monument, Elderslie

The monument was erected in 1912 and marks the birthplace of the Scottish Patriot, Sir William Wallace. It stands adjacent to the reconstructed foundation plan of the adjacent Wallace Buildings which dated from the 17th century.

Weaver's Cottage, Kilbarchan

This cottage, built in 1723, houses the last of the village's 800 looms and demonstrations are still given. It contains displays of weaving and domestic utensils, with Cottage garden and refreshments. Open April 1–May 31 and September 1–October 31 on Tuesdays, Thursdays, Saturdays and Sundays 2–5pm, June 1–August 31 from 2–5pm daily.

Public Transport

The City of Glasgow has one of the most advanced, fully integrated public transport systems in the whole of Europe. The Strathclyde Transport network consists of; the local British Rail network, the local bus services and the fully modernised Glasgow Underground, with links to Glasgow Airport and the Steamer and Car Ferry Services.
Note: Although the information in this section is correct at the time of printing it should be checked before use.

Bus Services and Tours

Long Distance Coach Service
Scottish Citylink Coaches Ltd
041-332 9191

Shorter Journeys
Tel: 041-332 9191 (0630-2300 Daily) for City Services and buses to Airdrie, Clydebank, Cumbernauld, Dumbarton, East Kilbride, Erskine, Hamilton, Johnstone, Kirkintilloch, Paisley, Wishaw
Buses leave from Anderston Cross Bus Station 041-248 7432.
for Ardrossan, Ayr, Blantyre, East Kilbride (via Busby), Edinburgh, Glasgow Airport, Gourock, Hamilton, Kilmarnock, Lanark, Largs, Motherwell, Paisley, Prestwick, Renfrew, Wemyss Bay, etc.
Buses leave from Buchanan Bus Station 041-332 7133.
for Aberfoyle, Airdrie, Bearsden, Blantyre, Callander, Clydebank, Crieff, Cumbernauld, Dundee, Dunfermline, East Kilbride (via

Bridgeton), Edinburgh, Glasgow Airport, Glencoe, Inverary, Leven, Milngavie, Motherwell, Perth. St. Andrews, Stirling, etc.
Day and Half Day Tours
Scottish City Link
Buchanan Bus Station.
041-332 8055

Haldane's of Cathcart, Delvin Road, G44. 041-637 2234.

Strathclyde Buses Ltd.
197 Victoria Road, G42 7AD
041-636 3190
(Glasgow City Bus Tour and Glimpses of Charles R. Mackintosh Architecture with C.R.M. Society) 041-636 3195

British Rail

Passenger enquiries: 041-204 2844.
Sleeper reservations: 041-221 2305.

Central Station
Inter-City electric services for English destinations, including Carlisle, Preston, Liverpool, Manchester (3 hours 35 minutes), Leeds, Nottingham, Crewe, Birmingham (4 hours 20 minutes), London (Euston) (5 hours). Also connections for Wales and West of England.
Scottish destinations in South and West include Ayr (for Burns country), Kilmarnock, Dumfries, Stranraer (for Ireland via Larne), Ardrossan and Largs. Electric trains include Gourock and Wemyss Bay (for Clyde steamers).

Queen Street Station
Trains for scenic West Highland Line to Oban, Fort William and Mallaig. Steamer connections to the Islands. Inter-City expresses for Edinburgh, connecting with trains to England including Newcastle, York, London (King's Cross). Services for North and East Scotland, including Fife, Stirling, Perth, Dundee, Aberdeen, Inverness, Wick, Thurso, Kyle of Lochalsh.
Electric trains: Dumbarton, Balloch (for Loch Lomond), Helensburgh.
City Rail Link Service bus connects Queen Street Station and Central Station.

Parks & Gardens

There are over 70 public parks within the city. The most famous is Glasgow Green. Abutting the north bank of the River Clyde, it was acquired in 1662. Of interest are the Winter Gardens attached to the People's Palace. Kelvingrove Park is an 85-acre park laid out by Sir Joseph Paxton in 1852. On the south side of the city is the 148-acre Queen's Park, Victoria Road, established 1857-94. Also of interest: Rouken Glen, Thornliebank, with a spectacular waterfall, walled garden, nature trail and boating facilities; Victoria Park, Victoria Park Drive, with its famous Fossil Grove flower gardens and yachting pond. In Great Western Road are the Botanic Gardens. Founded in 1817, the gardens' 42 acres are crammed with natural attractions, including the celebrated Kibble Palace glasshouse with its fabulous tree ferns, exotic plants and white marble Victorian statues.

The main public parks in Glasgow are:

Alexandra
671 Alexandra Parade, G31.

Bellahouston
Paisley Road West, G52.

Botanic Gardens
730 Gt. Western Road, G12.

Hogganfield Loch
Cumbernauld Road, G33.

Kelvingrove
Sauchiehall Street, G3.

King's
325 Carmunnock Road, G44.

Linn
Clarkston Road at Netherlee Road, G44.

Queen's
Victoria Road, G42.

Rouken Glen
Rouken Glen Road, G46.

Springburn
Broomfield Road, G21.

Tollcross
461 Tollcross Road, G32.

Victoria
Victoria Park Drive North, G14.

Kibble Palace

Strathclyde Further Education

Anniesland College
Hatfield Drive, Glasgow, G12 0YE.
041-357 3969

Ayr College
Dam Park, Ayr, KA8 0EU.
Ayr (0292) 265184

Barmulloch College
186 Rye Road, Glasgow, G21 3JY.
041-558 9071

Bell College of Technology
Almada Street, Hamilton,
Lanarkshire, ML3 0JB.
Hamilton (0698) 283100

Cambuslang College
Hamilton Road,
Cambuslang, Glasgow, G72 7BS.
041-641 6197

**Cardonald College of Further
Education**
690 Mosspark Drive, Glasgow,
G52 3AY.
041-883 6151

Central College of Commerce
300 Cathedral Street, G1 2TA.
041-552 3941

Clydebank College
Kilbowie Road, Clydebank,
Dunbartonshire, G81 2AA.
041-952 7771

Coatbridge College
Kildonan Street, Coatbridge,
Lanarkshire, ML5 3LS.
Coatbridge (0236) 22316

Cumbernauld College
Town Centre, Cumbernauld,
Glasgow, G67 1HU.
Cumbernauld (0236) 731811

**Glasgow College of Building and
Printing**
60 North Hanover Street, Glasgow,
G1 2BP.
041-332 9969

**Glasgow College of Food
Technology**
230 Cathedral Street, Glasgow,
G1 2TG.
041-552 3751

**Glasgow College of Nautical
Studies**
21 Thistle Street, Glasgow, G5 9XB.
041-429 3201

Glasgow College of Technology
Cowcaddens Road, Glasgow,
G4 0BA.
041-332 7090

James Watt College
Finnart Street, Greenock,
Renfrewshire, PA16 8HF.
Greenock (0475) 24433

John Wheatley College
1346-1364 Shettleston Road,
Glasgow G32 9AT
041-778 2426

Kilmarnock College
Holehouse Road, Kllmarnock,
Ayrshire, KA3 7AT.
Kilmarnock (0563) 23501

Langside College
50 Prospecthill Road, Glasgow,
G42 9LB.
041-649 4991

Motherwell College
Dalzell Drive, Motherwell,
Lanarkshire, ML4 2DD.
Motherwell (0698) 59641

Reid Kerr College, The
Renfrew Road, Paisley, Renfrewshire,
PA13 4DR
041-889 4225

Springburn College
110 Flemington Street, Glasgow,
G21 4BX.
041-558 9001

Stow College
43 Shamrock Street, Glasgow,
G4 9LD.
041-332 1786

University of Glasgow
University Avenue, Glasgow
041-339 8855

University of Strathclyde,
George Street, Glasgow
G11XQ
041 552 4400

Hospitals

**Greater Glasgow Health Board
(Adminstration)
112 Ingram St., Glasgow G1 1ET
041-552-6222**

Acorn Street Psychiatric Day Hospital
23 Acorn Street, Bridgeton,
Glasgow G40 4AA
041-556 4789

Baillieston Health Centre
20 Muirside Road,
Glasgow G69 7AD
041-771 0871

Belvidere Hospital
London Road, Glasgow G31 4PG
041-554 1855

Birdston Hospital, Milton of Campsie
Glasgow G65 8BY
041-776 6114

Blawarthill Hospital,
129 Holehouse Drive,
Knightswood.Glasgow G13 3TG
041-954 9547

Bridgeton Health Centre
201 Abercromby Street
Glasgow G40 2EA
041-554 1866

Broomhill & Lanfine Hospitals
Kirkintilloch, Glasgow G66 1RR
041-776 5141

Carsewell House (Psychiatric
Outpatient)
5 Oakley Terrace, Glasgow G31 2HX
041-554 6267

Castlemilk Health Centre
Dougrie Drive, Castlemilk,
Glasgow G45
041-634 3434

Canniesburn Hospital
Switchback Road, Bearsden,
Glasgow G61 1QL
041-942 2255

Charing Cross (Alcohol and Drug)
Day Centre, 8 Woodside Crescent,
Glasgow G3 7UL
041-332 5463

Children's Home Hospital
Strathblane, Glasgow G63 9EP
0360 70203

Clydebank Health Centre
Kilbowie Road, Clydebank G81 2TQ
041-952 2080

Cowglen Hospital
Boydstone Road, Glasgow G53 6XJ
041-632 9106

Darnley Hospital
755 Nitshill Road, Glasgow G53 7RR
041-881 1005

David Elder Infirmary
503 Langlands Road, Glasgow G51 4DY
041-445 2466

Douglas Inch Centre
2 Woodside Terrace,
Glasgow G3 7UY
041-332 3844

Drumchapel Hospital
129 Drumchapel Road,
Glasgow G15 6PX
041-944 2344

Duke Street Hospital
253 Duke Street, Glasgow G31 1HY
041-556 5222

Duntocher Hospital
Duntocher, Clydebank G81 5QU
Duntocher 74294

Easterhouse Health Centre
9 Auchinlea Road, Glasgow G34 9QU
041-771 0781

Gartloch Hospital, Gartloch Road,
Gartcosh, Glasgow G69 8EJ
041-771 0771

Gartnavel General Hospital
1053 Great Western Road,
Glasgow G12 0YN
041-334 8122

Gartnavel Royal Hospital
1055 Great Western Road,
Glasgow G12 0XH
041-334 6241

Glasgow Dental Hospital and School
378 Sauchiehall Street
Glasgow G2 3JZ
041-332 7020

Glasgow Eye Infirmary
3 Sandyford Place, Glasgow G3 7NB
041-204 0721

Glasgow Homeopathic Hospital
1000 Great Western Road,
Glasgow G12 0AA
041-339 0382

Glasgow Royal Infirmary
84 Castle Street, Glasgow G4 0SF
041-552 3535

Glasgow Royal Maternity Hospital
Rottenrow, Glasgow G4 0NA
041-552 3400

Glasgow School of Chiropody
757 Crookston Road,
Glasgow G53 7UA
041-883 0418

Glasgow School of Occupational
Therapy, 29 Sherbrooke Avenue,
Glasgow G41 4ER
041-427 3032

Gorbals Health Centre
45 Pine Place, Glasgow G5 0BQ
041-429 6291

Govan Health Centre
5 Drumoyne Road,
Glasgow G51 4BJ
041-440 1212

Govanhill Health Centre
233 Calder Street
Glasgow G42 7DR
041-424 3003

Knightswood Hospital
125 Knightswood Road,
Glasgow G12 2XG
041-954 9641

Lennox Castle Hospital
Lennoxtown, Glasgow G65 7LB
Lennoxtown 313000

Lenzie Hospital
Auchinloch Road, Kirkintilloch,
Glasgow G66 5DF
041-776 1208

Leverndale Hospital
510 Crookston Road
Glasgow G53 7TU
041-882 6255

Lightburn Hospital
Carntyne Road, Glasgow G32 6ND
041-774 5102

Maryhill Health Centre
41 Shawpark Street,
Glasgow G20 9DR
041-946 7151

Mearnskirk Hospital
Newton Mearns, Glasgow G77 5RZ
041-639 2251

Parkhead Health Centre
101 Salamanca Street,
Glasgow G31 5BA
041-556 5232

Parkhead Hospital
81 Salamanca Street,
Glasgow
041-554 7951

Philipshill Hospital
East Kilbride Road, Busby,
Glasgow G76 9HW
041-644 1144

Pollock Health Centre
21 Cowglen Road
Glasgow G53 6EQ
041-880 8899

Possilpark Health Centre
85 Denmark Street,
Glasgow G22 5EG
041-336 5311

Queen Mother's Hospital
Yorkhill, Glasgow G3 8SH
041-339 8888

Royal Hospital for Sick Children
129 Drumchapel Road
Glasgow G15 6PX
041-944 2344

Royal Hospital for Sick Children
Yorkhill, Glasgow G3 8SJ
041-339 8888

Royal Samaritan Hospital for Women
69 Coplaw Street, Glasgow G42 7JF
041-423 3033

Ruchill Hospital
Bilsland Drive, Glasgow G20 9NB
041-946 7120

Rutherglen Health Centre
130 Stonelaw Road, Rutherglen,
Glasgow G73 2PQ
041-647 7171

Rutherglen Maternity Hospital
120 Stonelaw Road, Rutherglen,
Glasgow G73 2PG
041-647 0011

Shettleston Health Centre
420 Old Shettleston Road,
Glasgow G32 7JZ
041-778 9191

Southern General Hospital
1345 Govan Road, Glasgow G51 4TF
041-445 2466

Springburn Health Centre
200 Springburn Way,
Glasgow G21 1TR
041-558 0101

Stobhill General Hospital
133 Balornock Road,
Glasgow G21 3UW
041-558 0111

Stoneyetts Hospital
Chryston, Glasgow G69 0JG
041-776 1026

Thornliebank Health Centre
20 Kennishead Road
Glasgow G46 8NY
041-620 2222

Townhead Health Centre
16 Alexandra Parade
Glasgow G31 2ES
041-552 3477

Victoria Geriatric Unit
Mansionhouse Road,
Glasgow G41 3DX
041-649 4511

Victoria Infirmary
Langside Road, Glasgow G42 9TY
041-649 4545

Waverley Park Hospital
Kirkintilloch, Glasgow G66 2HE
041-776 2461

Western Infirmary
Dumbarton Road, Glasgow G11 6NT
041-339 8822

Woodilee Hospital
Kirkintilloch, Glasgow G66 3UG
041-776 2451

Woodside Health Centre
Barr Street, Glasgow G20 7LR
041-332 9977

INDEX TO STREETS

General Abbreviations

All.	Alley	Ct.	Court	Mans.	Mansions	S.	South
App.	Approach	Dr.	Drive	Mkt.	Market	Sq.	Square
Arc.	Arcade	E.	East	Ms.	Mews	Sta.	Station
Av.	Avenue	Est.	Estate	Mt.	Mount	St.	Street
Bldgs.	Buildings	Esp.	Esplanade	N.	North	Ter.	Terrace
Boul.	Boulevard	Gdns.	Gardens	Par.	Parade	Trd.	Trading
Bri.	Bridge	Gra.	Grange	Pass.	Passage	Vills.	Villas
Circ.	Circus	Grn.	Green	Pk.	Park	Vw.	View
Cft.	Croft	Gro.	Grove	Pl.	Place	W.	West
Clo.	Close	Ho.	House	Prom.	Promenade	Wf.	Wharf
Cor.	Corner	Ind.	Industrial	Quad.	Quadrant	Wk.	Walk
Cotts.	Cottages	La.	Lane	Ri.	Rise	Yd.	Yard
Cres.	Crescent	Lo.	Lodge	Rd.	Road		

District Abbreviations

Bail.	Baillieston	Clark.	Clarkston	Giff.	Giffnock	Old K.	Old Kilpatrick
Barr.	Barrhead	Clyde.	Clydebank	John.	Johnstone	Pais.	Paisley
Bear.	Bearsden	Coat.	Coatbridge	Kilb.	Kilbarchan	Renf.	Renfrew
Bish.	Bishopbriggs	Cumb.	Cumbernauld	Kirk.	Kirkintilloch	Step.	Stepps
Blan.	Blantyre	Dalm.	Dalmuir	Lenz.	Lenzie	Thorn.	Thornliebank
Both.	Bothwell	E.K.	East Kilbride	Linw.	Linwood	Udd.	Uddingston
Chr.	Chryston	Gart.	Gartcosh	Neil.	Neilston		

NOTES

The figures and letters following a street name indicate the postal district for that street with the square and page number where it will be found in the atlas. Thus the postal district for Abbey Drive is G14, and it will be found in square H12 on page 19.

A street name followed by the name of another street in italics does not appear on the map, but will be found adjoining or near the latter.

101

Street		
Albert Ct. G41	M15	51
Albert Dr.		
Albert Dr. G41	N14	50
Albert Dr. G73	P19	65
Albert Dr., Bear.	E13	8
Albert Rd. G42	N16	51
Albert Rd., Clyde.	D 7	5
Albert Rd., Lenz.	D23	13
Albert Rd., Renf.	H 8	17
Alberta Ter. G12	H14	20
Saltoun St.		
Albion St. G1	K17	36
Albion St., Bail.	M24	55
Albion St., Pais.	L 6	30
Alcaig Rd. G52	N12	49
Alder Av., Lenz.	C22	12
Alder Ct., Barr.	R 8	59
Alder Pl. G43	P14	62
Alder Pl., John.	N 1	44
Alder Rd. G43	P14	62
Alder Rd., Cumb.	C 4	71
Alder Rd., Dalm.	C 6	4
Alderman Pl. G13	G11	19
Alderman Rd. G13	F 9	18
Aldersdyke Pl., Blan.	R26	68
Alderside Dr., Udd.	O27	57
Alexander St., Clyde.	E 7	5
Alexandra Av. G33	G23	25
Alexandra Av., Lenz.	D23	13
Alexandra Cross G31	K19	37
Duke St.		
Alexandra Ct. G31	K19	37
Roebank St.		
Alexandra Dr., Pais.	M 4	45
Alexandra Dr., Renf.	H 8	17
Alexandra Gdns., Lenz.	D23	13
Alexandra Par. G31	K19	37
Alexandra Park St. G31	K19	37
Alexandra Rd., Lenz.	D23	13
Alford St. G21	H17	22
Alfred Ter. G52	H14	20
Great Western Rd.		
Algie St. G41	O15	51
Alice St. G5	M17	52
Alice St., Pais.	N 6	46
Aline Ct., Barr.	Q 7	59
Allan Av., Renf.	J 9	32
Allan Pl. G40	M19	53
Allan St. G40	N19	53
Allander Gdns., Bish.	D18	10
Allander Rd., Bear.	D11	7
Allander St. G22	H17	22
Allands Av., Renf.	G 5	16
Allanfauld Rd., Cumb.	B 2	70
Allanton Av., Pais.	M 9	48
Allanton Dr. G52	L10	32
Allerton Gdns., Bail.	M24	55
Alleysbank G73	N19	53
Allison Dr. G72	P22	66
Allison Pl. G42	N16	51
Prince Edward St.		
Allison Pl. Gart.	H27	27
Allison St. G42	N16	51
Allnach Pl. G34	K27	41
Alloway Cres. G73	P18	64
Alloway Dr. G73	P18	64
Alloway Dr., Clyde.	D 8	5
Alloway Rd. G43	P14	62
Alma St. G40	L19	37
Almond Av., Renf.	J 9	32
Almond Cres., Pais.	N 3	45
Almond Dr., Lenz.	C22	12
Almond Rd. G33	G23	25
Almond Rd., Bear.	E11	7
Almond St. G33	J20	37
Almond Vale, Udd.	O28	57
Hamilton Vw.		
Alness Cres. G52	M12	49
Alpatrick Gdns., John.	M 1	44
Alpine Gro., Udd.	O27	57
Alsatian Av., Clyde.	E 8	5
Alston La. G40	L18	36
Claythorn St.		
Altnacreag Gdns., Chr.	D28	15
Alton Gdns. G12	H14	20
Great George St.		
Alton Rd., Pais.	M 8	47
Altyre St. G32	M21	54
Alva Gate. G52	N12	49
Alva Gdns. G52	N12	49
Alva Pl., Lenz.	D24	13
Alyth Cres., Clark.	S16	63
Alyth Gdns. G52	M12	49
Alyth Gdns., Clark.	S16	63
Ambassador Way, Renf.	J 8	31
Cockels Loan		
Amisfield St. G20	G15	21
Amochrie Dr., Pais.	O 4	45
Amochrie Rd., Pais.	N 3	45
Amulree Pl. G32	M22	54
Amulree St. G32	L22	38
Ancaster Dr. G13	G12	19
Ancaster La. G13	F11	19
Great Western Rd.		
Anchor Av., Pais.	M 7	47
Anchor Cres., Pais.	M 7	47
Anchor Dr., Pais.	M 7	47
Anchor Wynd, Pais.	M 7	47
Ancroft St. G20	H16	21
Anderson Dr., Renf.	H 8	17
Anderson Gdns., Blan.	R27	69
Station Rd.		
Anderson Quay G3	L15	35
Anderson St. G11	J13	34
Andrew Av., Lenz.	D23	13
Andrew Av., Renf.	H 9	18
Andrew Dr., Clyde.	F 8	17
Andrew Sillars Av. G72	P23	67
Andrews St., Pais.	L 6	30
Anglegate G14	H11	19
Angus Av. G52	M11	49
Angus Av., Bish.	F20	23
Angus Gdns., Udd.	O27	57
Angus La. G64	E20	11
Angus Oval G52	M10	48
Angus Pl. G52	M10	48
Angus St. G21	H18	22
Angus St., Clyde.	F 9	18
Angus Wk., Udd.	O28	57
Annan Dr. G73	O20	53
Annan Dr., Bear.	D11	7
Annan Dr., Pais.	N 3	45
Annan Pl., John.	O08	43
Annan St. G42	O16	51
Annandale St. G42	M16	51
Annbank St. G31	L18	36
Anne Av., Renf.	H 8	17
Anne Cres., Lenz.	D23	13
Annette St. G42	N16	51
Annfield Gdns., Blan.	R26	68
Annfield Pl. G31	K18	36
Annick Dr., Bear.	E11	7
Annick St. G32	L22	38
Annick St. G72	P23	67
Anniesdale Av. G33	G23	25
Anniesland Cres. G14	G10	18
Anniesland Mansions G13	G12	19
Ancaster Dr.		
Anniesland Rd. G13	G11	19
Anniesland Rd. G14	G10	18
Anson St. G40	M18	52
Anson Way, Renf.	J 8	31
Britannia Way		
Anstruther St. G32	L21	38
Antonine Gdns., Clyde.	C 7	5
Antonine Rd., Bear.	C10	6
Anworth St. G32	M22	54
Appin Rd. G31	K19	37
Appin Ter. G73	Q20	65
Lochaber Dr.		
Appin Way, Udd.	Q28	69
Bracken Ter.		
Appleby St. G22	H16	21
Applecross Gdns., Chr.	D27	15
Applecross St. G22	H16	21
Appledore Cres., Udd.	Q28	69
Apsley La. G11	J13	34
Apsley St. G11	J13	34
Aray St. G20	G14	20
Arbroath Av. G52	M10	48
Arcadia St. G40	L18	36
Arcadia St. G40	L18	36
Drake St.		
Arcan Cres. G15	E10	6
Archerfield Av. G32	N22	54
Archerfield Cres. G32	N22	54
Archerfield Dr. G32	N22	54
Archerfield Gro. G32	N22	54
Archerhill Av. G13	F 9	18
Archerhill Cotts. G13	F10	18
Archerhill Rd.		
Archerhill Cres. G13	F10	18
Archerhill Gdns. G13	F10	18
Archerhill Rd.		
Archerhill Rd. G13	F10	18
Archerhill Sq. G13	F10	18
Kelso St.		
Archerhill St. G13	F10	18
Archerhill Rd.		
Archerhill Ter. G13	F10	18
Archerhill Rd.		
Ard Pl. G42	O18	52
Ard Rd., Renf.	H 7	17
Ard St. G32	M22	54
Ardagie Dr. G32	O23	55
Ardagie Pl. G32	O23	55
Ardbeg Av. G73	Q21	66
Ardbeg Av., Bish.	E20	11
Ardbeg St. G42	N16	51
Ardconnel St. G46	Q12	61
Arden Av. G46	R12	61
Arden Dr., Giff.	R13	62
Arden Pl. G46	R12	61
Stewarton Rd.		
Ardencraig Cres. G44	R17	64
Ardencraig Dr. G45	R18	64
Ardencraig La. G45	R17	64
Ardencraig Rd.		
Ardencraig Quad. G45	R18	64
Ardencraig Rd. G45	R17	64
Ardencraig St. G45	R19	65
Ardencraig Ter. G45	R18	64
Ardenlea Rd., Udd.	O27	57
Ardenlea St. G40	M19	53
Ardery St. G11	J13	34
Apsley St.		
Ardessie Pl. G20	G14	20
Ardessie St. G23	E14	8
Torrin Rd.		
Ardfern St. G32	M22	54
Ardgay Pl. G32	M22	54
Ardgay St. G32	M22	54
Ardgay Way G73	Q19	65
Ardgour Dr., Linw.	L 1	28
Ardgowan Av., Pais.	M 6	46
Ardgowan Dr., Udd.	O27	57
Ardgowan St., Pais.	N 6	46
Ardholm St. G32	L22	38
Ardhu Pl. G15	D 9	6
Ardlamont Sq., Linw.	L 2	28
Ardlaw St. G51	L12	33
Ardle Rd. G43	P15	63
Ardlui St. G32	M21	54
Ardmaleish Cres. G45	R18	64
Ardmaleish Rd. G45	R17	64
Ardmaleish St. G45	R18	64
Ardmaleish Ter. G45	R18	64
Ardmay Cres. G44	O17	52
Ardmillan St. G33	K21	38
Ardmore Oval, Pais.	L 4	29
Ardmore St. G31	K19	37
Ardmory Av. G42	O17	52
Ardmory La. G42	O18	52
Ardnacross Dr. G33	J23	39
Ardnahoe Av. G42	O17	52
Ardnahoe Pl. G42	O17	52
Ardneil Rd. G51	L12	33
Ardnish St. G51	L12	33
Ardo Gdns. G51	L13	34
Ardoch Gro. G72	P21	66
Ardoch Rd., Bear.	C13	8
Ardoch St. G22	H17	22
Ardoch Way, Chr.	E27	15
Braeside Av.		
Ardshiel Rd. G51	K12	33
Ardsloy La. G14	H10	18
Ardsloy Pl.		
Ardsloy Pl. G14	H10	18
Ardtoe Cres. G33	G24	25
Ardtoe Pl. G33	G24	25
Arduthie Rd. G51	K12	33
Ardwell Rd. G52	M12	49
Argosy Way, Renf.	J 8	31
Britannia Way		
Argyle St. G3	J14	34
Argyle St., Pais.	M 5	46
Argyll Arc. G2	K16	35
Argyll Av., Renf.	H 7	17
Argyll Rd., Bear.	B12	7

Argyll Rd., Clyde. E 8 5
Arisaig Dr. G52 M12 49
Arisaig Dr., Bear. D13 8
Arisaig Pl. G52 M12 49
Ark La. G31 K18 36
Arkle Ter. G72 Q21 66
Arkleston Cres., Pais. K 7 31
Arkleston Rd., Pais. K 7 31
Arklet Rd. G51 L12 33
Arklie Av., Bear. B12 7
Tweedsmuir Cres.
Arlington St. G3 J15 35
Armadale Ct. G31 K19 37
Armadale Path G31 K19 37
Armadale Pl. G31 K19 37
Armadale St. G31 K19 37
Armour Pl., John. M 1 44
Armour St. G31 L18 36
Armour St., John. M 1 44
Arngask Rd. G51 K12 33
Arnhall Pl. G52 M12 49
Arnholm Pl. G52 M12 49
Arnisdale Pl. G34 K25 40
Arnisdale Rd. G34 K25 40
Arnisdale Way G73 Q19 65
Shieldaig Dr.
Arniston St. G32 K21 38
Arnol Pl. G33 K24 39
Arnold Av., Bish. E19 11
Arnold St. G20 G16 21
Arnott Way G72 P22 66
Arnprior Gdns., Chr. E27 15
Braeside Av.
Arnprior Quad. G45 Q17 64
Arnprior Rd. G45 Q17 64
Arnprior St. G45 Q17 64
Arnside Av., Giff. Q14 62
Arnthern St. G72 P23 67
Arnwood Dr. G12 G13 20
Aron Ter. G72 Q21 66
Aros Dr. G52 N12 49
Arran Dr. G52 M12 49
Arran Dr., Cumb. D 1 70
Arran Dr., Giff. R13 62
Arran Dr., John. N08 43
Arran Dr., Pais. O 6 46
Arran La., Chr. E28 15
Burnbrae Av.
Arran Pl., Clyde. E 8 5
Arran Pl., Linw. L 1 28
Arran Rd., Renf. J 8 31
Arran Ter. G73 P18 64
Arranthrue Cres., Renf. H 8 17
Arranthrue Dr., Renf. H 8 17
Arriochmill Rd. G20 H14 20
Kelvin Dr.
Arrochar Ct. G23 F15 21
Sunningdale Rd.
Arrochar Dr. G23 E14 8
Arrochar St. G23 F14 20
Arrol Pl. G40 M19 53
Arrol St. G52 K 9 32
Arrowchar Ct. G23 F15 21
Arrowchar St.
Arrowchar St. G23 F14 20
Arrowsmith Av. G13 F11 19
Arthur Av., Barr. R 7 59
Arthur Rd., Pais. O 6 46
Arthur St. G3 J14 34
Arthur St., Pais. L 5 30
Arthurlie Av., Barr. R 8 59
Arthurlie Dr., Giff. R14 62
Arthurlie St. G51 K12 33
Arthurlie St., Barr. R 8 59
Arundel Dr. G42 O16 51
Arundel Dr., Bish. D19 11
Asbury Ct., Linw. L 2 28
Ascaig Cres. G52 N12 49
Ascog Rd., Bear. E12 7
Ascog St. G42 N16 51
Ascot Av. G12 G12 19
Ascot Ct. G12 G13 20
Ash Gro., Bish. E19 11
Ash Gro., Lenz. C22 12
Ash Gro., Udd. O28 57
Douglas Cres.
Ash Pl., John. N 1 44
Ash Rd., Bail. M25 56
Ash Rd., Cumb. A 4 71
Ash Rd., Dalm. C 6 4

Ash Wk. G73 Q20 65
Ashburton Rd. G12 G13 20
Ashby Cres. G13 E12 7
Ashcroft Dr. G44 P18 64
Ashdale Dr. G52 M12 49
Ashdene Rd. G22 F16 21
Ashfield St. G22 H17 22
Ashfield, Bish. D19 11
Ashgill Pl. G22 G17 22
Ashgill Rd. G22 G16 21
Ashgrove St. G40 N19 53
Ashgrove, Bail. L27 41
Ashkirk Dr. G52 M12 49
Ashlea Dr., Giff. Q14 62
Ashley La. G3 J15 35
Woodlands Rd.
Ashley St. G3 J15 35
Ashmore Rd. G43 P15 63
Ashton Gdns. G12 J14 34
Ashton Rd.
Ashton La. G12 J14 34
University Av.
Ashton Pl. G12 H14 20
Byres Rd.
Ashton Rd. G12 J14 34
University Av.
Ashton Rd. G73 N19 53
Ashton Ter. G12 J14 34
Ashton Rd.
Ashton Way G78 O 3 45
Ashtree Rd. G43 O14 50
Ashvale Cres. G21 H18 22
Ashvale Row E. G21 H18 22
Ashvale Row
Ashvale Row W. G21 H18 22
Ashvale Row
Aspen Pl., John. N 1 44
Athelstane Dr., Cumb. D 1 70
Athelstane Rd. G13 F11 19
Athena Way, Udd. O28 57
Athol Av. G52 K 9 32
Athol Gdns., Bear. B12 7
Athol Ter., Udd. N27 57
Lomond Rd.
Athole Gdns. G12 H14 20
Athole La. G12 H14 20
Saltoun St.
Atholl Cres., Pais. L 9 32
Atholl Dr., Giff. S14 62
Atholl Gdns. G73 Q21 66
Atholl Gdns., Bish. D19 11
Atholl La., Chr. E28 15
Atholl Pl., Linw. L 1 28
Atlas Pl. G21 H18 22
Atlas Rd. G21 H18 22
Atlas St., Clyde. F 7 17
Attlee Av., Clyde. E 8 5
Attlee Pl., Clyde. E 8 5
Attlee Av.
Attow Rd. G43 P13 62
Auburn Dr., Barr. R 8 59
Auburn Pl. G78 L20 37
Auchans Rd., Linw. J 1 28
Auchencrow St. G34 K26 40
Auchendale, Lenz. C24 13
Auchengeich Rd., Chr. D26 14
Auchengill Path G34 J26 40
Auchengill Rd.
Auchengill Pl. G34 J26 40
Auchengill Rd. G34 J26 40
Auchenglen Dr., Chr. E27 15
Auchenlodment Rd., N 1 44
John.
Auchentorlie Quad., M 7 47
Pais.
Auchentorlie St. G11 J12 33
Auchentoshan Av., C 6 4
Clyde.
Auchentoshan Ter. G21 J18 36
Auchentoshen Cotts., C 5 4
Old K.
Auchinairn Rd., Bish. F18 22
Auchinbee Loop Rd., B 1 70
Cumb.
Auchinlea Rd. G34 J24 39
Auchinleck Av. G33 G21 24
Auchinleck Cres. G33 G21 24
Auchinleck Dr. G33 G21 24
Auchinleck Gdns. G33 G21 24
Auchinleck Rd. G33 F21 24

Auchinleck Rd., Clyde, B 7 5
Auchinleck Ter., Clyde. B 7 5
Auchinleck Rd.
Auchinloch Rd., Lenz. D23 13
Auchinloch St. G21 H18 22
Auchmannoch Av., Pais. L 9 32
Auckengreoch Av., O08 43
John.
Auckengreoch Rd., O08 43
John.
Auckland Pl., Dalm. D 5 4
Auckland St. G22 H16 21
Auld Kirk Rd. G72 Q23 67
Auld Rd., The, Cumb. B 3 71
Auld St., Dalm. D 6 4
Auldbar Rd. G52 M12 49
Auldbar Ter., Pais. N 7 47
Auldburn Rd. G43 P13 62
Auldearn Rd. G21 F20 23
Auldgirth Rd. G52 M12 49
Auldhouse Av. G42 P13 62
Harriet St.
Auldhouse Rd. G43 P13 62
Auldhouse Ter. G43 P14 62
Auldhouse Rd.
Aultbea St. G22 F16 21
Aultmore Rd. G33 K24 39
Aurs Cres., Barr. R 8 59
Aurs Dr., Barr. R 8 59
Aurs Pl., Barr. R 8 59
Aurs Rd., Barr. Q 8 59
Aursbridge Dr., Barr. R 8 59
Austen La. G13 G12 19
Skaterig La.
Austen La. G13 G12 19
Woodend Dr.
Austen Rd. G13 G12 19
Avenel Rd. G13 E12 7
Avenue End Rd. G33 H22 24
Avenue St. G40 L19 37
Avenue St. G73 N19 53
Avenue, The, Kilb. N07 42
Low Barholm
Avenuehead Rd., Chr. D27 15
Avenuehead Rd., Gart. F28 27
Avenuepark St. G20 H15 21
Aviemore Gdns., Bear. C13 8
Aviemore Rd. G52 N12 49
Avoch Dr. G46 Q12 61
Avoch St. G34 J25 40
Avon Av., Bear. D13 8
Avon Dr. G64 F19 23
Avon Dr., Linw. L 1 28
Avon Rd., Bish. F19 23
Avon Rd., Giff. R13 62
Avon St. G5 L15 35
Avonbank Rd. G73 O18 52
Avondale Dr., Pais. L 7 31
Avondale St. G33 J22 38
Avonhead Av. G67 D 1 70
Avonhead Gdns. G67 D 1 70
Avonhead Pl. G67 D 1 70
Avonhead Rd. G67 D 1 70
Avonspark St. G21 H19 23
Aylmer Rd. G43 P15 63
Ayr Rd., Giff. R13 62
Ayr St. G21 H18 22
Aytoun Rd. G41 M14 50

Back Causeway G31 L20 37
Back Sneddon St., Pais. L 6 30
Backmuir Rd. G15 D10 6
Bagnell St. G21 G18 22
Bailie Dr., Bear. B11 7
Baillie Dr., Both. Q28 69
Baillieston Rd. G32 M23 55
Baillieston Rd., Udd. N25 56
Bain Sq. G40 L18 36
Bain St.
Bain St. G40 L18 36
Bainsford St. G32 L21 38
Baird Av. G52 K 9 32
Baird Dr., Bear. C11 7
Baird St. G4 J17 36
Bairdsbrae G4 H16 21
Possil Rd.
Baker Pl. G41 N15 51
Baker St.
Baker St. G41 N15 51
Bakewell Rd., Bail. L25 40

Name	Grid	Page
Balaclava St. G2	L16	35
McAlpine St.		
Balado Rd. G33	K24	39
Balbeg St. G51	L12	33
Balbeggie Pl. G32	M23	55
Balbeggie St. G32	M23	55
Balblair Rd. G52	N12	49
Balcarres Av. G12	G14	20
Balcomie St. G33	J22	38
Balcurvie Rd. G34	J25	40
Baldinnie Rd. G34	K25	40
Baldorran Cres., Cumb.	B 1	70
Baldoven Cres. G33	K24	39
Baldovie Rd. G52	M11	49
Baldragon Rd. G34	J25	40
Baldric Rd. G13	G11	19
Baldwin Av. G13	E11	7
Balerno Dr. G52	M12	49
Balfluig St. G34	J24	39
Balfour St. G20	G14	20
Balfron Rd. G51	K12	33
Balfron Rd., Pais.	L 8	31
Balgair Dr., Pais.	L 7	31
Balgair St. G22	G16	21
Balgair Ter. G32	L22	38
Balglass St. G22	H16	21
Balgonie Av. G78	N 4	45
Balgonie Av., Pais.	N 4	46
Balgonie Dr., Pais.	N 5	46
Balgonie Rd. G52	M12	49
Balgonie Woods, Pais.	N 5	46
Balgownie Cres., Thorn.	R13	62
Balgray Cres., Barr.	R 9	60
Balgraybank St. G21	H19	23
Balgrayhill Rd. G21	G18	22
Balintore St. G32	L22	38
Baliol La. G3	J15	35
Woodlands Rd.		
Baliol St. G3	J15	35
Ballaig Av., Bear.	C11	7
Ballaig Cres. G33	G23	25
Ballantay Quad. G45	Q19	65
Ballantay Rd. G45	Q19	65
Ballantay Ter. G45	Q19	65
Ballantyne Rd. G52	K10	32
Ballater Dr., Bear.	E12	7
Ballater Dr., Pais.	N 7	47
Ballater Dr., Renf.	F 5	16
Ballater St. G5	L17	36
Ballayne Dr., Chr.	E28	15
Ballindalloch Dr. G31	K19	37
Balloch Gdns. G52	M12	49
Balloch Vw., Cumb.	C 2	70
Ballochmill Rd. G73	O20	53
Ballogie Rd. G44	O16	51
Balmarino Pl. G64	E20	11
Balmartin Rd. G23	E14	8
Balmeg Av., Giff.	S14	62
Balmerino Pl., Bish.	F20	23
Angus Av.		
Balmoral Cres. G42	N16	51
Queens Dr.		
Balmoral Cres., Renf.	G 6	16
Balmoral Dr. G32	O22	54
Balmoral Dr., Bear.	E13	8
Balmoral Dr., G72	P21	66
Balmoral Gdns., Blan.	R26	68
Balmoral Gdns., Udd.	N27	57
Balmoral Rd., John.	N 1	44
Balmoral St. G14	H10	18
Balmore Pl. G22	G16	21
Balmore Rd. G23	C15	9
Balmore Sq. G22	G16	21
Balmuildy Rd., Bish. G23	D16	9
Balornock Rd. G21	G19	23
Balruddery Pl. G64	F20	23
Balshagray Av. G11	H12	19
Balshagray Cres. G11	J12	19
Balshagray La. G11	H12	19
Balshagray Pl. G11	H12	19
Balshagray Dr.		
Baltic Ct. G40	M19	53
Baltic St.		
Baltic La. G40	M19	53
Baltic Pl. G40	M18	52
Baltic St. G40	M19	53
Balure St. G31	K20	37
Balvaird Cres. G73	O19	53
Balvaird Dr. G73	O19	53
Balveny St. G33	J23	39
Balvicar Dr. G42	N15	51
Balvicar St. G42	N15	51
Balvie Av. G15	E10	6
Balvie Av., Giff.	R14	62
Banavie Rd. G11	H13	20
Banchory Av. G43	P13	62
Banchory Av., Renf.	F 5	16
Banchory Cres., Bear.	E13	8
Banff St. G33	J22	38
Bangorshill St. G46	Q12	61
Bank Rd. G32	O23	55
Bank St. G12	J15	35
Bank St. G72	P22	66
Bank St., Barr.	R 8	59
Bank St., Pais.	M 6	30
Bankbrae Av. G53	P10	60
Bankend St. G33	J22	38
Bankfoot Dr. G52	M10	48
Bankfoot Rd. G52	M10	48
Bankfoot Rd., Pais.	L 4	29
Bankglen Rd. G15	D10	6
Bankhall St. G42	N16	51
Bankhead Av. G13	G10	18
Bankhead Dr. G73	O19	53
Bankhead Rd. G73	P18	64
Bankhead Rd., Waterside	B25	14
Bankier St. G40	L18	36
Banknock St. G32	L21	38
Bankside Av., John.	M09	43
Banktop Pl., John.	M09	43
Banling Green Rd. G44	P16	63
Clarkston Rd.		
Bannatyne Av. G31	K19	37
Banner Dr. G13	E11	7
Banner Rd. G13	E11	7
Bannercross Av., Bail.	L25	40
Bannercross Dr., Bail.	L23	40
Bannercross Gdns., Bail.	L25	40
Bannercross Dr.		
Bannerman Pl., Clyde.	E 8	5
Bannerman St., Clyde.	E 7	5
Bantaskin St. G20	F14	20
Banton Pl. G33	K25	40
Barassie Cres., Cumb.	A 2	70
Barassie Ct., Both.	R27	69
Barbae Pl., Udd.	Q28	69
Hume Dr.		
Barbreck Rd. G42	N15	51
Pollokshaws Rd.		
Barcaldine Av., Chr.	E25	14
Barcaple St. G21	H18	22
Barclay Av., John.	N 1	44
Barclay Sq., Renf.	J 7	31
Barclay St. G21	G18	22
Balgrayhill Rd.		
Barcraigs Dr., Pais.	O 6	46
Bard Av. G13	F10	18
Bardowie St. G22	H16	21
Bardrain Av., John.	N 2	44
Bardrain Rd., Pais.	O 5	46
Bardrill Dr., Bish.	E18	10
Bardykes Rd., Blan.	R26	68
Barfillan Dr. G52	L12	33
Barfillan Rd. G52	L12	33
Bargaran Rd. G53	M10	48
Bargarron Dr., Pais.	K 7	31
Bargeddie St. G33	J20	37
Barhill Cres., Kilb.	N07	42
Barholm Sq. G33	J23	39
Barke Rd., Cumb.	B 3	71
Barlanark Av. G32	K23	39
Barlanark Pl. G32	L23	39
Hallhill Rd.		
Barlanark Pl. G33	K24	39
Barlanark Rd. G33	K23	39
Barlia Dr. G45	Q18	64
Barlia St. G45	Q18	64
Barlia Ter. G45	Q18	64
Barloch St. G22	H17	22
Barlogan Av. G52	L12	33
Barlogan Quad. G52	L12	33
Barmill Rd. G43	P13	62
Barmulloch Rd. G21	H19	23
Barn Grn. G78	M07	42
Barnard Gdns., Bish.	D19	11
Barnard Ter. G40	M19	53
Barnbeth Rd. G53	N10	48
Barnes Rd. G20	G16	21
Barnes St., Barr.	R 7	59
Barnflat St. G73	N19	53
Barnkirk Av. G15	D10	6
Barns St., Clyde.	E 8	5
Barnsford Av., Renf.	H 4	16
Barnsford Rd., Pais.	J 4	29
Barnton St. G32	K21	38
Barnwell Ter. G51	K12	33
Barochan Cres., Pais.	M 4	45
Barochan Rd. G53	M10	48
Baron Rd., Pais.	L 7	31
Baron St., Renf.	J 8	31
Baronald Dr. G12	G13	20
Baronald Gate G12	G13	20
Baronald St. G73	N19	53
Baronhill, Cumb.	A 3	71
Barons Court Dr., John.	M 3	45
Barons Court Gdns.,	M 3	45
John.		
Barons Court Rd., John.	M 3	45
Barons Gate, Both.	Q27	69
Barr Cres., Clyde.	C 7	5
Barr Pl., Pais.	M 5	46
Barr St. G20	H16	21
Barra Av., Renf.	J 8	31
Barra St. G20	F14	20
Barrachnie Cres., Bail.	L24	39
Barrachnie Rd., Bail.	L24	39
Barrack St. G4	L18	36
Barrhead Rd. G43	O 9	48
Barrhead Rd., Pais.	M 7	47
Barrie Quad., Clyde.	D 7	5
Barrie Rd. G52	K10	32
Barrington Dr. G4	J15	35
Barrisdale Rd. G20	F14	20
Barrisdale Way G73	Q19	65
Barrland Dr., Giff.	Q14	62
Barrland St. G41	M16	51
Barrochan Rd., John.	M09	43
Barrowfield St. G40	L19	37
Barrwood St. G33	J21	38
Barshaw Dr., Pais.	L 7	31
Barshaw Pl., Pais.	L 8	31
Barshaw Rd. G52	L 9	32
Barterholm Rd., Pais.	N 6	46
Bartholomew St. G40	M19	53
Bartiebeith Rd. G33	K24	39
Basset Av. G13	F10	18
Basset Cres. G13	F10	18
Bath La. G2	K16	35
Blythswood St.		
Bath La. W. G3	K15	35
North St.		
Bath St. G2	K16	35
Bathgate St. G31	L19	37
Bathgo Av., Pais.	M 9	48
Batson St. G42	N16	51
Battle Pl. G41	O15	51
Battleburn St. G32	M22	54
Battlefield Av. G42	O16	51
Battlefield Cres. G42	O16	51
Battlefield Gdns.		
Battlefield Gdns. G42	O16	51
Battlefield Rd. G42	O16	51
Bavelaw St. G33	J23	39
Bayfield Av. G15	D10	6
Bayfield Ter. G15	D10	6
Beaconsfield Rd. G12	G13	20
Beard Cres., Gart.	G27	27
Beardmore Cotts., Renf.	G 5	16
Beardmore St., Dalm.	D 5	4
Beardmore Way, Dalm.	D 5	4
Bearford Dr. G52	L10	32
Bearsden Rd. G13	F12	19
Beaton Rd. G41	N15	51
Beattock St. G31	L20	37
Beatty St., Dalm.	D 4	4
Beaufort Av. G43	P14	62
Beaufort Gdns., Bish.	E18	10
Beauly Dr., Pais.	N 3	45
Beauly Pl. G20	G14	20
Beauly Pl., Bish.	E20	11
Beauly Pl., Chr.	E26	14
Beauly Rd., Bail.	M25	56
Beaumont Gate G12	J14	34
Bedale Rd., Bail.	M24	55
Bedford Av., Clyde.	E 8	5
Onslow Dr.		
Bedford La. G5	L16	35
Bedford Row G5	L16	35
Dunmore St.		

Name	Map	Pg
Bedford St. G5	L16	35
Bedlay Ct., Chr.	D28	15
Bedlay St. G21	H18	22
Linsburn St.		
Bedlay St. G21	H18	22
Petershill Rd.		
Bedlay Wk., Chr.	D28	15
Beech Av. G41	M13	50
Beech Av. G72	P21	66
Beech Av. G73	Q20	65
Beech Av., Bail.	L25	40
Beech Av., Bear.	C13	8
Beech Av., John.	N 2	44
Beech Av., Pais.	N 7	47
Beech Av. North Av. G72	P21	66
Beech Dr., Dalm.	C 7	5
Beech Gdns., Bail.	L25	40
Beech Gro., Barr.	R 8	59
Arthurlie Av.		
Beech Pl., Bish.	F19	23
Beech Rd., Bish.	F19	23
Beech Rd., John.	N08	43
Beech Rd., Lenz.	C23	13
Beechcroft Pl., Blan.	R27	69
Beeches Av., Clyde.	C 6	4
Beeches Rd., Clyde.	C 6	4
Beeches Ter., Clyde.	C 7	4
Beechgrove St. G40	N19	53
Beechlands Av., Giff.	R15	63
Beechmount Cotts. G14	G 9	18
Dumbarton Rd,		
Beechmount Rd., Lenz.	D23	13
Beechwood Av. G11	H12	19
Beechwood Dr.		
Beechwood Av. G73	P20	65
Beechwood Ct., Bear.	D12	7
Beechwood Dr. G11	H12	19
Beechwood Dr., Renf.	J 7	31
Beechwood La., Bear.	D12	7
Beechwood Ct.		
Beechwood Pl. G11	H12	19
Beechwood Dr.		
Beechwood Rd., Cumb.	C 2	70
Beil Dr. G13	F 9	18
Beith Rd., John.	O07	42
Beith St. G11	J13	34
Belgrave La. G12	H15	21
Belgrave Ter.		
Belgrave Ter. G12	H15	21
Belhaven Cres. La. G12	H14	20
Lorraine Dr.		
Belhaven Ter. G12	H14	20
Belhaven Ter. W. G12	H14	20
Bell St. G1	L17	36
Bell St., Clyde.	F 8	17
Bell St., Renf.	H 8	17
Bellahouston Dr. G52	M12	49
Bellahouston La. G52	M12	49
Bellairs Pl., Blan.	R26	68
Belleisle Av., Udd.	O27	57
Belleisle St. G42	N16	51
Bellevue Pl. G21	J18	36
Bellfield Cres., Barr.	Q 7	59
Bellfield St. G31	L19	37
Bellfield St., Barr.	Q 7	59
Bellgrove St. G31	L18	36
Bellrock Cres. G33	K22	38
Bellrock St. G33	K22	38
Bellscroft Av. G73	O18	52
Bellshaugh La. G12	G14	20
Bellshaugh Pl. G12	G14	20
Bellshaugh Rd. G12	G14	20
Bellshill Rd., Both.	R28	69
Bellshill Rd., Udd.	P27	69
Belltrees Cres., Pais.	M 4	45
Bellwood St. G41	O15	51
Belmar Ct., Linw.	L 2	28
Belmont Av., Udd.	O27	57
Belmont Cres. G12	H15	21
Belmont Dr. G73	O19	53
Belmont Dr., Barr.	R 8	59
Belmont Dr., Giff.	Q13	62
Belmont La. G12	H14	20
Great Western Rd.		
Belmont Rd. G21	G18	22
Belmont Rd. G72	Q21	66
Belmont Rd., Pais.	L 7	31
Belmont St. G12	H15	21
Belmont St., Clyde.	F 7	17
Belses Dr. G52	L11	33
Belstane Pl., Udd.	Q28	69
Appledore Cres.		
Belsyde Av. G15	E10	6
Beltane St. G3	K15	35
Beltrees Av. G53	N10	48
Beltrees Cres. G53	N10	48
Beltrees Rd. G53	N10	48
Belvidere Cres., Bish.	D19	11
Belvoir Pl., Bish.	S26	68
Bemersyde Av. G43	P13	62
Bemersyde Rd. G78	O 3	45
Bemersyde, Bish.	E20	11
Ben Alder Dr., Pais.	N 8	47
Ben Buie Way, Pais.	N 8	47
Ben Ledi Av., Pais.	N 8	47
Ben Lui Dr., Pais.	N 8	47
Ben More Dr., Pais.	N 8	47
Ben Nevis Rd., Pais.	N 8	47
Ben Venue Way, Pais.	N 8	47
Ben Wyvis Dr., Pais.	N 8	47
Benalder St. G11	J14	34
Benarty Gdns., Bish.	E19	11
Bencroft Dr. G44	P18	64
Bengairn St. G31	K20	37
Bengal Pl. G43	O14	50
Christian St.		
Bengal St. G43	O14	50
Benhar Pl. G33	K21	38
Benholme St. G32	M21	54
Benhope Av., Pais.	N 8	47
Benlawers Dr., Pais.	N 8	47
Benloyal Av., Pais.	N 8	47
Benmore St. G21	G18	22
Bennan Sq. G42	N17	52
Benston Pl., John.	N09	43
Benston Rd., John.	N09	43
Bentall St. G5	M17	52
Bentinck St. G3	J15	35
Bents Rd., Bail.	L25	40
Benvane Av., Pais.	N 8	47
Benvie Gdns., Bish.	E19	11
Benview St. G20	H15	21
Benview Ter., Pais.	N 7	47
Berelands Cres. G73	O18	52
Berelands Pl. G73	O18	52
Beresford Av. G14	H12	19
Berkeley St. G3	K15	35
Berkeley Terrace La. G3	J15	35
Elderslie St.		
Berkley Dr., Blan.	R26	68
Bernard Path G40	M19	53
Bernard St. G40	M19	53
Bernard Ter. G40	M19	53
Berneray St. G22	F17	22
Berridale Av. G44	P16	63
Berriedale Av., Bail.	M25	56
Berryburn Rd. G21	H20	23
Berryhill Dr., Giff.	R13	62
Berryhill Rd., Cumb.	C 2	70
Berryhill Rd., Giff.	R13	62
Berryknowes Av. G52	L11	33
Berryknowes La. G52	L11	33
Berryknowes Rd. G52	M11	49
Berryknowes Rd., Chr.	F26	26
Bertram St. G41	N15	51
Bertrohill Ter. G33	K23	39
Stepps Rd.		
Bervie St. G51	L12	33
Berwick Cres., Linw.	K 1	28
Berwick Dr. G52	M10	48
Berwick Dr. G73	O20	53
Betula Dr., Dalm.	C 7	5
Bevan Gro., John.	O08	43
Beverley Rd. G43	P14	62
Bevin Av., Clyde.	E 8	5
Bideford Cres. G32	M23	55
Biggar Pl. G31	L19	37
Biggar St. G31	L19	37
Bigton St. G33	J22	38
Bilbao St. G45	M17	52
Bilsland Dr. G20	G15	21
Binend Rd. G53	O11	49
Binnie Pl. G40	L18	36
Binniehill Rd., Cumb.	B 1	70
Binns Rd. G33	J23	39
Birch Cres., John.	N 1	44
Birch Dr., Lenz.	C23	13
Birch Gro., Udd.	O28	57
Burnhead St.		
Birch Knowle, Bish.	F19	23
Birch Rd., Dalm.	C 7	5
Birch Vw., Bear.	C13	8
Birchfield Dr. G14	H10	18
Birchlea Dr., Giff.	Q14	62
Birchwood Av. G32	M24	55
Birchwood Dr., Pais.	N 4	45
Birchwood Pl. G32	M24	55
Birdston Rd. G21	G20	23
Birgidale Av. G45	R17	64
Birgidale Rd. G45	R17	64
Birgidale Ter. G45	R17	64
Birkdale Ct., Both.	R27	69
Birken Rd., Lenz.	D24	13
Birkenshaw St. G31	K19	37
Birkenshaw Way, Pais.	K 6	30
Abbotsburn Way		
Birkhall Av. G52	M 9	48
Birkhall Av., Renf.	F 5	16
Birkhall Dr., Bear.	E12	7
Birkhill Av., Bish.	D19	11
Birkhill Gdns., Bish.	D20	11
Birkmyre Rd. G51	L12	33
Birks Rd., Renf.	J 7	31
Tower Dr.		
Birkwood St. G40	N19	53
Birmingham Rd., Renf.	J 7	31
Birnam Av., Bish.	D19	11
Birnam Cres., Bear.	C13	8
Birnam Gdns., Bish.	E19	11
Birnam Rd. G31	M20	53
Birness Dr. G43	O14	50
Birness St. G43	O14	50
Birnie Ct. G21	H20	23
Birnie Rd. G21	H20	23
Birnock Av., Renf.	J 9	32
Birsay Rd. G22	F16	21
Bishop Gdns., Bish.	E18	10
Bishop St. G2	K16	35
Bishopmill Pl. G21	H20	23
Bishopmill Rd. G21	H20	23
Bisset Cres., Clyde.	C 6	4
Black St. G4	J17	36
Blackburn Sq., Barr.	R 8	59
Blackburn St. G51	L14	34
Blackburn St. G51	L15	35
Blackbyres Rd., Barr.	P 8	59
Blackcraig Av. G15	D10	6
Blackcroft Gdns. G32	M23	55
Blackcroft Rd. G32	M23	55
Blackfaulds Rd. G73	O18	52
Blackford Cres. G32	M23	55
Blackford Pl. G32	M23	55
Blackford Rd., Pais.	M 7	47
Blackfriars St. G1	K17	36
Blackhall La., Pais.	M 6	46
Blackhall St., Pais.	M 6	46
Blackhill Cotts. G23	E16	9
Blackhill Pl. G33	J20	37
Blackhill Rd. G23	E14	8
Blackie St. G3	J14	34
Blacklands Pl., Lenz.	D24	13
Blacklaw La., Pais.	L 6	30
Blackstone Av. G53	O11	49
Blackstone Cres. G53	N11	49
Blackstone Rd., Candren	K 3	29
Blackstoun Av., Linw.	L 1	28
Blackstoun Oval, Pais.	L 4	29
Blackstoun Rd., Pais.	L 4	29
Blackthorn Av., Lenz.	C22	12
Blackthorn Gro., Lenz.	C22	12
Blackthorn Rd., Cumb.	B 4	71
Blackthorn St. G22	G18	22
Blackwood Av., Linw.	L 1	28
Blackwood St. G13	F12	19
Blackwood St., Barr.	R 7	59
Blackwoods Cres., Chr.	E27	15
Blacurvie Rd. G34	J25	40
Bladda La., Pais.	M 6	46
Blades Ct., Gart.	G28	27
Bladnoch Dr. G15	E11	7
Moraine Av.		
Blaeloch Av. G45	R17	64
Blaeloch Dr. G45	R17	64
Blaeloch Ter. G45	R17	64
Blair Cres., Bail.	M25	56
Blair Rd., Pais.	L 9	32
Blair St. G32	L21	38
Blairatholl Av. G11	H13	20
Blairatholl Gdns. G11	H13	20

Name	Grid	Page
Blairbeth Dr. G44	O16	51
Blairbeth Rd. G73	P19	65
Blairbeth Ter. G73	Q19	65
Blairdardie Rd. G15	E10	6
Blairdenan Av., Chr.	D28	15
Blairgowrie Rd. G52	M11	49
Blairhall Av. G41	O15	51
Blairhill Av., Chr. &	C25	14
Waterside		
Blairlogie St. G33	J22	38
Blairston Av., Both.	R28	69
Blairston Gdns., Both.	R28	69
Blairston Av.		
Blairtum Dr. G73	P19	65
Blairtummock Rd. G32	K23	39
Blake Rd., Cumb.	C 3	71
Blane St. G4	J17	36
Blantyre Cres., Clyde.	B 6	4
Blantyre Farm Rd.,	R26	68
Blan. & Udd.		
Blantyre Mill Rd., Both.	R27	69
Blantyre Rd., Both.	R28	69
Blantyre St. G3	J14	34
Blaven Ct., Bail.	M26	56
Bracadale Rd.		
Blawarthill St. G14	G 9	18
Blenheim Av. G33	G23	25
Blenheim Ct. G33	G24	25
Blenheim Av.		
Blenheim La. G33	G24	25
Blesdale Ct., Clyde.	E 7	5
Blochairn Rd. G21	J19	37
Bluevale St. G31	L19	37
Blyth Pl. G32	L23	39
Blyth Rd., G33	L24	39
Blythswood Av., Renf.	H 8	17
Blythswood Dr., Pais.	L 6	30
Blythswood Rd., Renf.	G 8	17
Blythswood Sq. G2	K16	35
Blythswood St. G2	K16	35
Boclair Av., Bear.	D12	7
Boclair Cres., Bear.	D13	8
Boclair Cres., Bish.	E19	11
Boclair Rd., Bear.	D13	8
Boclair Rd., Bish.	E19	11
Boclair St. G13	F12	19
Boden St. G40	M19	53
Bodmin Gdns., Chr.	D27	15
Gartferry Rd.		
Bogany Ter. G45	R18	64
Bogbain Rd. G34	K25	40
Boghall Rd., Udd.	N25	56
Boghall St. G33	J22	38
Boghead Rd., Lenz.	D22	12
Bogleshole Rd. G72	O21	54
Bogmoor Rd. G51	K11	33
Bogside Pl., Bail.	K26	40
Whamflet Av.		
Bogside Rd. G33	G22	24
Bogside St. G40	M19	53
Bogton Av. G44	Q15	63
Bogton Avenue La. G44	Q15	63
Bogton Av.		
Boleyn Rd. G41	N15	51
Bolivar Ter. G42	O17	52
Bolton Dr. G42	O16	51
Bon Accord St., Clyde.	F 7	17
Bonawe St. G20	H15	21
Kirkland St.		
Boness St. G40	M19	53
Bonhill St. G22	H16	21
Bonnar St. G40	M19	53
Bonnaughton Rd., Bear.	C10	6
Bonnyholm Av. G53	M10	48
Bonnyrigg Dr. G43	P13	62
Bonyton Av. G13	G 9	18
Boon Dr. G15	E10	6
Boquhanran Pl., Clyde.	D 7	5
Albert Av.		
Boquhanran Rd., Clyde	E 6	4
Borden La. G13	G12	19
Borden Rd. G13	G12	19
Boreland Dr. G13	F10	18
Boreland Pl. G13	G10	18
Borgie Cres. G72	P22	66
Borland Rd., Bear.	D13	8
Borron St. G4	H17	22
Borthwick St. G33	J22	38
Boswell Sq. G52	K 9	32
Botanic Cres. G20	H14	20
Bothlyn Cres., Gart.	F27	27
Bothlynn Dr. G33	G23	25
Bothlynn Rd., Chr.	F26	26
Bothwell La. G2	K16	35
West Campbell St.		
Bothwell Park Rd. G71	R28	69
Bothwell Rd., Udd. &	P27	69
Both.		
Bothwell St. G72	P21	66
Bothwell Ter. G12	J15	35
Bank St.		
Bothwick Way, Pais.	O 3	45
Crosbie Dr.		
Boundary Rd. G73	N18	52
Bourne Cres., Renf.	F 5	16
Bourne Ct., Renf.	F 5	16
Bourock Sq., Barr.	R 9	60
Bourtree Dr. G73	Q20	65
Bouverie St. G14	G 9	18
Bouverie St. G73	O18	52
Bowden Dr. G52	L10	32
Bower St. G12	H15	21
Bowerwalls St., Barr.	Q 9	60
Bowes Cres., Bail.	M24	55
Bowfield Av. G52	L 9	32
Bowfield Cres. G52	L 9	32
Bowfield Dr. G52	L 9	32
Bowfield Pl. G52	L 9	32
Bowfield Ter. G52	L 9	32
Bowfield Cres.		
Bowhouse Way G73	Q19	65
Westland Dr.		
Bowling Green La. G14	H11	19
Bowling Green Rd. G14	H11	19
Bowling Green Rd. G32	M23	55
Bowling Green Rd. G44	P16	63
Bowman St. G42	N16	51
Bowmont Gdns. G12	H14	20
Bowmont Hill, Bish.	D19	11
Bowmont Ter. G12	H14	20
Bowmore Gdns. G73	Q21	66
Bowmore Gdns., Udd.	O27	57
Bowmore Rd. G52	L12	33
Boyd St. G42	N16	51
Boydstone Pl. G46	P12	61
Boydstone Rd. G43	P12	61
Boyle St., Clyde.	F 8	17
Boyleston Rd., Barr.	Q 7	59
Boyndie Path G34	K25	40
Boyndie St. G34	K25	40
Brabloch Cres., Pais.	L 6	30
Bracadale Dr., Bail.	M26	56
Bracadale Gdns., Bail.	M26	56
Bracadale Gro., Bail.	M26	56
Bracadale Rd., Bail.	M26	56
Bracken Rd., Barr.	P 7	59
Bracken St. G22	G16	21
Bracken Ter., Udd.	Q28	69
Brackenbrae Av., Bish.	E18	10
Brackenbrae Rd., Bish.	E18	10
Brackenrig Rd. G46	R12	61
Brackla Av. G13	F 9	18
Bracora Pl. G20	G14	20
Glenfinnan Dr.		
Bradan Av. G13	F 9	18
Bradda Av. G73	Q20	65
Bradfield Av. G12	G14	20
Brae Av., Clyde.	B 7	5
Brae Cres., Clyde.	B 7	5
Braeface Rd., Cumb.	C 2	70
Braefield Dr., Thorn.	Q13	62
Braefoot Cres., Pais.	O 6	46
Braehead Rd., Clyde.	B 7	5
Braehead Rd., Cumb.	B 3	71
Braehead Rd., Pais.	P 5	58
Braehead St. G5	M17	52
Braemar Av., Dalm.	D 6	4
Braemar Cres., Bear.	E12	7
Braemar Dr., John.	N 1	44
Braemar Rd. G73	Q21	66
Braemar Rd., Renf.	G 5	16
Braemar St., G42	O15	51
Braemar Vw., Dalm.	C 6	4
Braemount Av., Pais.	P 5	58
Braes Av., Clyde.	F 8	17
Braeside Av. G73	O20	53
Braeside Av., Chr.	E27	15
Braeside Cres., Bail.	L27	41
Braeside Cres., Barr.	R 9	60
Braeside Dr., Barr.	R 8	59
Braeside Pl. G72	Q22	66
Braeside St. G20	H15	21
Braid Sq. G4	J16	35
Braid St. G4	J16	35
Braidbar Farm Rd., Giff.	Q14	62
Braidbar Rd., Giff.	Q14	62
Braidcraft Rd. G53	N11	49
Braidfauld Gdns. G32	M21	54
Braidfauld Pl. G32	N21	54
Braidfauld St. G32	N21	54
Braidfield Rd., Clyde.	C 7	5
Braidholm Cres., Giff.	Q14	62
Braidholm Rd., Giff.	Q14	62
Braidpark Cres., Giff.	Q14	62
Braidpark Dr., Giff.	Q14	62
Braids Rd., Pais.	N 6	46
Bramley Pl., Lenz.	D24	13
Branchock Av. G72	Q23	67
Brand St. G51	L14	34
Brandon Gdns. G72	P21	66
Brandon St. G31	L18	36
Branscroft G78	M07	42
Brassey St. G20	G15	21
Breadalbane Gdns. G73	Q20	65
Breadalbane St. G3	K15	35
Brech Av., Bail.	L27	41
Brechin Rd., Bish.	E20	11
Brechin St. G3	K15	35
Breck Av. G78	O 2	44
Brediland Rd., Linw.	L 1	28
Brediland Rd., Pais.	N 3	45
Bredisholm Dr., Bail.	M26	56
Bredisholm Rd., Bail.	M27	57
Bredisholm Ter., Bail.	M26	56
Brenfield Av. G44	Q15	63
Brenfield Dr. G44	Q15	63
Brentwood Av. G53	Q10	60
Brentwood Dr. G53	Q10	60
Brentwood Sq. G53	Q10	60
Brentwood Sq. G53	Q10	60
Brentwood Dr.		
Brereton St. G42	N17	52
Bressey Rd. G33	L24	39
Breval Cres., Clyde.	B 7	5
Brewery St., John.	M09	43
Brewster Av., Pais.	K 7	31
Briar Dr., Clyde.	D 7	5
Briar Neuk, Bish.	F19	23
Briar Rd. G43	P14	62
Briarlea Dr., Giff.	Q14	62
Briarwood Ct. G32	N24	55
Brick La., Pais.	L 6	30
Bridge of Weir Rd.	L08	43
Kilb. & Linw.		
Bridge St., Dalm.	D 6	4
Bridge St., G72	P22	66
Bridge St., Linw.	L 2	28
Bridge St., Pais.	M 6	46
Bridgebar St., Barr.	Q 9	60
Bridgeburn Dr., Chr.	E27	15
Bridgegate G1	L17	36
Bridgend Rd. G53	O11	49
Bridgeton Cross G40	L18	36
Brigham Pl. G23	F15	21
Broughton Rd.		
Brighton Pl. G51	L13	34
Brighton St. G51	L13	34
Brightside Av., Udd.	P28	69
Brisbane St. G42	O16	51
Brisbane St., Dalm.	D 5	4
Britannia Way, Clyde.	E 7	5
Britannia Way, Renf.	J 8	31
Briton St. G51	L13	34
Broad Pl. G40	L18	36
Broad St.		
Broad St. G40	L18	36
Broadford St. G4	J17	36
Harvey St.		
Broadholm St. G22	G16	21
Broadleys Av., Bish.	D18	10
Broadlie Dr. G13	G10	18
Broadloan, Renf.	J 8	31
Broadwood Dr. G44	P16	63
Brock Oval G53	P11	61
Brock Pl. G53	O11	49
Brock Rd. G53	O11	49
Brock Ter. G53	P11	61
Brock Way G67	C 3	71
North Carbrain Rd.		

Brockburn Rd. G53	N10	48	Brownside Rd.	P20	65	Burnbrae Av., Linw.	L 2	28
Brockburn Ter. G53	O11	49	G72 & G73			*Bridge St.*		
Brockville St. G32	L21	38	Bruce Av., John.	O09	43	Burnbrae Ct., Lenz.	D23	13
Brodick Sq. G64	F19	23	Bruce Av., Pais.	K 7	31	*Auchinloch Rd.*		
Brodick St. G21	J19	37	Bruce Rd. G41	M15	51	Burnbrae Dr. G73	P20	65
Brodie Park Av., Pais.	N 6	46	Bruce Rd., Pais.	L 7	31	*East Kilbride Rd.*		
Brodie Pl., Renf.	J 7	31	Bruce Rd., Renf.	J 7	31	Burnbrae Rd., John.	M 2	44
Brodie Rd. G21	F20	23	Bruce St., Clyde.	E 7	5	Burnbrae Rd., Lenz.	E24	13
Brogknowe, Udd.	O26	56	Bruce Ter., Blan.	R27	69	Burnbrae St. G21	H19	23
Glasgow Rd.			Brucefield Pl. G34	K26	40	Burnbrae, Clyde.	C 7	5
Brook St. G40	L18	36	Brunstance Rd. G34	J25	40	Burncleuch Av., G72	Q22	66
Brooklands Av., Udd.	O27	57	Brunswick Ho., Dalm.	C 5	4	Burncrooks Ct., Clyde.	C 6	4
Brooklea Dr., Giff.	P14	62	*Perth Cres.*			Burndyke Ct. G51	K14	34
Brookside St. G40	L19	37	Brunswick St. G1	K17	36	Burndyke Sq. G51	K14	34
Broom Cres., Barr.	P 7	59	Brunton St. G44	P16	63	Burndyke St. G51	K13	34
Broom Dr., Clyde.	D 7	5	Brunton Ter. G44	Q15	63	Burnett Rd. G33	K24	39
Broom Gdns., Lenz.	C22	12	Bruntsfield Av. G53	Q10	48	Burnfield Av., Giff.	Q13	62
Broom Rd. G43	P14	62	Bruntsfield Gdns. G53	Q10	60	Burnfield Cotts., Giff.	Q13	62
Broom Rd. G67	A 4	71	Brydson Pl., Linw.	L 1	28	Burnfield Dr. G43	Q13	62
Broom Ter., John.	N 1	44	*Fulwood Av.*			Burnfield Gdns., Giff.	Q14	62
Broomdyke Way, Pais.	K 5	30	Buccleuch Av. G52	K 9	32	*Burnfield Rd.*		
Broomfield Av. G21	H19	23	Buccleuch La. G3	J16	35	Burnfield Rd., Giff.	P13	62
Broomfield Rd.			*Scott St.*			Burnfoot Cres. G73	P20	65
Broomfield Av. G72	O20	53	Buccleuch St. G3	J16	35	Burnfoot Cres., Pais.	O 5	46
Broomfield Pl. G21	G18	22	Buchan St. G5	L16	35	Burnfoot Dr. G52	L10	32
Broomfield Rd.			*Norfolk St.*			Burngreen Ter., Cumb.	A 3	71
Broomfield Rd. G21	G18	22	Buchan Ter., G72	Q21	66	Burnham Rd. G14	H10	18
Broomfield Ter., Udd.	N27	57	Buchanan Cres. G64	F20	23	Burnham Ter. G14	H10	18
Broomhill Av. G11	J12	33	Buchanan Dr. G64	F20	23	*Burnham Rd.*		
Broomhill Av. G32	O22	54	Buchanan Dr. G72	P21	66	Burnhead Rd. G43	P15	63
Broomhill Cres. G11	H12	19	Buchanan Dr. G73	P19	65	Burnhead Rd., Cumb.	C 1	70
Broomhill Dr. G11	H12	19	Buchanan Dr., Bear.	D13	8	Burnhead St., Udd.	O28	57
Broomhill Dr. G73	P19	65	Buchanan Dr., Bish.	F20	23	Burnhill Quadrant G73	O18	52
Broomhill Gdns. G11	H12	19	Buchanan Dr., Lenz.	D23	13	Burnhill St. G73	O18	52
Broomhill La. G11	H12	19	Buchanan Gdns. G32	N24	55	Burnhouse St. G20	G14	20
Broomhill Path G11	J12	33	Buchanan St. G1	K16	35	Burnmouth Ct. G33	L24	39
Broomhill Pl. G11	H12	19	Buchanan St., Bail.	M25	56	*Pendeen Rd.*		
Broomhill Rd. G11	J12	33	Buchanan St., John.	N09	43	Burnpark Av., Udd.	O26	56
Broomhill Ter. G11	J12	33	Buchlyvie Path G34	K25	40	Burns Dr., John.	O09	43
Broomieknowe Dr. G73	P19	65	Buchlyvie Rd., Pais.	L 9	32	Burns Gro., Thorn.	R13	62
Broomieknowe Rd. G73	P19	65	Buchlyvie St. G34	K25	40	Burns Rd., Cumb.	C 3	71
Broomielaw G1	L16	35	Buckingham Bldgs.	H14	20	Burns St. G4	J16	35
Broomknowe Pl. G66	D24	13	G12			Burns St., Dalm.	D 6	4
Broomknowe, Cumb.	B 1	70	*Great Western Rd.*			Burnside Av., Barr.	Q 7	59
Broomknowes Rd. G21	H19	23	Buckingham Dr. G32	O22	54	Burnside Cres., Clyde.	B 7	5
Broomlands Av., Renf.	F 5	16	Buckingham Dr. G73	O20	53	Burnside Ct., Dalm.	D 6	4
Broomlands Cres., Renf.	F 5	16	Buckingham St. G12	H14	20	*Scott St.*		
Broomlands Gdns., Renf.	F 5	16	Buckingham Ter. G12	H14	20	Burnside Gate G73	P20	65
Broomlands Rd., Cumb.	D 3	71	*Great Western Rd.*			Burnside Gdns., Kilb.	N 7	42
Broomlands St., Pais.	M 5	46	Bucklaw Gdns. G52	M11	49	Burnside Rd. G73	P20	65
Broomlands Way, Renf.	F 6	16	Bucklaw Pl. G52	M11	49	Burnside Rd., John.	N 2	44
Broomlea Cres., Renf.	F 5	16	Bucklaw Ter. G52	M11	49	Burnside Ter. G72	Q24	67
Broomley Dr. G46	R14	62	Buckley St. G22	G17	22	Burntbroom Dr., Bail.	M24	55
Broomley La., Giff.	R14	62	Bucksburn Rd. G21	H20	23	Burntbroom Gdns.,	M24	55
Broomloan Ct. G51	L13	34	Buddon St. G40	M20	53	Bail.		
Broomloan Pl. G51	L13	34	Budhill Av. G32	L22	38	Burntbroom Rd.,	M24	55
Broomloan Rd. G51	L13	34	Bulldale St. G14	G 9	18	Udd. & Bail.		
Broompark Circus G31	K18	36	Bullionslaw Dr. G73	P20	65	Burntbroom St. G33	K23	39
Broompark Dr. G31	K18	36	Bulloch Av., Giff.	R14	62	Burntshields Rd.,	N06	42
Broompark Dr., Renf.	F 5	16	Bullwood Av. G53	N 9	48	Kilb.		
Broompark St. G31	K18	36	Bullwood Ct. G53	N 9	48	Burr Gdns., Bish.	E20	11
Broomton Rd. G21	F20	23	Bullwood Dr. G53	N 9	48	*Solway Rd.*		
Broomward Dr., John.	M 1	44	Bullwood Gdns. G53	N 9	48	Burrells La. G4	K18	36
Brora Dr., Bear.	D13	8	Bullwood Pl. G53	N 9	48	*High St.*		
Brora Dr., Giff.	R14	62	Bunessan St. G52	L12	33	Burrelton Rd. G43	P15	63
Brora Dr., Renf.	H 9	18	Bunhouse Rd. G3	J14	34	Burton La. G43	N16	51
Brora Gdns., Bish.	E19	11	Burgh Hall La. G11	J13	34	*Langside Rd.*		
Brora La. G31	J20	37	*Fortrose St.*			Bushes Av., Pais.	N 5	46
Brora St.			Burgh Hall St. G11	J13	34	Busheyhill St. G72	P22	66
Brora Rd., Bish.	E19	11	Burgh La. G12	H14	20	Bute Av., Renf.	J 8	31
Brora St. G33	J20	37	*Vinicombe St.*			Bute Cres., Bear.	E12	7
Broughton Dr. G23	F15	21	Burghead Dr. G51	K12	33	Bute Cres., Pais.	O 5	46
Broughton Gdns. G23	E15	9	Burghead Pl. G51	K12	33	Bute Dr., John.	N08	43
Broughton Rd. G23	F15	21	Burgher St. G31	L20	37	Bute Gdns. G12	J14	34
Brown Av., Clyde.	F 8	17	Burleigh Rd., Udd.	O28	69	Bute Gdns. G44	Q16	53
Brown Rd., Cumb.	C 2	70	Burleigh St. G51	K13	34	Bute Ter. G73	P19	65
Brown St. G2	K16	35	Burlington Av. G12	G13	20	Bute Ter., Udd.	O28	57
Brown St., Pais.	L 5	30	Burmola St. G22	H16	21	Butterbiggins Rd. G42	M16	51
Brown St., Renf.	J 7	31	Burmouth Rd. G33	L24	39	Butterfield Pl. G41	N15	51
Brownhill Rd. G43	Q13	62	Burn Gdns., Blan.	R26	68	*Pollokshaws Rd.*		
Brownlie St. G42	O16	51	Burn Ter. G72	O21	54	Byrebush Rd. G53	N11	49
Browns La., Pais.	M 6	46	Burn Vw., Cumb.	B 4	71	Byres Av., Pais.	L 7	31
Brownsdale Rd. G73	O18	52	Burnacre Gdns., Udd.	O27	57	*Byres Cres.*		
Brownside Av. G72	P21	66	Burnbank Dr., Barr.	R 8	59	Byres Cres., Pais.	L 7	31
Brownside Av., Barr.	P 7	59	Burnbank Gdns. G20	J15	35	Byres Rd. G11	J14	34
Brownside Av., Pais.	O 5	46	Burnbank Pl. G4	K18	36	Byres Rd., John.	N 2	44
Brownside Cres., Barr.	P 7	59	*Drygate*			Byron La., Udd.	R28	69
Brownside Dr. G13	G 9	18	Burnbank Ter. G20	J15	35	*Shelly Dr.*		
Brownside Dr., Barr.	P 7	59	Burnbrae Av., Bear.	B13	8	Byron La. G11	J12	33
Brownside Gro., Barr.	P 7	59	Burnbrae Av., Chr.	E28	15	*Sandeman St.*		

Byron St. G11	J12	33
Byron St., Clyde.	D 6	4
Byshot St. G22	H17	22
Cable Depot Rd., Dalm.	E 6	4
Cadder Ct., Bish.	C19	11
Cadder Gro. G20	F15	21
Cadder Rd.		
Cadder Pl. G20	F15	21
Cadder Rd. G20	F15	21
Cadder Rd., Bish.	C19	11
Cadder Way, Bish.	C19	11
Cadoc St., G72	P22	66
Cadogan St. G2	K16	35
Cadzow Av., Giff.	S13	62
Cadzow Dr., G72	P21	66
Caird Dr. G11	J13	34
Cairn Av., Renf.	J 9	32
Cairn Dr., Linw.	L 1	28
Cairn La., Pais.	K 5	30
Mosslands Rd.		
Cairn St. G21	G18	22
Cairnban St. G51	L11	33
Cairnbrook Rd. G34	K26	40
Cairncraig St. G31	M20	53
Cairndow Av. G44	Q15	63
Cairndow Ct. G44	Q15	63
Cairngorm Cres., Barr.	R 8	59
Cairngorm Cres., Bear.	C10	6
Cairngorm Cres., Pais.	N 6	46
Cairngorm Rd. G43	P14	62
Cairnhill Circus G52	M 9	48
Cairnhill Dr. G52	M 9	48
Cairnhill Pl. G52	M 9	48
Cairnhill Circus		
Cairnhill Rd. G61	E12	7
Cairnlea Dr. G51	L13	34
Cairnmuir Rd. G72	R21	66
Cairns Av. G72	P22	66
Cairns Rd. G72	Q22	66
Cairnsmore Pl. G15	E 9	6
Cairnsmore Rd. G15	E 9	6
Cairnswell Av. G72	Q23	67
Cairnswell Pl. G72	Q23	67
Cairntoul Dr. G14	G10	18
Cairntoul Pl. G14	G10	18
Calcots Path G34	J26	40
Auchengill Rd.		
Calcots Pl. G34	J26	40
Caldarvan St. G22	H16	21
Calder Av., Barr.	R 8	59
Calder Dr. G72	P22	66
Calder Gate, Bish.	D18	10
Calder Pl., Bail.	M25	56
Calder Rd., Pais.	L 4	29
Calder Rd., Udd.	P26	68
Calder St. G42	N16	51
Calderbank Vw., Bail.	M26	56
Calderbraes Av., Udd.	O27	57
Caldercuilt Rd. G20	F14	20
Caldercuilt St. G20	F14	20
Calderpark Av., Udd.	N25	56
Calderpark Cres., Udd.	N25	56
Caldervale, Udd.	P26	68
Calderwood Av., Bail.	M25	56
Calderwood Dr., Bail.	M25	56
Calderwood Gdns., Bail.	M25	56
Calderwood Rd. G73	O20	53
Calderwood Rd., G43	P14	62
Caldwell Av. G13	G10	18
Caldwell Av., Linw.	L 1	28
Caledon La. G12	J14	34
Highburgh Rd.		
Caledon St. G12	J14	34
Caledonia Av. G5	M17	52
Caledonia Av. G73	O19	53
Caledonia Dr., Bail.	M25	56
Caledonia Rd. G5	M17	52
Caledonia Rd., Bail.	M25	56
Caledonia St. G5	M17	52
Caledonia St., Dalm.	E 6	4
Caledonia St., Pais.	L 5	30
Caledonian Circuit G72	P23	67
Caledonian Cotts., Both.	R28	69
Caledonian Cres. G12	H14	20
Great Western Rd.		
Caledonian Cres. G12	J15	35
Caledonian Mans. G12	H14	20
Great Western Rd.		
Caledonian Pl. G72	P24	67

Caley Brae, Udd.	P27	69
Calfhill Rd. G53	M10	48
Calfmuir Rd.,	C25	14
Chr. & Waterside		
Calgary St. G4	J17	36
Callander St. G20	H16	21
Callieburn Rd., Bish.	F19	23
Cally Av. G15	D10	6
Calside, Pais.	N 6	46
Calside Av., Pais.	M 5	46
Calton Entry G40	L18	36
Gallowgate		
Calvay Cres. G33	K23	39
Calvay Pl. G33	L24	39
Calvay Rd. G33	K23	39
Cambourne Rd., Chr.	D27	15
Cambridge Av., Clyde.	D 7	5
Cambridge Dr. G20	G14	20
Glenfinnan Dr.		
Cambridge La. G3	J16	35
Cambridge St.		
Cambridge Rd., Renf.	J 8	31
Cambridge St.	K16	35
Camburn St. G32	L21	38
Cambus Pl. G32	J23	39
Cambusdoon Rd. G32	J23	39
Cambuskenneth Gdns.	L24	39
Cambuskenneth Pl. G32	J23	39
Cambuslang Rd. G32	O21	54
Cambuslang Rd.	N19	53
G72 & G73		
Cambusmore Pl. G32	J23	39
Camden St. G5	M17	52
Camelon St. G32	L21	38
Cameron Dr., Bear.	D13	8
Cameron Dr., Udd.	O28	57
Cameron Sq., Clyde.	C 8	5
Glasgow Rd.		
Cameron St. G20	H16	21
Cameron St. G52	K 9	32
Cameron St., Clyde	F 8	17
Camlachie St. G31	L19	37
Camp Rd. G73	N18	52
Camp Rd., Bail.	L25	40
Campbell Dr., Barr.	R 8	59
Campbell Dr., Bear.	C11	7
Campbell St. G20	F14	21
Campbell St., John.	N09	43
Campbell St., Renf.	H 8	17
Camperdown St. G20	H16	21
Garscube Rd.		
Camphill Av. G41	O15	51
Camphill, Pais.	M 5	46
Camps Cres., Renf.	J 9	32
Campsie Av., Barr.	R 8	59
Campsie Dr., Bear.	B12	7
Campsie Dr., Pais.	K 7	31
Campsie Dr., Pais.	O 5	46
Campsie Pl., Chr.	F26	26
Campsie St. G21	G18	22
Campsie Vw., Bail.	L27	41
Campsie Vw., Chr.	F26	26
Campsie Vw., Cumb.	B 3	71
Campsie Vw. G33	H23	25
Campston Pl. G33	J22	38
Camstradden Dr. E., Bear.	D11	7
Camstradden Dr. W., Bear.	D11	7
Camus Pl. G15	D 9	6
Canal Av., John.	M 1	44
Canal Rd., John.	N09	43
Canal St. G4	J17	36
Canal St., Clyde.	F 7	17
Canal St., John.	M 2	44
Canal St., Pais.	M 5	46
Canal St., Renf.	H 8	17
Canal Ter., Pais.	M 6	46
Canberra Av., Dalm.	D 5	4
Cander Rigg, Bish.	D19	11
Candleriggs G1	L17	36
Candren Rd., Linw.	L 2	28
Candren Rd., Pais.	M 4	45
Canmore Pl. G31	M20	53
Canmore St. G31	M20	53
Cannich Dr., Pais.	N 7	47
Canniesburn Rd., Bear.	D11	7
Canniesburn Sq., Bear.	E12	7
Macfarlane Rd.		
Canniesburn Toll, Bear.	D12	7

Canonbie St. G34	J26	40
Canting Way G51	K14	34
Capelrig St. G46	Q12	61
Caplaw Rd., Pais.	P 5	58
Caplethill Rd.,	O 6	46
Pais. & Barr.		
Caprington St. G33	J22	38
Cara Dr. G51	K12	33
Caravelle Way, Renf.	J 8	31
Friendship Way		
Carberry Rd. G41	N14	50
Carbeth St. G22	H16	21
Carbisdale St. G22	G18	22
Carbost St. G23	E14	8
Torgyle St.		
Carbrook St. G21	J19	37
Carbrook St., Pais.	M 5	46
Cardarrach St. G21	H19	23
Cardell Dr., Pais.	M 4	45
Cardell Rd., Pais.	M 4	45
Carding La. G3	K15	35
Argyle St.		
Cardonald Dr. G52	M10	48
Cardonald Gdns. G52	M10	48
Cardonald Place Rd.	M10	48
G52		
Cardow Rd. G21	H20	23
Cardowan Dr. G33	G23	25
Cardowan Rd. G33	G24	25
Cardowan Rd. G33	L21	38
Cardrona St. G33	H22	24
Cardross Ct. G31	K18	36
Cardross St. G31	K18	36
Cardwell St. G41	M16	51
Cardyke St. G21	H19	23
Careston Pl., Bish.	E20	11
Carfin St. G42	N16	51
Carfrae St. G3	K14	34
Cargill St. G31	M21	54
Cargill St. G64	F19	23
Carham Cres. G52	L11	33
Carham Dr. G52	L11	33
Carillon Rd. G51	L14	34
Carisbrooke Cres., Bish.	D19	11
Carlaverock Rd. G43	P14	62
Carleith Av., Clyde.	C 6	4
Carleith Quad. G51	K11	33
Carleith Ter., Clyde.	C 6	4
Carleith Av.		
Carleston St. G21	H18	22
Carleton Dr., Giff.	Q14	62
Carleton Gate, Giff.	Q14	62
Carlibar Av. G13	G 9	18
Carlibar Dr., Barr.	Q 8	59
Carlibar Gdns., Barr.	Q 8	59
Commercial Rd.		
Carlibar Rd., Barr.	Q 7	59
Carlile La., Pais.	L 6	30
New Sneddon St.		
Carlile Pl., Pais.	L 6	30
Carlisle St. G21	H17	22
Carlowrie Av., Blan.	R26	68
Carlton Ct. G5	L16	35
Carlton Pl. G5	L16	35
Carlton Ter. G20	H15	21
Wilton St.		
Carlyle Av. G52	K 9	32
Carlyle Rd., Pais.	L 6	30
Carlyle Ter. G73	N19	53
Carmaben Rd. G33	K24	39
Carment Dr. G41	O14	50
Carment La. G41	O14	50
Carmichael Pl. G42	O15	51
Carmichael St. G51	L13	34
Carmunnock By-pass	R17	64
G44		
Carmunnock La. G44	P16	63
Madison Av.		
Carmunnock Rd. G44	O16	51
Carmyle Av. G32	N22	54
Carna Dr. G44	P17	64
Carnarvon St. G3	J15	35
Carnbooth Ct. G42	R18	64
Carnbroe St. G20	J16	35
Carnegie Rd. G52	L10	32
Carnock Cres., Barr.	R 7	59
Carnock St. G53	O11	49
Carnoustie Cres., Bish.	E20	11
Carnoustie Ct., Both.	R27	69
Carnoustie St. G5	L15	35

Churchill Way, Bish.	E18	10
Kirkintilloch Rd.		
Circus Dr. G31	K18	36
Circus Pl. G31	K18	36
Circus Place La. G31	K18	36
Circus Pl.		
Civic Way, Lenz.	B23	13
Kirkintilloch Rd.		
Clachan Dr. G51	K12	33
Skipness Dr.		
Claddens Pl., Lenz.	D24	13
Claddens Quad. G22	G17	22
Claddens St. G22	G16	21
Claddens Wynd G66	D24	13
Claddon Vw., Clyde.	D 8	5
Kirkoswald Dr.		
Clair Rd., Bish.	E20	11
Clairmont Gdns. G3	J15	35
Clare St. G21	J19	37
Claremont Av., Giff.	R14	62
Claremont Pl. G3	J15	35
Claremont Ter.		
Claremont St. G3	K15	35
Claremont Ter. G3	J15	35
Claremont Terrace La.	J15	35
G3		
Clifton St.		
Clarence Dr. G11	H13	20
Clarence Gdns. G11	H13	20
Clarence St., Clyde.	D 8	5
Clarence St., Pais.	L 7	31
Clarendon La., G20	J16	35
Clarendon St.		
Clarendon Pl. G20	J16	35
Clarendon St. G20	J16	35
Clarion Cres. G13	F10	18
Clarion Rd. G13	F10	18
Clark St. G41	L15	35
Tower St.		
Clark St., Dalm.	D 6	4
Clark St., John.	M09	43
Clark St., Pais.	L 5	30
Clark St., Renf.	H 7	17
Clarkston Av. G44	Q15	63
Clarkston Rd. G44	R15	63
Clathic Av., Bear.	D13	8
Claude Av. G72	Q24	67
Claude Rd., Pais.	L 7	31
Claudhall Av., Gart.	F27	27
Clavens Rd. G52	L 9	32
Claverhouse Pl., Pais.	M 7	47
Claverhouse Rd. G52	K 9	32
Clavering St. E., Pais.	L 5	30
Well St.		
Clavering St. W., Pais.	L 5	30
King St.		
Clayhouse Rd. G33	G24	25
Claypotts Pl. G33	J22	38
Claypotts Rd. G33	J22	38
Clayslaps Rd. G3	J14	34
Argyle St.		
Claythorn Av. G40	L18	36
Claythorn Circus G40	L18	36
Claythorn Av.		
Claythorn Ct. G40	L18	36
Claythorn Pk.		
Claythorn Pk. G40	L18	36
Claythorn Ter. G40	L18	36
Claythorn Pk.		
Clayton Ter. G31	K18	36
Cleddans Cres., Clyde.	C 8	5
Cleddans Rd., Clyde.	C 8	5
Cleddens Ct., Bish.	E10	11
Cleeves Pl. G53	P10	60
Cleeves Quadrant G53	P10	60
Cleeves Rd. G53	P10	60
Cleghorn St. G22	H16	21
Cleland La. G5	L17	36
Cleland St.		
Cleland St. G5	L17	36
Clelland Av., Bish.	F19	23
Clerwood St. G32	L20	37
Cleveden Cres. G12	G13	20
Cleveden Cres. La. G12	G13	20
Cleveden Dr.		
Cleveden Dr. G12	G13	20
Cleveden Dr. G73	P20	65
Cleveden Gdns. G12	G14	20
Cleveden Pl. G12	G13	20
Cleveden Rd. G12	G13	20
Cleveland St. G3	K15	35
Cliff Rd. G3	J15	35
Clifford Gdns. G51	L13	34
Clifford La. G51	L14	34
Gower St.		
Clifford Pl. G51	L14	34
Clifford St.		
Clifford St. G51	L13	34
Clifton Pl. G3	J15	35
Clifton St.		
Clifton Rd., Giff.	Q13	62
Clifton St. G3	J15	35
Clifton Ter. G72	Q21	66
Clifton Ter., John.	N 1	44
Clincart Rd. G42	O16	51
Clincarthill Rd. G73	O19	53
Clinton Av., Udd.	P27	69
Clippens Rd., Linw.	L 1	28
Cloan Av. G15	E10	6
Cloan Cres., Bish.	D19	11
Cloberhill Rd. G13	E11	7
Cloch St. G33	K22	38
Clochoderick Av., Kilb.	N07	42
Mackenzie Dr.		
Clonbeith St. G33	J24	39
Closeburn St. G22	G17	22
Cloth St., Barr.	R 8	59
Clouden Rd., Cumb.	C 3	71
Cloudhowe Ter., Blan.	R26	68
Clouston Ct. G20	H15	21
Clouston La. G20	H14	20
Clouston St.		
Clouston St. G20	H14	20
Clova Pl., Udd.	P27	69
Clova St. G46	Q12	61
Clover Av., Bish.	E18	10
Cloverbank St. G21	J19	37
Clovergate, Bish.	E18	10
Clunie Rd. G52	M12	49
Cluny Av., Bear.	E13	8
Cluny Dr., Bear.	E13	8
Cluny Dr., Pais.	L 7	31
Cluny Gdns. G14	H12	19
Cluny Gdns., Bail.	M25	56
Cluny Vill. G14	H11	19
Westland Dr.		
Clutha St. G51	L15	35
Paisley Rd. W.		
Clyde Av., Barr.	R 8	59
Clyde Av., Both.	R27	69
Clyde Cres., Blan.	S26	68
Clyde Ct., Dalm.	D 6	4
Little Holm		
Clyde Pl. G5	L16	35
Clyde Pl. G72	Q23	67
Clyde Pl., John.	O08	43
Clyde Rd., Pais.	K 7	31
Clyde St. G1	L16	35
Clyde St., Clyde.	F 8	17
Clyde St., Renf.	G 8	17
Clyde Ter., Both.	R28	69
Clyde Vale G71	R28	69
Clyde Vw. G71	R28	69
Clyde Vw., Pais.	N 7	47
Clydebrae Dr. G71	R28	69
Clydebrae St. G51	K13	34
Clydeford Dr. G32	M21	54
Clydeford Dr., Udd.	O26	56
Clydeford Rd. G72	O22	54
Clydeham Ter., Clyde.	F 8	17
Clydeholm Rd. G14	J11	33
Clydeneuk Dr., Udd.	O26	56
Clydesdale Av.,	J 7	31
Pais. & Renf.		
Clydeside Expressway	H11	19
G14		
Clydeside Rd. G73	N18	52
Clydesmill Dr. G32	O22	54
Clydesmill Gro. G32	O22	54
Clydesmill Pl. G32	O22	54
Clydesmill Rd. G32	O22	54
Clydeview G11	J13	34
Dumbarton Rd.		
Clydeview La. G11	J12	33
Broomhill Ter.		
Clydeview Ter. G32	O23	55
Clydeview Ter. G40	M18	52
Newhall St.		
Clynder St. G51	L13	34
Clyth Dr., Giff.	R14	62
Coalhill St. G31	L19	37
Coatbridge Rd., Bail.	L27	41
Coatbridge Rd., Gart.	H27	27
Coates Cres. G53	O11	49
Coats Cres., Bail.	L25	40
Coats Dr., Pais.	M 4	45
Coatshill Av., Blan.	R26	68
Cobbleriggs Way, Udd.	P27	69
Cobinshaw St. G32	L22	38
Cobinton Pl. G38	J22	38
Coburg St. G5	L16	35
Coburg St. G5	L16	35
Bedford St.		
Cochno Rd., Clyde.	B 7	5
Cochno St., Clyde.	F 8	17
Cochran St., Pais.	M 6	46
Cochrane St. G1	K17	36
Cochrane St., Barr.	R 7	59
Cochranemill Rd., John.	N08	43
Cockels Loan, Renf.	J 7	31
Cockenzie St. G32	L22	38
Cockmuir St. G21	H19	23
Cogan Rd. G43	P14	62
Cogan St. G43	O14	50
Cogan St., Barr.	R 7	59
Colbert St. G40	M18	52
Colbreggan Cr., Clyde.	C 8	5
St. Helena Cres.		
Colbreggan Gdns.,	C 8	5
Clyde.		
Colchester Dr. G12	G13	20
Coldingham Av. G14	G 9	18
Coldstream Dr. G73	P20	65
Coldstream Dr., Pais.	N 4	45
Coldstream Pl. G21	H17	22
Keppochhill Rd.		
Coldstream Rd., Clyde.	E 7	5
Colebrook St. G72	P22	66
Colebrook Ter. G12	H15	21
Colebrooke St.		
Colebrooke La. G12	H15	21
Colebrooke St.		
Colebrooke Pl. G12	H15	21
Belmont St.		
Colebrooke St. G12	H15	21
Coleridge, Udd.	Q28	69
Colfin St. G34	J26	40
Colgrain St. G20	G16	21
Colinbar Circle, Barr.	R 7	59
Colinslee Av., Pais.	N 6	46
Colinslee Cres., Pais.	N 6	46
Colinslee Dr., Pais.	N 6	46
Colinslie Rd. G53	O11	49
Colinton Pl. G32	K22	38
Colintraive Av. G33	H21	24
Coll Av., Renf.	J 8	31
Coll Pl. G21	J19	37
Coll St. G21	J19	37
Colla Gdns., Bish.	E20	11
College La. G1	L17	36
High St.		
College St. G1	K17	36
Collessie Dr. G33	J23	39
Collier St., John.	M09	43
Collina St. G20	G14	20
Collins St. G4	K18	36
Collins St., Clyde.	C 8	5
Collylin Rd., Bear.	D12	7
Colmonell Av. G13	F 9	18
Colonsay Av., Renf.	J 8	31
Colonsay Rd. G52	L12	33
Colonsay Rd., Pais.	O 5	46
Colquhoun Av. G52	K10	32
Colquhoun Dr., Bear.	C11	7
Colston Av., Bish.	F18	22
Colston Dr., Bish.	F18	22
Colston Gdns., Bish.	F18	22
Colston Path, Bish.	F18	22
Colston Gdns.		
Colston Pl., Bish.	F18	22
Colston Rd., Bish.	F18	22
Coltmuir St. G22	G16	21
Coltness La. G33	K23	39
Coltness St. G33	K23	39
Coltpark Av., Bish.	F18	22
Coltpark La., Bish.	F18	22
Coltsfoot Dr. G53	Q10	60
Columba Path , Clyde.	E 8	5
Onslow Rd.		
Columba St. G51	K13	34

Street	Grid	Page
Colvend Dr. G73	Q19	65
Colvend St. G40	M18	52
Colville Dr. G73	P20	65
Colwood Av. G53	Q10	60
Colwood Gdns. G53	Q10	60
Colwood Rd.		
Colwood Path G53	Q10	60
Parkhouse Rd.		
Colwood Pl. G53	Q10	60
Colwood Sq. G53	Q10	60
Colwood Av.		
Comedie Rd. G33	H24	25
Comely Park St. G31	L19	37
Comley Pl. G31	L19	37
Gallowgate		
Commerce St. G5	L16	35
Commercial Ct. G5	L17	36
Commercial Rd. G5	M17	52
Commercial Rd., Barr.	Q 8	59
Commonhead Rd. G34	K26	40
Commonhead Rd., Bail.	K27	41
Commore Av., Barr.	R 8	59
Commore Dr. G13	F10	18
Comrie Rd. G33	G23	25
Comrie St. G32	M22	54
Cona St. G46	Q12	61
Conan Ct. G72	P23	67
Condorrat Ring Rd., Cumb.	D 1	70
Congleton St. G53	P 9	60
Nitshill Rd.		
Congress Rd. G3	K15	35
Conifer Pl., Lenz.	C22	12
Conisborough Path G34	J24	39
Balfluig St.		
Conisborough Rd. G34	J24	39
Connal St. G40	M19	53
Conniston St. G32	K21	38
Conon Av. Bear.	D11	7
Consett La. G33	K23	39
Consett St. G33	K23	39
Consett La.		
Contin Pl. G12	G14	20
Convair Way, Renf.	J 8	31
Lismore Av.		
Conval Way, Pais.	K 5	30
Abbotsburn Way		
Cook St. G5	L16	35
Coopers Well La. G11	J14	34
Dumbarton Rd.		
Coopers Well St. G11	J14	34
Dumbarton Rd.		
Copland Pl. G51	L13	34
Copland Quad. G51	L13	34
Copland Rd. G51	L13	34
Coplaw St. G42	M16	51
Copperfield La., Udd.	O28	57
Hamilton Vw.		
Corbett St. G32	M22	54
Corbiston Way, Cumb.	C 3	71
Cordiner St. G44	O16	51
Corkerhill Gdns. G52	M12	49
Corkerhill Pl. G52	N11	49
Corkerhill Rd. G52	N11	49
Corlaich Av. G42	O18	52
Corlaich Dr. G42	O18	52
Corn St. G4	J16	35
Cornaig Rd. G53	O10	48
Cornalee Gdns. G53	O10	48
Cornalee Pl. G53	O10	48
Cornalee Rd. G53	O10	48
Cornhill St. G21	G19	23
Cornoch St. G23	E14	8
Torrin Rd.		
Cornock Cres., Clyde.	D 7	5
Cornock St., Clyde.	D 7	5
Cornwall Av. G73	P20	65
Cornwall St. G41	L14	34
Coronation Pl., Gart.	F27	27
Coronation Way, Bear.	E13	8
Corpach Pl. G34	J26	40
Corran St. G33	K21	38
Corrie Dr., Pais.	M 9	48
Corrie Gro. G44	Q15	63
Corrie Pl., Lenz.	D24	13
Corrour Rd. G43	O14	50
Corse Rd. G52	L 9	32
Corsebar Av., Pais.	N 5	46
Corsebar Cres. Pais.	N 5	46
Corsebar Dr., Pais.	N 5	46
Corsebar La. G78	N 4	45
Balgonie Av.		
Corsebar Rd., Pais.	N 5	46
Corseford Av., John.	O08	43
Corsehill Pl. G34	K26	40
Corsehill St. G34	K26	40
Corselet Rd. G53	Q10	60
Corsewall Av. G32	M24	55
Corsford Dr. G53	P11	61
Corsock St. G31	K20	37
Corston St. G33	K20	37
Cortachy Pl., Bish.	E20	11
Coruisk Way	O 3	45
Spencer Dr.		
Coruisk Way, Pais.	O 3	45
Spencer Dr.		
Corunna St. G3	K15	35
Coshneuk Rd. G33	G22	24
Cottar St. G20	F15	21
Cotton Av., Linw.	L 1	28
Cotton Rd. G40	N19	53
Cotton St., Pais.	M 6	46
Coulters La. G40	L18	36
Countess Wk., Bail.	L28	41
County Av. G72	O20	53
County Pl., Pais.	L 6	30
Moss St.		
County Sq., Pais.	L 6	30
Couper St. G4	J17	36
Courthill Av. G44	P16	63
Coustonhill St. G43	O14	50
Pleasance St.		
Coustonholm Rd. G43	O14	50
Coventry Dr. G31	K19	37
Cowal Dr., Linw.	L 1	28
Cowal Rd. G20	F14	20
Cowal St. G20	F14	20
Cowan Clo., Barr.	Q 8	59
Cowan Cres.	R 8	59
Cowan La. G12	J15	35
Cowan St.		
Cowan Rd., Cumb.	A 1	70
Cowan St. G12	J15	35
Cowan Wilson Av., Blan.	S26	68
Cowcaddens Rd. G2	J16	35
Cowden Dr., Bish.	D19	11
Cowden St. G51	K11	33
Cowdenhill Circus G13	F11	19
Cowdenhill Pl. G13	F11	19
Cowdenhill Rd. G13	F11	19
Cowdie St., Pais.	K 5	30
Cowdray Cres., Renf.	H 8	17
Cowell Vw., Clyde.	D 7	5
Granville St.		
Cowglen Pl. G53	O11	49
Cowglen Rd.		
Cowglen Rd. G53	O11	49
Cowglen Ter. G53	O11	49
Cowie St. G41	L15	35
Cowlairs Rd. G21	H18	22
Coxhill St. G21	H17	22
Coxton Pl. G33	J23	39
Coylton Rd. G43	P15	63
Craggan Dr. G14	G 9	18
Cragielea St. G31	K19	37
Crags Av., Pais.	N 6	46
Crags Cres., Pais.	N 6	46
Crags Rd., Pais.	N 6	46
Craig Rd. G44	P16	63
Craig Rd., Linw.	K 1	28
Craigallian Av. G72	Q23	67
Craiganour La. G43	P14	62
Craiganour Pl. G43	P14	62
Craigard Pl. G73	Q21	66
Inverclyde Gdns.		
Craigbank Dr. G53	P10	60
Craigbank St. G22	H17	22
Craigbarnet Cres. G33	H22	24
Craigbo Av. G23	E14	8
Craigbo Ct. G23	F14	20
Craigbo Dr. G23	F14	20
Craigbo Pl. G23	F14	20
Craigbo Rd. G23	F14	20
Craigbo St. G23	E14	8
Craigbog Av., John.	N08	43
Craigdonald Pl., John.	M09	43
Craigellan Rd. G43	P14	62
Craigenbay Cres., Lenz.	C23	13
Craigenbay Rd., Lenz.	D23	13
Craigenbay St. G21	H19	23
Craigencart Ct., Clyde.	C 6	4
Gentle Row		
Craigend Dr., Coat.	M29	57
Craigend Rd. G13	G12	19
Craigend St. G13	G12	19
Craigendmuir Rd. G33	H24	25
Craigendmuir St. G33	J20	37
Craigendon Oval, Pais.	P 5	58
Craigendon Rd., Pais.	P 5	58
Craigends Dr., Kilb.	M07	42
High Barholm		
Craigenfeoch Av., John.	N08	43
Craigfaulds Av., Pais.	N04	45
Craigflower Gdns. G53	Q10	60
Craigflower Rd. G53	Q10	60
Craighalbert Rd. G68	B 1	70
Craighall Rd. G4	J16	35
Craighead Av. G33	H20	23
Craighead St., Barr.	R 7	59
Craighead Way, Barr.	R 7	59
Craighouse St. G33	J22	38
Craigie Pk. G66	C24	13
Craigie St. G42	N16	51
Craigiebar Dr., Pais.	O 5	46
Craigieburn Gdns. G20	F13	20
Craigieburn Rd., Cumb.	C 2	70
Craigiehall Pl. G51	L14	34
Craigielea Dr., Pais.	L 5	30
Craigielea Rd. G81	B 6	4
Craigielea Rd., Renf.	H 8	17
Craigielinn Av., Pais.	P 5	58
Craigievar St. G33	J24	39
Craigleith St. G32	L21	38
Craiglockhart St. G33	J23	39
Craigmaddie Ter. La. G3	K15	35
Derby St.		
Craigmillar Rd. G42	O16	51
Craigmont Dr. G20	G15	21
Craigmont St. G20	G15	21
Craigmore Rd., Bear.	B10	6
Craigmore St. G31	L20	37
Craigmount Av., Pais.	P 5	58
Craigmuir Cres. G52	L 9	32
Craigmuir Pl. G52	L 9	32
Craigmuir Rd.		
Craigmuir Rd. G52	L 9	32
Craigneil St. G33	J24	39
Craignestock St. G40	L18	36
Craignethan Gdns. G11	J13	34
Lawrie St.		
Craignure Rd. G73	Q19	65
Craigpark Dr. G31	K19	37
Craigpark G31	K19	37
Craigpark Ter. G31	K19	37
Craigpark		
Craigpark Way, Udd.	O28	57
Newton Dr.		
Craigs Av., Clyde.	C 8	5
Craigston Pl., John.	N09	43
Craigston Rd., John.	N09	43
Craigton Av., Barr.	R 9	60
Craigton Dr. G51	L12	33
Craigton Dr., Barr.	R 9	60
Craigton Pl. G51	L12	33
Craigton Pl., Blan.	R26	68
Craigton Rd. G51	L12	33
Craigvicar Gdns. G32	L23	39
Hailes Av.		
Craigview Av., John.	O08	43
Craigwell Av. G73	P20	65
Crail St. G31	L20	37
Cramond Av., Renf.	J 9	32
Cramond St. G5	N17	52
Cramond Ter. G32	L22	38
Cranberry Rd. G12	G13	20
Cranbrooke Dr. G20	F14	20
Cranhill St. G33	J20	37
Cranston St. G3	K15	35
Cranworth La. G12	H14	20
Great George St.		
Cranworth St. G12	H14	20
Crarae Av., Bear.	E12	7
Crathie Dr. G11	J13	34
Crathie La. G11	J13	34
Exeter Dr.		
Craw Rd., Pais.	M 5	46
Crawford Av., Lenz.	D23	13
Crawford Cres., Blan.	R26	68
Crawford Cres., Udd.	O27	57

Street	Grid	Page
Crawford Ct., Giff.	R13	62
Milverton Rd.		
Crawford Dr. G15	E 9	6
Crawford La. G11	J13	34
Crawford Path G11	J13	34
Crawford St.		
Crawford St. G11	J13	34
Crawfurd Dr., Pais.	L 4	29
Crawford Gdns. G73	Q19	65
Crawfurd Rd. G73	Q19	65
Crawriggs Av., Lenz.	C23	13
Crebar Dr., Barr.	R 8	59
Crebar St. G46	Q12	61
Credon Gdns. G73	Q20	65
Cree Av., Bish.	E20	11
Cree Gdns. G32	L21	38
Kilmany Dr.		
Creran St. G40	L18	36
Tobago St.		
Crescent Ct., Dalm.	D 6	4
Swindon St.		
Crescent Rd. G13	G10	18
Cresswell La. G12	H14	20
Great George St.		
Cresswell St. G12	H14	20
Cressy St. G11	K12	33
Crest Av. G13	F10	18
Crestlea Av., Pais.	O 6	46
Creswell Ter., Udd.	O27	57
Kylepark Dr.		
Crichton Ct. G42	R18	64
Crichton St. G21	H18	22
Crieff Ct. G3	K15	35
North St.		
Criffell Gdns. G32	M23	55
Criffell Rd. G32	M23	55
Crimea St. G2	K16	35
Crinan Gdns., Bish.	E19	11
Crinan Rd., Bish.	E19	11
Crinan St. G31	K19	37
Cripps Av., Clyde.	E 8	5
Croft Rd. G73	P22	66
Croft Wynd, Udd.	P28	69
Croftbank Av. G71	R28	69
Croftbank Cres., Both.	R28	69
Croftbank Cres., Udd.	P27	69
Croftbank St. G21	H18	22
Croftbank St., Udd.	P27	69
Croftburn Dr. G44	Q17	64
Croftcroighn Rd. G33	J22	38
Croftend Av. G44	P18	64
Croftfoot Rd. G44	Q17	64
Croftfoot Cotts., Gart.	G28	27
Croftfoot Cres. G45	Q19	65
Croftfoot Dr. G45	Q18	64
Croftfoot Quad. G45	Q18	64
Croftfoot Rd. G45	Q17	64
Croftfoot St. G45	Q19	65
Croftfoot Ter. G45	Q18	64
Crofthead St., Udd.	P27	69
Crofthill Av., Udd.	P27	69
Crofthill Rd. G44	P17	64
Crofthouse Dr. G44	Q18	64
Croftmont Av. G44	Q18	64
Croftmoraig Av., Chr.	D28	15
Crofton Av. G44	Q17	64
Croftpark Av. G44	Q17	64
Croftpark Rd., Clyde.	B 7	5
Croftside Av. G44	Q18	64
Croftspar Av. G32	L23	39
Croftspar Dr. G32	L23	39
Croftspar Pl. G32	L23	39
Croftwood Av. G44	Q17	64
Croftwood, Bish.	D19	11
Cromart Pl., Chr.	E26	14
Cromarty Av. G43	P15	63
Cromarty Av., Bish.	E20	11
Cromarty Gdns., Clark.	R16	63
Crombie Gdns., Bail.	M25	56
Cromdale St. G51	L12	33
Cromer La., Pais.	K 5	30
Abbotsburn Way		
Cromer St. G20	G15	21
Cromer Way, Pais.	K 5	30
Mosslands Rd.		
Crompton Av. G44	P16	63
Cromwell La. G20	J16	35
Cromwell St.		
Cromwell St. G20	J16	35
Cronberry Quad. G52	M 9	48
Cronberry Ter. G52	M 9	48
Crookedshields Rd. G72	R22	66
Crookston Av. G52	M10	48
Crookston Ct. G52	M10	48
Crookston Dr. G52	M 9	48
Crookston Gdns. G52	M 9	48
Crookston Gro. G52	M10	48
Crookston Pl. G52	M 9	48
Crookston Quad. G52	M 9	48
Crookston Rd. G52	N10	48
Crookston Ter. G52	M10	48
Crookston Rd.		
Crosbie Dr. G78	O 3	45
Crosbie St. G20	F14	20
Crosbie Woods, Pais.	N 4	45
Cross Arthurlie St.,	R 7	59
Barr.		
Cross Rd., Pais.	N 4	45
Cross St. G32	N23	55
Cross St., Pais.	M 5	46
Cross, The, G1	L17	36
Cross, The, Pais.	L 6	30
Crossbank Av. G42	N18	52
Crossbank Dr. G42	N18	52
Crossbank Rd. G42	N17	52
Crossbank Ter. G42	N17	52
Crossflat Cres., Pais.	L 7	31
Crossford Dr. G23	E15	9
Crosshill Av. G42	N16	51
Crosshill Av., Lenz.	C23	13
Crosshill Dr. G73	P19	65
Crosshill Rd.,	C20	11
Bish. & Lenz.		
Crosshill Sq., Bail.	M26	56
Crosslee St. G52	L12	33
Crosslees Ct., Thorn.	Q12	61
Main St.		
Crosslees Dr., Thorn.	Q12	61
Crosslees Pk., Thorn.	Q12	61
Crosslees Rd., Thorn.	R12	61
Crossloan Pl. G51	K12	33
Crossloan Rd. G51	K12	33
Crossloan Ter. G51	K12	33
Crossmill Av., Barr.	Q 8	59
Crossmyloof Gdns.	N14	50
G41		
Crosspoint Dr. G23	E15	9
Invershiel Rd.		
Crosstobs Rd. G53	N10	48
Crovie Rd. G53	O10	48
Crow Ct., The, Bish.	E18	10
Kenmure Av.		
Crow La. G13	G12	19
Crow Rd. G11	H12	19
Crow Wood Rd., Chr.	F25	26
Crowflats Rd., Udd.	P27	69
Lady Isle Cres.		
Crowhill Rd. G64	F18	22
Crowhill St. G22	G17	22
Crowlin Cres. G33	K22	38
Crown Av., Clyde.	D 7	5
Crown Circuit G12	H13	20
Crown Rd. S.		
Crown Circus G12	H13	20
Crown Ct. G1	K17	36
Virginia St.		
Crown Gdns. G12	H13	20
Crown Rd. N.		
Crown Mansions G11	H13	20
North Gardner St.		
Crown Rd. N. G12	H13	20
Crown Rd. S. G12	H13	20
Crown St. G5	M17	52
Crown St., Bail.	M24	55
Crown Ter. G12	H13	20
Crown Rd. S.		
Crownpoint Rd. G40	L18	36
Crowpoint Rd. G40	L19	37
Alma St.		
Crowwood Ter., Chr.	F25	26
Croy Pl. G21	G20	23
Rye Rd.		
Croy Pl. G21	G20	23
Croy Rd.		
Croy Rd. G21	G20	23
Cruachan Av., Renf.	J 8	31
Cruachan Cres., Pais.	O 6	46
Cruachan Dr., Barr.	R 8	59
Cruachan Rd. G73	Q20	65
Cruachan Rd., Bear.	B10	6
Ledi Dr.		
Cruachan St. G46	Q12	61
Cruachan Way, Barr.	R 8	59
Cruden St. G51	L12	23
Crum Av., Thorn.	Q13	62
Crusader Av. G13	E11	7
Cubie St. G40	L18	36
Cuilhill Rd., Bail.	K27	41
Cuillin Way, Barr.	R 8	59
Cuillins Rd. G73	Q20	65
Cuillins, The, Udd.	N26	56
Culbin Dr. G13	F 9	18
Cullen St. G32	M22	54
Cullins, The, Chr.	D28	15
Culloden St. G31	K19	37
Culrain Gdns. G32	L22	38
Culrain St. G32	L22	38
Culross La. G32	M23	55
Culross St. G32	M23	55
Cult Rd., Lenz.	D24	13
Cults St. G51	L12	33
Culzean Cres., Bail.	M25	56
Huntingtower Rd.		
Culzean Dr. G32	M23	39
Cumberland Ct. G1	L17	36
Gallowgate		
Cumberland La. G5	M16	51
Cumberland St.		
Cumberland Pl. G5	M17	52
Cumberland Pl., Pais.	M 6	46
Laigh Kirk La.		
Cumberland St. G5	L16	35
Cumberland St. G5	M17	52
Cumbernauld Rd. G31	K20	37
Cumbrae Ct., Clyde.	E 7	5
Montrose St.		
Cumbrae Rd., Pais.	O 6	46
Cumbrae Rd., Renf.	J 8	31
Cumbrae St. G33	K22	38
Cumlodden Dr. G20	F14	20
Cumming Dr. G42	O16	51
Cumnock Dr., Renf.	R 8	59
Cunard St., Clyde.	F 8	17
Cunningham Dr., Clyde.	C 6	4
Cunningham Dr., Giff.	Q15	63
Cunningham Rd. G73	O20	53
Cambuslang Rd.		
Cunningham Rd., G52	K 9	32
Cunningham Rd., Kilb.	M07	42
Curfew Rd. G13	E11	7
Curle St. G14	J11	33
Curlew Pl., John.	O08	43
Curling Cres. G44	O17	52
Currie St. G20	G15	21
Curtis Av. G44	O17	52
Curzon St. G20	G15	21
Cut, The, Udd.	P27	69
Cuthbert St., Udd.	O28	57
Oakdene Av.		
Cuthbertson St. G42	N16	51
Cuthelton Dr. G31	M21	54
Cuthelton St.		
Cuthelton St. G31	M20	53
Cuthelton Ter. G31	M20	53
Cypress Av., Blan.	S26	68
Cypress Av., Udd.	O28	57
Myrtle Rd.		
Cypress St., Lenz.	C22	12
Cypress St. G22	G17	22
Cyprus Av., John.	N 1	44
Cyprus St., Clyde.	F 8	17
Cyril St., Pais.	M 7	47
Daer Av., Renf.	J 9	32
Dairsie Gdns., Bish.	F20	23
Dairsie St. G44	Q15	63
Daisy St. G42	N16	51
Dakota Way, Renf.	J 8	31
Friendship Way		
Dalbeth Rd. G32	N21	54
Dalchurn Path G34	K25	40
Dalchurn Pl.		
Dalchurn Pl. G34	K25	40
Dalcraig Cres., Blan.	R26	68
Dalcross La. G11	J14	34
Byres Rd.		
Dalcross St. G11	J14	34
Dalcruin Gdns. G69	D28	15
Daldowie Av. G32	M23	55

Name	Ref		
Dale Path G40	M18	52	
Dale St. G40	M18	52	
Dale Way G73	Q19	65	
Daleview Av. G12	G13	20	
Dalfoil Ct. G52	M 9	48	
Dalgarroch Av. G13	F 9	18	
Dalgleish Av., Clyde.	C 6	4	
Dalhousie Gdns., Bish.	E18	10	
Dalhousie La. G3	J16	35	
Scott St.			
Dalhousie La. W. G3	J16	35	
Buccleuch St.			
Dalhousie Rd., Kilb.	N07	42	
Dalhousie St. G3	J16	35	
Dalilea Dr. G34	J26	40	
Dalilea Dr.			
Dalilea Path G34	J26	40	
Dalilea Pl. G34	J26	40	
Dalintober St. G5	L16	35	
Dalkeith Av. G41	M13	50	
Dalkeith Av., Bish.	D19	11	
Dalkeith Rd., Bish.	D19	11	
Dalmahoy St. G32	K21	38	
Dalmally St. G20	H15	21	
Dalmarnock Ct. G40	M19	53	
Baltic St.			
Dalmary Dr., Pais.	L 7	31	
Dalmeny Av., Giff.	Q14	62	
Dalmeny Dr., Barr.	R 7	59	
Dalmeny St. G5	N18	52	
Dalmuir Ct., Dalm.	D 6	4	
Stewart St.			
Dalnair St. G3	J14	34	
Dalness Pass. G32	M22	54	
Ochil St.			
Dalness St. G32	M22	54	
Dalnottar Hill Rd.,	C 4	4	
Old.K.			
Dalreoch Av., Bail.	L26	40	
Dalriada St. G40	M20	53	
Dalry Av., Udd.	O28	57	
Myrtle Rd.			
Dalry St. G32	M22	54	
Dalserf Cres., Giff.	R13	62	
Dalserf St. G31	L19	37	
Dalsetter Av. G15	E 9	6	
Dalsetter Pl. G15	E10	6	
Dalsholm Rd. G20	F13	20	
Dalskeith Av., Pais.	L 4	29	
Dalskeith Cres., Pais.	L 4	29	
Dalskeith Rd., Pais.	M 4	45	
Dalswinton Pl. G34	K26	40	
Dalswinton St.			
Dalswinton St. G34	K26	40	
Dalton Av., Clyde.	E 9	6	
Dalton St. G31	L21	38	
Dalveen Av., Udd.	O27	57	
Dalveen Ct., Barr.	R 8	59	
Dalveen St. G32	L21	38	
Dalveen Way G73	Q20	65	
Dalwhinnie Av., Blan.	R26	68	
Daly Gdns., Blan.	R27	69	
Dalziel Dr. G41	M14	50	
Dalziel Quadrant G41	M14	50	
Dalziel Dr.			
Dalziel St. G52	K 9	32	
Damshot Cres. G53	N11	49	
Damshot Rd. G53	O11	49	
Danes Cres. G14	G10	18	
Danes Dr. G14	G10	18	
Danes La. S. G14	H11	19	
Dunglass Av.			
Dargarvel Av. G41	M13	50	
Darkwood Cres., Pais.	L 4	29	
Darleith St. G32	L21	38	
Darluith Rd., Linw.	L 1	28	
Darnaway Av. G33	J23	39	
Darnaway St. G33	J23	39	
Darnick St. G21	H19	23	
Hobden St.			
Darnley Cres., Bish.	D18	10	
Darnley Gdns. G41	N15	51	
Darnley Pl. G41	N15	51	
Darnley Rd.			
Darnley Rd. G41	N15	51	
Darnley Rd., Barr.	Q 9	60	
Darnley St. G41	N15	51	
Darroch Way, Cumb.	B 3	71	
Dartford St. G22	H16	21	
Darvaar Rd., Renf.	J 8	31	
Darvel Cres., Pais.	M 8	47	
Darvel St. G53	P 9	60	
Darwin Pl., Dalm.	D 5	4	
Dava St. G51	K13	34	
Davaar Rd., Pais.	O 6	46	
Davaar St. G40	M19	53	
Daventry Dr. G12	G13	20	
David Pl., Bail.	M24	55	
David Pl., Pais.	K 7	31	
Killarn Way			
David St. G40	L19	37	
David Way, Pais.	K 7	31	
Killarn Way			
Davidson Gdns. G14	H11	19	
Westland Dr.			
Davidson Quad., Clyde.	B 6	4	
Davidson St. G40	N19	53	
Davidson St., Clyde.	F 9	18	
Davidston Pl., Lenz.	D24	13	
Davieland Rd., Giff.	R13	62	
Daviot St. G51	L11	33	
Dawes La. N. G14	H11	19	
Upland Dr.			
Dawson Pl. G4	H16	21	
Dawson Rd.			
Dawson Rd. G4	H16	21	
Dealston Rd., Barr.	Q 7	59	
Dean Park Dr. G72	Q23	67	
Dean Park Rd., Renf.	J 9	32	
Dean St., Clyde.	E 8	5	
Deanbrae St., Udd.	P27	69	
Deanfield Quad. G52	L 9	32	
Deanpark Av., Udd.	Q28	69	
Deans Av. G72	Q23	67	
Deanside La. G4	K17	36	
Rotton Row			
Deanside Rd., Renf.	K10	32	
Deanston Dr. G41	O15	51	
Deanwood Av. G44	Q15	63	
Deanwood Rd. G44	Q15	63	
Debdale Cotts. G13	G12	19	
Whittingehame Dr.			
Dechmont Av. G72	Q23	67	
Dechmont Gdns., Blan.	R26	68	
Dechmont Gdns., Udd.	N27	57	
Dechmont Pl. G72	Q23	67	
Dechmont Rd., Udd.	N27	57	
Dechmont St. G31	M20	53	
Dechmont Vw., Udd.	O28	57	
Hamilton Vw.			
Dee Av. G78	N 3	45	
Dee Av., Renf.	H 9	18	
Dee Dr., Pais.	N 3	45	
Dee Pl., John.	O08	43	
Dee St. G33	J20	37	
Deepdene Rd., Bear.	E11	7	
Deepdene Rd., Chr.	E28	15	
Delburn St. G31	M20	53	
Delhi Av., Dalm.	D 5	4	
Delhmont Vw., Udd.	O28	57	
Hamilton Vw.			
Delny Pl. G33	K24	39	
Delvin Rd., G44	P16	63	
Denbeck St. G32	L21	38	
Denbrae St. G32	L21	38	
Dene Wk., Bish.	F20	23	
Denewood Av., Pais.	O 5	46	
Denham St. G22	H16	21	
Denholme Dr., Giff.	R14	62	
Denkenny Sq. G15	D 9	6	
Denmark St. G22	H17	22	
Denmilne Path G34	K26	40	
Denmilne Pl. G34	K26	40	
Denmilne St. G34	K26	40	
Derby St. G3	K15	35	
Derby Terrace La. G3	K15	35	
Derby St.			
Derwent St. G22	H16	21	
Despard Av. G32	M24	55	
Despard Gdns. G32	M24	55	
Deveron Av., Giff.	R14	62	
Deveron Rd., Bear.	E11	7	
Deveron St. G33	J20	37	
Devol Cres. G53	O10	48	
Devon Gdns. G12	H13	20	
Hyndland Rd.			
Devon Gdns., Bish.	D18	10	
Devon Pl. G42	M16	51	
Devon St. G5	M16	51	
Devondale Av., Blan.	R26	68	
Devonshire Gdns. G12	H13	20	
Devonshire Gdns. La.	H13	20	
G12			
Hyndland Rd.			
Devonshire Ter. G12	H13	20	
Devonshire Ter. La. G12	H13	20	
Hughenden Rd.			
Diana Av. G13	F10	18	
Dick St. G20	H15	21	
Henderson St.			
Dickens Av., Clyde.	D 6	4	
Dilwara Av. G14	J12	33	
Dimity St., John.	N09	43	
Dinard Dr., Giff.	Q14	62	
Dinart St. G33	J20	37	
Dinduff St. G34	J26	40	
Dingwall St. G3	K14	34	
Kelvinhaugh St.			
Dinmont Pl. G41	N15	51	
Norham St.			
Dinmont Rd. G41	N14	50	
Dinwiddie St. G21	J20	37	
Dipple Pl. G15	E10	6	
Dirleton Av. G41	O15	51	
Dirleton Dr., Pais.	N 4	45	
Dirleton Gate, Bear.	E11	7	
Divernia Way, Barr.	S 8	59	
Dixon Av. G42	N16	51	
Dixon Rd. G42	N17	52	
Dixon St. G1	L16	35	
Dixon St., Pais.	M 6	46	
Dobbies Loan G4	J16	35	
Dobbies Loan Pl. G4	K17	36	
Dochart Av., Renf.	J 9	32	
Dochart St. G33	J21	38	
Dock St., Clyde.	F 8	17	
Dodhill Pl. G13	G10	18	
Dodside Gdns. G32	M23	55	
Dodside Pl. G32	M23	55	
Dodside St. G32	M23	55	
Dolan St., Bail.	L25	40	
Dollar Ter. G20	F14	20	
Crosbie St.			
Dolphin Rd. G41	N14	50	
Don Av., Renf.	J 9	32	
Don Dr., Pais.	N 3	45	
Don Pl., John.	O08	43	
Don St. G33	K20	37	
Donald Way, Udd.	O28	57	
Donaldson Dr., Renf.	H 8	17	
Ferguson St.			
Donaldswood Rd., Pais.	O 5	46	
Doncaster St. G20	H16	21	
Doon Cres., Bear.	D11	7	
Doon Side, Cumb.	C 3	71	
Doon St., Clyde.	D 8	5	
Doonfoot Rd. G43	P14	62	
Dora St. G40	M19	53	
Dorchester Av., G12	G13	20	
Dorchester Ct. G12	G13	20	
Dorchester Av.			
Dorchester Pl. G12	G13	20	
Dorian Dr., Clark.	S14	62	
Dorlin Rd. G33	G24	25	
Dormanside Rd. G53	M10	48	
Dornal Av. G13	F 9	18	
Dornford Av. G32	N23	55	
Dornford Rd. G32	N23	55	
Dornie Dr. G32	O23	55	
Dornie Dr. G46	Q12	61	
Dornoch Av., Giff.	R14	62	
Dornoch Pl., Bish.	E20	11	
Dornoch Pl., Chr.	E26	14	
Dornoch Rd., Bear.	E11	7	
Dornoch St. G40	L18	36	
Dorset Sq. G3	K15	35	
Dorset St.			
Dorset St. G3	K15	35	
Dosk Av. G13	F 9	18	
Dosk Pl. G13	F 9	18	
Douglas Av. G32	N22	54	
Douglas Av. G73	P20	65	
Douglas Av., Giff.	R14	62	
Douglas Av., John.	N 1	44	
Douglas Av., Lenz.	C23	13	
Douglas Ct., Lenz.	C23	13	
Douglas Dr. G15	E 9	6	
Douglas Dr. G72	P21	66	
Douglas Dr., Bail.	L24	39	
Douglas Dr., Both.	R28	69	

Street	Ref	Page
Douglas Gdns., Bear.	D12	7
Douglas Gdns., Giff.	R14	62
Douglas Gdns., Lenz.	C23	13
Douglas Gdns., Udd.	P27	69
Douglas La. G2	K16	35
West George St.		
Douglas Park Cres.,	C13	8
Bear.		
Douglas Pl., Bear.	C12	7
Douglas Pl., Lenz.	C23	13
Douglas St.,	K 7	31
Pais. & Renf.		
Douglas St. G2	K16	35
Douglas St., Pais.	L 5	30
Douglas St., Udd.	O28	57
Douglas Ter. G41	M15	51
Shields Rd.		
Douglas Ter., Pais.	J 6	30
Douglaston Rd. G23	E15	9
Dougray Pl., Barr.	R 8	59
Dougrie Dr. G45	Q17	64
Dougrie Pl. G45	Q18	64
Dougrie Rd. G45	R17	64
Dougrie St. G45	Q18	64
Dougrie Ter. G45	Q17	64
Doune Cres., Bish.	D19	11
Doune Gdns. G20	H15	21
Doune Quad. G20	H15	21
Dove St. G53	P10	60
Dovecot G43	O14	50
Shawhill Rd.		
Dovecothall St., Barr.	Q 8	59
Dowanfield Rd., Cumb.	C 2	70
Dowanhill Pl. G11	J14	34
Old Dumbarton Rd.		
Dowanhill St. G11	J14	34
Dowanside La. G12	H14	20
Byres Rd.		
Dowanside Rd. G12	H14	20
Dowanvale Ter. G11	J13	34
White St.		
Down St. G21	H18	22
Downcraig Dr. G45	R17	64
Downcraig Rd. G45	R17	64
Downcraig Ter. G45	R17	64
Downfield Gdns., Both.	R27	69
Downfield St. G32	M21	54
Downiebrae Rd. G73	N19	53
Dowrie Cres. G53	N10	48
Dows Pl. G4	H16	21
Possil Rd.		
Drainie St. G34	K25	40
Westerhouse Rd.		
Drake St. G40	L18	36
Drakemire Av. G45	Q17	64
Drakemire Dr. G45	Q17	64
Dreghorn St. G31	K20	37
Drem Pl. G11	J13	34
Merkland St.		
Drimnin Rd. G33	G24	25
Drive Gdns., John.	M 3	45
Drive Rd. G51	K12	33
Drochil St. G34	J25	40
Drumbeg Dr. G53	P10	60
Drumbeg Pl. G53	P10	60
Drumbottie Rd. G21	G19	23
Drumby Cres., Clark.	S14	62
Drumby Dr., Clark.	S14	62
Drumcavel Rd.,	F26	26
Chr. & Gart.		
Drumchapel Gdns. G15	E10	6
Drumchapel Pl. G15	E10	6
Drumchapel Rd. G15	E10	6
Drumclog Gdns. G33	G21	24
Auchinleck Av.		
Drumclutha Dr., Both.	R28	69
Drumcross Rd. G53	N11	49
Drumhead Pl. G32	N21	54
Drumhead Rd. G32	N21	54
Drumilaw Rd. G73	P19	65
Drumilaw Way G73	P19	65
Drumlaken Av. G23	E14	8
Drumlaken Ct. G23	E14	8
Drumlaken St. G23	E14	8
Drumlanrig Av. G34	J26	40
Drumlanrig Pl. G34	J26	40
Drumlanrig Quad. G34	J26	40
Drumlochy Rd. G33	J22	38
Drummond Av. G73	O18	52
Drummond Dr., Pais.	M 8	47
Drummond Gdns. G13	G12	19
Crow Rd.		
Drummore Rd. G15	D10	6
Drummyne Pl. G51	L12	33
Drumoyne Circus		
Drumover Dr. G31	M21	54
Drumoyne Av. G51	K12	33
Drumoyne Circus G51	L12	33
Drumoyne Dr. G51	K12	33
Drumoyne Quad. G51	L12	33
Drumoyne Rd. G51	L12	33
Drumoyne Sq. G51	K12	33
Drumpark St. G46	Q12	61
Drumpark St., Coat.	M28	57
Dunnachie Dr.		
Drumpeller Rd., Bail.	M25	56
Drumpellier Av., Bail.	M25	56
Drumpellier Pl., Bail.	M25	56
Drumpellier St. G33	J20	37
Drumreoch Dr. G42	O18	52
Drumreoch Pl. G42	O18	52
Drumry Pl. G15	E 9	6
Drumry Rd. E. G15	E 9	6
Drumry Rd., Clyde.	D 7	5
Drums Av., Pais.	L 5	30
Drums Cres., Pais.	L 5	30
Drums Rd. G53	M10	48
Drumsack Av., Chr.	F26	26
Drumsargard Rd. G73	P20	65
Drumshaw Dr. G32	O23	55
Drumvale Dr., Chr.	E27	15
Drury St. G2	K16	35
Dryad St. G46	P12	61
Dryborough Av., John.	N 4	45
Dryburgh Av. G73	O19	53
Dryburgh Gdns. G20	H15	21
Dryburgh Rd., Bear.	C11	7
Dryburn Av. G52	L10	32
Drygate G4	K18	36
Drygrange Rd. G33	J23	39
Drymen Pl., Lenz.	D23	13
Drymen Rd., Bear.	C11	7
Drymen St. G52	L12	33
Morven St.		
Drymen Wynd, Bear.	D12	7
Drynoch Pl. G22	F16	21
Duart Dr., John.	N 1	44
Duart St. G20	F14	20
Dubs Rd., Barr.	Q 9	60
Dubton Path G34	J25	40
Dubton St. G34	J25	40
Duchall Pl. G14	H10	18
Duchess Pl. G73	O20	53
Duchess Rd. G73	N20	53
Duchray Dr., Pais.	M 9	48
Duchray La. G31	J20	37
Duchray St.		
Duchray St. G33	J20	37
Ducraig St. G32	L22	38
Dudhope St. G33	J23	39
Dudley Dr. G12	H13	20
Duffus Pl. G32	O23	55
Duffus St. G34	J25	40
Duffus Ter. G32	O23	55
Duisdale Rd. G32	O23	55
Duke St., G4	K18	36
Duke St., Linw.	L 2	28
Duke St., Pais.	N 6	46
Dukes Gate, Both.	Q27	69
Dukes Rd., Bail.	L28	41
Dukes Rd. G72 & G73	P20	65
Dulnain St. G72	P24	67
Dulsie Rd. G21	G20	23
Dumbarton Rd. G11	G 9	18
Dumbarton Rd., Clyde.	C 6	4
Dumbarton Rd., Old.K.	D 5	4
Dalm. & Clyde.		
Dumbreck Av. G41	M13	50
Dumbreck Ct. G41	M13	50
Dumbreck Pl., Lenz.	D24	13
Dumbreck Rd. G41	M13	50
Dumbreck Rd. G41	M13	50
Dumbreck Sq. G41	M13	50
Dumbreck Av.		
Dunagoil St. G45	R17	64
Dunagoil St. G45	R18	64
Dunagoil Ter. G45	R18	64
Dunalastair Dr. G33	G22	24
Dunalistair Av. G33	G22	24
Dunan Pl. G33	K24	39
Dunard Rd. G73	O19	53
Dunard St. G20	H15	21
Dunard Way, Pais.	K 5	30
Mosslands Rd.		
Dunaskin St. G11	J14	34
Dunbar Av. G73	O20	53
Dunbar Av., John.	O09	43
Dunbar Rd., Pais.	N 4	45
Dunbeith Pl. G20	G14	20
Dunblane St. G4	J16	35
Dunbrach Rd., Cumb.	B 1	70
Duncan Av. G14	H11	19
Duncan La. G14	H11	19
Duncan Av.		
Duncan La. N. G14	H11	19
Ormiston Av.		
Duncan St., Clyde.	D 7	5
Duncansby Rd. G33	L23	39
Dunchatt St. G31	K18	36
Dunchattan Pl. G31	K18	36
Duke St.		
Dunchurch Rd., Pais.	L 8	31
Dunclutha Dr., Both.	R28	69
Dunclutha St. G40	N19	53
Duncombe St. G20	F14	20
Duncombe Vw., Clyde.	D 8	5
Kirkoswald Dr.		
Duncraig Cres., John.	O08	43
Duncrub Dr., Bish.	E18	10
Duncruin St. G20	F14	20
Duncryne Av. G32	M23	55
Duncryne Gdns. G32	M24	55
Duncryne Pl., Bish.	F18	22
Dundas La. G1	K17	36
Dundas St. G1	K17	36
Dundasvale Ct. G4	J16	35
Maitland St.		
Dundasvale Rd. G4	J16	35
Maitland St.		
Dundee Dr. G52	M10	48
Dundonald Av., John.	N08	43
Dundonald Rd. G12	H14	20
Dundonald Rd., Pais.	K 7	31
Dundrennan Rd. G42	O15	51
Dunearn Pl., Pais.	M 7	47
Dunearn St. G4	J15	35
Dunegoin St. G51	K13	34
Sharp St.		
Dunellan Dr., Clyde.	B 7	5
Dunellan St. G52	L12	33
Dungeonhill Rd. G34	K26	40
Dunglass Av. G14	H11	19
Dunglass La. N. G14	H11	19
Verona Av.		
Dungoil Av., Cumb.	B 1	70
Dungoil Rd., Lenz.	D24	13
Dungoyne St. G20	F14	20
Dunira St. G32	M21	54
Dunivaig St. G33	K24	39
Dunkeld Av. G73	O19	53
Dunkeld Dr., Bear.	D13	8
Dunkeld Gdns., Bish.	E19	11
Dunkeld La., Chr.	E28	15
Burnbrae Av.		
Dunkeld St. G31	M20	53
Dunkenny Pl. G15	D 9	6
Dunkenny Rd. G15	D 9	6
Dunlop Cres., Both.	R28	69
Dunlop Cres., Renf.	H 8	17
Hairst St.		
Dunlop St. G1	L17	36
Dunlop St. G72	P24	67
Dunlop St., Linw.	L 2	28
Dunlop St., Renf.	H 8	17
Hairst St.		
Dunmore La. G5	L16	35
Norfolk St.		
Dunmore St. G5	L16	35
Dunmore St., Clyde.	F 8	17
Dunn St. G40	M19	53
Dunn St., Clyde.	C 6	4
Dunn St., Dalm.	D 6	4
Dunn St., Pais.	M 7	47
Dunnachie Dr., Coat.	M28	57
Dunnichen Pl., Bish.	E20	11
Dunning St. G31	M20	53
Dunolly St. G21	J19	37
Dunottar St. G33	J22	38
Dunottar St., Bish.	E20	11
Dunphail Dr. G34	K26	40
Dunphail Rd. G34	K26	40

Name	Grid	Page
Dunragit St. G31	K20	37
Dunrobin Av., John.	N 1	44
Dunrobin St. G31	L19	37
Dunrod St. G32	M22	54
Dunside Dr. G53	P10	60
Dunskaith Pl. G34	K26	40
Dunskaith St. G34	K26	40
Dunsmuir St. G51	K13	34
Dunster Gdns., Bish.	D19	11
Dunswin Av., Dalm.	D 6	4
Dunswin Ct., Dalm.	D 6	4
Dunswin Av.		
Dunsyre Pl. G23	E15	9
Dunsyre Pl. G23	F15	21
Broughton Rd.		
Dunsyre St. G33	K21	38
Duntarvie Cres. G34	K26	40
Duntarvie Pl. G34	K25	40
Duntarvie Quad. G34	K26	40
Duntarvie Rd. G34	K25	40
Dunterle Ct., Barr.	Q 8	59
Dunterlie Av. G13	G10	18
Duntiglennan Rd., Clyde.	C 7	5
Duntocher Rd.,	D 6	4
Dalm. & Clyde.		
Duntocher Rd., Bear.	C10	6
Duntocher Rd., Clyde.	C 7	5
Duntocher St. G21	H18	22
Northcroft Rd.		
Duntreath Av. G13	F 9	18
Duntroon St. G31	K19	37
Dunure Dr. G73	P18	64
Dunure St. G20	F14	20
Dunvegan Av., John.	N 2	44
Dunvegan Ct. G13	G10	18
Kintillo Dr.		
Dunvegan Dr., Bish.	D19	11
Dunvegan Quad., Renf.	H 7	17
Kirklandneuk Rd.		
Dunvegan St. G51	K13	34
Sharp St.		
Dunwan Av. G13	F 9	18
Dunwan Pl. G13	F 9	18
Durban Av., Dalm.	D 5	4
Durness Av., Bear.	C13	8
Durno Path G33	K24	39
Duror St. G32	L22	38
Durris Gdns. G32	M23	55
Durrockstock Cres., Pais.	O 3	45
Durward Av. G41	N14	50
Durward Cres., Pais.	N 3	45
Durwood Ct. G41	N14	50
Duthil St. G51	L11	33
Dyce La. G11	J13	34
Dyers La. G1	L17	36
Turnbull St.		
Dyers Wynd, Pais.	L 6	30
Gilmour St.		
Dyke Pl. G13	F10	18
Dyke Rd. G13	G 9	18
Dyke St., Bail.	L26	40
Dykebar Av. G13	G10	18
Dykebar Cres., Pais.	N 7	47
Dykefoot Dr. G53	O11	49
Dykehead La. G33	K23	39
Dykehead Rd., Bail.	L27	41
Dykehead St. G33	K23	39
Dykemuir Pl. G21	H19	23
Dykemuir Quadrant G21	H19	23
Dykemuir St.		
Dykemuir St. G21	H19	23
Eagle Cres., Bear.	C10	6
Eagle St. G4	J17	36
Eaglesham Ct. G51	L15	35
Blackburn St.		
Eaglesham Pl. G51	L15	35
Earl Haig Rd. G52	K 9	32
Earl Pl. G14	H11	19
Earl St. G14	H10	18
Earlbank Av. G14	H11	19
Earlbank La. N. G14	H11	19
Dunglass Av.		
Earlbank La. N. G14	H11	19
Vancouver Rd.		
Earlbank La. S. G14	H11	19
Verona Av.		
Earls Ct., Chr.	E27	15
Longdale Rd.		
Earls Gate, Both.	Q27	69
Earls Hill G68	B 1	70
Earlsburn Rd., Lenz.	D24	13
Earlspark Av. G43	O15	51
Earn Av., Bear.	D13	8
Earn Av., Renf.	J 9	32
Almond Av.		
Earn St. G33	J21	38
Earnock St. G33	H20	23
Earnside St. G32	L22	38
Easdale Dr. G32	M22	54
East Av., Renf.	H 8	17
East Av., Udd.	P29	69
East Barns St., Clyde.	F 8	17
East Bath La. G2	K16	35
Sauchiehall St.		
East Buchanan St., Pais.	L 6	30
East Campbell St. G1	L18	36
East Fulton Holdings,	K 1	28
Linw.		
East Greenlees Av. G72	Q23	67
East Greenlees Cres.	Q22	66
G72		
East Greenlees Dr. G72	Q22	66
East Greenlees Rd. G72	Q22	66
East Hallhill Rd., Bail.	L25	40
East Kilbride Expressway	R22	66
G72		
East Kilbride Rd. G73	P20	65
East La., Pais.	M 7	47
East Reid St. G73	O20	53
East Springfield Ter.,	F19	23
Bish.		
East St., Kilb.	M07	42
East Thomson St.,	D 7	5
Clyde.		
East Whitby St. G31	M20	53
Eastburn Rd. G21	G19	23
Eastcote Av. G14	H12	19
Eastcroft G73	O19	53
Eastcroft Ter. G21	H19	23
Easter Av., Udd.	P27	69
Easter Garngaber Rd.	C24	13
G66		
Easter Ms., Udd.	P27	69
Church St.		
Easter Queenslie Rd.	K24	39
G33		
Eastercraigs G31	K19	37
Easterhill Pl. G32	M21	54
Easterhill St. G32	M21	54
Easterhouse Path G34	K26	40
Easterhouse Pl. G34	K26	40
Easterhouse Quad. G34	K26	40
Easterhouse Rd. G34	K26	40
Eastfield Av. G72	P21	66
Eastfield Rd. G21	H18	22
Eastgate, Gart.	G28	27
Eastmuir St. G32	L22	38
Eastvale Pl. G3	K14	34
Eastwood Av. G41	O14	50
Eastwood Av., Giff.	R14	62
Eastwood Cres., Thorn.	Q12	61
Eastwood Ct., Thorn.	Q12	61
Main St.		
Eastwood Rd., Chr.	E27	15
Eastwood Vw. G72	P24	67
Eastwoodmains Rd.,	R14	62
Giff. & Clark.		
Easwald Bank, Kilb.	N07	42
Eccles St. G22	G18	22
Eckford St. G32	M22	54
Eday St. G22	G17	22
Edderton Pl. G33	K25	40
Eddleston Pl. G72	P24	67
Eddlewood Path G33	K24	39
Eddlewood Rd. G33	K24	39
Edelweiss Ter. G11	J13	34
Gardner St.		
Eden La. G33	J20	37
Eden Pk., Both.	R27	69
Eden Pl. G72	P23	67
Eden Pl., Renf.	J 9	32
Eden St. G33	J20	37
Edenwood St. G33	L21	38
Edgam Dr. G52	L11	33
Edgefauld Av. G21	H18	22
Edgefauld Dr. G21	H18	22
Edgefauld Pl. G21	G18	22
Balgrayhill Rd.		
Edgefauld Rd. G21	H18	22
Edgehill La. G11	H13	20
Marlborough Av.		
Edgehill Rd. G11	H13	20
Edgehill Rd., Bear.	C12	7
Edgemont St. G41	O15	51
Edina St. G31	K19	37
Edinbeg Av. G42	O18	52
Edinbeg Pl. G42	O18	52
Edington Gdns., Chr.	D27	15
Edington St. G4	J16	35
Edison St. G52	K 9	32
Edmiston Dr. G51	L12	33
Edmiston Dr., Linw.	L 1	28
Edmiston St. G31	M20	53
Edmondstone Ct., Clyde.	F 8	17
Yokerburn Ter.		
Edrom Path G32	L21	38
Edrom St.		
Edrom St. G32	L21	38
Edward Av., Renf.	H 9	18
Edward St. G3	K14	34
Lumsden St.		
Edward St., Bail.	L27	41
Edward St., Clyde.	F 8	17
Edwin St. G51	L14	34
Edzell Ct. G14	J11	33
Edzell St.		
Edzell Dr., John.	N 2	44
Edzell Gdns., Bish.	F20	23
Edzell Pl. G14	J11	33
Edzell St.		
Edzell St. G14	J11	33
Egidia Av., Giff.	R13	62
Egilsay Cres. G22	F17	22
Egilsay Pl. G22	F17	22
Egilsay St. G22	F17	22
Egilsay Ter. G22	F17	22
Eglinton Ct. G5	L16	35
Eglinton Dr., Giff.	R14	62
Eglinton La. G5	M16	51
Eglinton St.		
Eglinton St. G5	M16	51
Egunton Ct. G5	M16	51
Cumberland St.		
Eighth St., Udd.	N27	57
Eildon Dr., Barr.	R 8	59
Eileen Gdns., Bish.	E19	11
Elba La. G31	L20	37
Elcho St. G40	L18	36
Elder Gro., Udd.	O28	57
Burnhead St.		
Elder St. G51	K12	33
Elderpark Gdns. G51	K12	33
Elderpark Gro. G51	K12	33
Elderpark St. G51	K12	33
Elderslie St. G3	J15	35
Eldon Gdns., Bish.	E18	10
Eldon Pl., John.	N 1	44
Eldon St. G3	J15	35
Eldon Ter. G11	J13	34
Caird Dr.		
Elgin Dr., Linw.	L 1	28
Elgin St. G40	L19	37
Elibank St. G33	J22	38
Elie St. G11	J14	34
Elizabeth Cres., Thorn.	Q13	62
Elizabeth St. G51	L14	34
Elizabethan Way, Renf.	J 8	31
Cockels Loan		
Ellangowan Rd. G41	O14	50
Ellergreen Rd., Bear.	D12	7
Ellerslie St., John.	M 1	44
Ellesmere St. G22	H16	21
Ellinger Ct., Dalm.	D 6	4
Scott St.		
Elliot Av. G78	O 3	45
Elliot Av., Giff.	R14	62
Elliot Dr., Giff.	Q14	62
Elliot La. G3	K15	35
Elliot St.		
Elliot Pl. G3	K15	35
Elliot St. G3	K15	35
Ellisland Av., Clyde.	D 8	5
Ellisland Cres. G73	P18	64
Ellisland Rd. G43	P14	62
Ellisland Rd., Cumb.	C 3	71
Ellismuir Farm Rd., Bail.	M26	56
Ellismuir Pl., Bail.	M26	56
Ellismuir Rd., Bail.	M26	56
Elliston Av. G53	P11	61

Elliston Dr. G53 P11 61
Elliston Pl. G53 P11 61
 Ravenscraig Dr.
Elm Av., Lenz. C23 13
Elm Av., Renf. H 8 17
Elm Bank, Bish. E19 11
Elm Dr., John. O09 43
Elm Gdns., Bear. C12 7
Elm Rd. G73 Q19 65
Elm Rd., Dalm. C 7 5
Elm Rd., Pais. N 7 47
Elm St. G14 H11 19
Elm Wk., Bear. C12 7
Elmbank Av., Udd. O28 57
Elmbank Cres. G2 K16 35
Elmbank La. G3 K15 35
 North St.
Elmbank St. G2 K16 35
Elmbank Street La. G3 K15 35
 North St.
Elmfoot St. G5 N17 52
Elmore Av. G44 P16 63
Elmore La. G44 P16 63
Elmslie Ct., Bail. M25 56
Elmvale Row E. G21 H18 22
 Elmvale Row
Elmvale Row G21 H18 22
Elmvale Row W. G21 H18 22
 Elmvale Row
Elmvale St. G21 G18 22
Elmwood Av. G11 H12 19
Elmwood Ct., Both. R28 69
 Blantyre Mill Rd.
Elmwood Gdns. G11 H12 19
 Randolph Rd.
Elmwood Gdns., Kirk. C22 12
Elmwood La. G11 H11 19
 Elmwood Av.
Elmwood Ter. G11 H12 19
 Crow Rd.
Elphin St. G23 E14 8
 Invershiel Rd.
Elphinstone Pl. G51 K14 34
Elrig Rd. G44 P16 63
Elspeth Gdns., Bish. E19 11
Eltham St. G22 H16 21
Elvan Ct. G32 L21 38
 Edrom St.
Elvan St. G32 L21 38
Embo Dr. G13 G10 18
Emerson Rd., Bish. E19 11
Emerson St. G20 G16 21
Emily Pl. G31 L18 36
Endfield Av. G12 G13 20
Endrick Bank, Bish. D19 11
Endrick Dr., Pais. L 7 31
Endrick St. G21 H17 22
Endsleigh Gdns. G11 H13 20
 Partickhill Rd.
Ennerdale St. G32 L21 38
Ensay St. G22 F17 22
Enterkin St. G32 M21 54
Ericht Rd. G43 P14 62
Eriska Av. G14 G10 18
Erradale St. G22 F16 21
Erriboll Pl. G22 F16 21
Erriboll St. G22 F16 21
Errogie St. G34 K25 40
Erskine Av. G41 M13 50
Erskine Sq. G52 K 9 32
Erskine Vw., Clyde. D 7 5
 Singer St.
Erskinefauld Rd., Linw. L 1 28
Ervie St. G34 K26 40
Esk Av., Renf. J 9 32
Esk Dr., Pais. N 3 45
Esk St. G14 G 9 18
Esk Way, Pais. N 3 45
Eskbank St. G32 L22 38
Eskdale Dr. G73 O20 53
Eskdale Rd., Bear. E11 7
Eskdale St. G42 N16 51
Esmond St. G3 J14 34
Espedair St., Pais. M 6 46
Essenside Av. G15 E11 7
Essex Dr. G14 H12 19
Essex La. G14 H12 19
Esslemont Av. G14 G10 18
Estate Quad. G32 O23 55

Estate Rd. G32 O23 55
Etive Av., Bear. D13 8
Etive Cres., Bish. E19 11
Etive Ct., Clyde. C 8 5
Etive Dr., Giff. R14 62
Etive St. G32 L22 38
Eton Gdns. G12 J15 35
 Oakfield Av.
Eton La. G12 J15 35
 Great George St.
Eton Pl. G12 J15 35
 Oakfield Av.
Eton Ter. G12 J15 35
 Oakfield Av.
Ettrick Av., Renf. J 9 32
Ettrick Cres. G73 O20 53
Ettrick Ct. G72 Q24 67
 Gateside Av.
Ettrick Oval, Pais. O 3 45
Ettrick Pl. G43 O14 50
Ettrick Ter., John. O08 43
Ettrick Way, Renf. J 9 32
Evan Cres., Giff. R14 62
Evan Dr., Giff. R14 62
Evanton Dr. G46 R12 61
Evanton Pl. G46 Q12 61
 Evanton Dr.
Everard Dr. G21 F18 22
Everard Pl. G21 F18 22
Everard Quad. G21 F18 22
Everglades, The, Chr. F25 26
Eversley St. G32 M22 54
Everton Rd. G53 N11 49
Ewart Pl. G3 K14 34
 Kelvinhaugh St.
Ewing Pl. G31 L20 37
Ewing St. G73 O19 53
Ewing St., Kilb. M07 42
Exchange Pl. G1 K17 36
 Buchanan St.
Exeter Dr. G11 J13 34
Exeter La. G11 J13 34
 Exeter Dr.
Eynort St. G22 F16 21

Fagan Ct., Blan. R27 69
Faifley Rd., Clyde. C 7 5
Fairbairn Cres., Thorn. R13 62
Fairbairn Path G40 M19 53
 Ruby St.
Fairbairn St. G40 M19 53
 Dalmarnock Rd.
Fairburn St. G32 M21 54
Fairfax Av. G44 P17 64
Fairfield Gdns. G51 K12 33
Fairfield Pl. G51 K12 33
Fairfield Pl. G71 R28 69
Fairfield St. G51 K12 33
Fairhaven Dr. G23 F14 20
Fairhill Av. G53 O11 49
Fairholm St. G32 M21 54
Fairley St. G51 L13 34
Fairlie Park Dr. G11 J13 34
Fairway Av., Pais. O 5 46
Fairways, Bear. C10 6
Fairyknowe Gdns. G71 R28 69
Falcon Cres., Pais. L 4 29
Falcon Rd., John. O08 43
Falcon Ter. G20 F14 20
Falfield St. G5 M16 51
Falkland Cres., Bish. F20 23
Falkland Mansions G12 H13 20
 Clarence Dr.
Falkland St. G12 H13 20
Falloch Rd., Bear. E11 7
Fallside Rd., Both. R28 69
Falside Av., Pais. N 6 46
Falside Rd. G32 M22 54
Falside Rd., Pais. N 5 46
Fara St. G23 F15 21
Farie St. G73 O19 53
Farm Ct., Both. Q28 69
 Fallside Rd.
Farm La., Udd. P28 69
 Myers Cres.
Farm Pk., Lenz. D23 13
Farm Rd. G41 M13 50
Farm Rd., Blan. R26 68
Farm Rd., Clyde. C 7 5
Farm Rd., Dalm. D 5 4

Farme Cross G73 N19 53
Farmeloan Rd. G73 O19 53
Farmington Av. G32 L23 39
Farmington Gate G32 L23 39
Farmington Gdns. G32 L23 39
Farmington Gro. G32 L23 39
Farne Dr. G44 Q16 63
Farnell St. G4 J16 35
Farrier Ct., John. M09 43
Faskally Av., Bish. D18 10
Faskin Cres. G53 O 9 48
Faskin Pl. G53 O 9 48
Faskin Rd. G53 O 9 48
Fasque Pl. G15 D 9 6
Fastnet St. G33 K22 38
Faulbswood Cres., Pais. N 4 45
Fauldhouse St. G5 M17 52
Faulds Gdns., Bail. L26 40
Faulds, Bail. L26 40
Fauldshead Rd., Renf. H 8 17
Fauldspark Cres., Bail. L26 40
Fauldswood Cres., Pais. N 4 45
Fauldswood Dr., Pais. N 4 45
Fearnmore Rd. G20 F14 20
Fendoch St. G32 M22 54
Fenella St. G32 L22 38
Fennsbank Av. G73 Q20 65
Fenwick Dr., Barr. R 8 59
Fenwick Pl., Giff. R13 62
Fenwick Rd., Giff. R14 62
Fereneze Av., Barr. Q 7 59
Fereneze Av., Pais. K 7 31
Ferenze Cres. G13 F10 18
Ferenze Dr., Pais. O 5 46
Fergus Ct. G20 H15 21
Fergus Dr. G20 H15 21
Ferguslie Park Av., Pais. L 4 29
Ferguslie Park Cres., Pais. M 4 45
Ferguslie Pk. L 3 29
Ferguslie Wk., Pais. M 4 45
Ferguslie, Pais. M 4 45
Ferguson Av., Renf. H 8 17
Ferguson St., John. M09 43
Ferguson St., Renf. H 8 17
Fergusson Rd., Cumb. C 2 70
Ferguston Rd., Bear. D12 7
Fern Av., Bish. F19 23
Fern Av., Lenz. C23 13
Fern Dr., Barr. Q 7 59
Fern Hill Grange G71 R28 69
Fernan St. G32 L21 38
Fernbank Av. G72 Q23 67
Fernbank St. G22 G18 22
Fernbrae Rd. G46 Q20 65
Fernbrae Way G73 Q19 65
Ferncroft Dr. G44 P17 64
Ferndale Ct. G23 F14 20
 Rothes Dr.
Ferndale Dr. G23 F14 20
Ferndale Gdns. G23 F14 20
Ferndale Pl. G23 F14 20
 Rothes Drive
Ferness Oval G21 F20 23
Ferness Pl. G21 F20 23
Ferness Rd. G21 G20 23
Ferngrove Av. G12 G13 20
Fernhill Rd. G73 O19 65
Fernleigh Pl., Chr. E27 15
Fernleigh Rd. G43 P14 62
Fernslea Av. G72 S26 68
Ferry Rd. G3 K13 34
Ferry Rd., Both. R28 69
Ferry Rd., Renf. H 8 17
Ferry Rd., Udd. P26 68
Ferryden St. G14 J12 33
Fersit St. G43 P14 62
Fetlar Dr. G44 P17 64
Fettercairn Av. G15 D 9 6
Fettercairn Gdns., Bish. E20 11
Fettes St. G33 K21 38
Fidra St. G33 K21 38
Fielden Pl. G40 L19 37
Fielden St. G40 L19 37
Fieldhead Dr. G43 P13 62
Fieldhead Sq. G43 P13 62
Fife Av. G52 M10 48
Fife Cres., Both. R28 69
Fifeway, Bish. F20 23

Street	Grid	Pg
Fifth Av. G12	G12	19
Fifth Av. G33	G22	24
Fifth Av., Lenz.	E23	13
Fifth Av., Renf.	J 8	31
Finart Dr., Pais.	N 7	47
Finch Pl., John.	OO8	43
Findhorn Av., Renf.	H 9	18
Findhorn Cres., Pais.	N 3	45
Findhorn St. G33	K20	37
Findochty St. G33	J23	39
Fingal La. G20	F14	20
Fingal St.		
Fingal St. G20	F14	20
Fingask St. G32	M23	55
Finglas Av., Pais.	N 7	47
Fingleton Av., Barr.	R 8	59
Finhaven St. G32	M21	54
Finlarig St. G34	K26	40
Finlas St. G22	H17	22
Finlay Dr. G31	K19	37
Finlay Dr., Linw.	L 1	28
Finnart Sq. G40	M18	52
Finnart St. G40	M18	52
Finnieston Pl. G3	K15	35
Finnieston St.		
Finnieston St. G3	K15	35
Finsbay St. G51	L12	33
Fintry Av., Pais.	O 6	46
Fintry Cres., Barr.	R 8	59
Fintry Cres., Bish.	E20	11
Fintry Dr. G44	O17	52
Fir Pl. G72	P23	67
Caledonian Circuit		
Fir Pl., Bail.	M25	56
Fir Pl., John.	N 1	44
Firbank Ter., Barr.	R 9	60
Firdon Cres. G15	E10	6
Firhill Rd. G20	H16	21
Firhill St. G20	H16	21
Firpark Pl. G31	K18	36
Firpark St.		
Firpark Rd., Bish.	F19	23
Firpark St. G31	K18	36
Firpark Ter. G31	K18	36
Ark La.		
First Av. G33	H22	24
First Av. G44	R15	63
First Av., Bear.	D13	8
First Av., Lenz.	E23	13
First Av., Renf.	J 8	31
First Av., Udd.	O27	57
First Gdns. G41	M13	50
First St., Udd.	O27	57
First Ter., Clyde.	D 7	5
Firwood Dr. G44	P17	64
Fisher Cres., Clyde.	C 7	5
Fisher Ct. G31	K18	36
Fishers Rd., Renf.	G 8	17
Fishescoates Av. G73	Q20	65
Fishescoates Gdns. G73	P20	65
Fishescoates Rd.		
Fishescoates Rd. G73	P20	65
Fitzalan Dr., Pais.	L 7	31
Fitzalan Rd., Renf.	J 7	31
Fitzroy La. G3	K15	35
Claremont St.		
Fitzroy Pl. G3	K15	35
Claremont St.		
Fitzroy Pl. G3	K15	35
Sauchiehall St.		
Flax Rd., Udd.	P28	69
Fleet Av., Renf.	J 9	32
Fleet St. G32	M22	54
Fleming Av., Chr.	F26	26
Fleming Av., Clyde.	F 8	17
Fleming Rd., Cumb.	C 2	70
Fleming St. G31	L19	37
Fleming St., Pais.	K 6	30
Flemington Rd. G72	R24	67
Flemington St. G21	H18	22
Fleurs Av. G41	M13	50
Fleurs Rd. G41	M13	50
Floors St., John.	N09	43
Floorsburn Cres., John.	N09	43
Flora Gdns., Bish.	E20	11
Florence Dr., Giff.	R14	62
Florence Gdns. G73	Q20	65
Florence St. G5	L17	36
Florence St. G73	M17	52
Florentine Pl. G12	J15	35
Gibson St.		
Florentine Ter. G12	J15	35
Southpark Av.		
Florida Av. G42	O16	51
Florida Cres. G42	O16	51
Florida Dr. G42	O16	51
Florida Gdns., Bail.	L25	40
Florida Sq. G42	O16	51
Florida St. G42	O16	51
Fochabers Dr. G52	L11	33
Fogo Pl. G20	G14	20
Forbes Dr. G40	L18	36
Forbes Pl., Pais.	M 6	46
Forbes St. G40	L18	36
Ford Rd. G12	H14	20
Fordneuk St. G40	L19	37
Fordoun St. G34	K26	40
Fordyce St. G11	J13	34
Fore St. G14	H11	19
Forehouse Rd., Kilb.	MO6	42
Forest Dr., Udd.	Q28	69
Forest Gdns., Lenz.	D22	12
Forest Pl., Lenz.	D22	12
Forest Pl., Pais.	N 6	46
Brodie Park Av.		
Forest Rd., Cumb.	C 4	71
Forest Vw., Cumb.	B 4	71
Forfar Av. G52	M10	48
Forfar Cres., Bish.	F20	23
Forgan Gdns., Bish.	F20	23
Forge St. G21	J19	37
Forglen St. G34	J25	40
Formby Dr. G23	E14	8
Forres Av. G46	Q14	62
Forres Gate, Giff.	R14	62
Forres Av.		
Forres St. G23	E15	9
Tolsta St.		
Forrest St. G40	L19	37
Forrestfield St. G21	J19	37
Fortevoit Av., Bail.	L26	40
Fortevoit Pl., Bail.	L26	40
Forth Av., Pais.	N 3	45
Forth Av., Renf.	J 8	31
Third Av.		
Forth Pl., John.	OO8	43
Forth Rd. G61	C11	7
Forth Rd., Bear.	E11	7
Forth St. G41	M15	51
Fortingall Av. G12	G14	20
Grandtully Dr.		
Fortingall Pl. G12	G14	20
Fortrose St. G11	J13	34
Foswell Pl. G15	C 9	6
Fotheringay La. G41	N15	51
Beaton Rd.		
Fotheringay Rd. G41	N14	50
Foulis La. G13	G12	19
Foulis St. G13	G12	19
Foundry La., Barr.	R 7	59
Main St.		
Foundry Open G31	L19	37
Fountain St. G31	L18	36
Fountainwell Av. G.21	J17	36
Fountainwell Dr. G21	J17	36
Fountainwell Pl. G21	J17	36
Fountainwell Rd. G21	J17	36
Fountainwell Sq. G21	J18	36
Fountainwell Ter. G21	J18	36
Fourth Av., G33	G22	24
Fourth Av., Lenz.	E23	13
Fourth Av., Renf.	J 8	31
Third Av.		
Fourth Gdns. G41	M13	50
Fourth St., Udd.	N27	57
Fox La. G1	L17	36
Fox St. G1	L16	35
Foxbar Cres., Pais.	O 3	45
Foxbar Dr. G13.	G10	18
Foxbar Dr. G78.	O 3	45
Foxbar Rd., Pais.	O 3	45
Foxes Gro. G66	C24	13
Foxhills Pl. G23	E15	9
Foxley St. G.32	N23	55
Foyers Ct. G13	G10	18
Kirkton Av.		
Foyers Ter. G21	H19	23
Francis St. G5	M16	51
Frankfield Rd. G33	G24	25
Frankfield St. G33	J20	37
Frankfort St. G41	N15	51
Franklin St. G40	M18	52
Fraser Av. G73	O20	53
Fraser Av., John.	N 1	44
Fraser St. G72	P21	66
Fraserbank St. G21	H17	22
Keppochhill Rd.		
Frazer St. G31	L20	37
Freeland Dr. G53	P10	60
Freeland Dr., Renf.	G 5	16
Freelands Cres., Old K	C 5	4
Freelands Ct., Old K.	C 5	4
Freelands Pl., Old K.	D 5	4
Freelands Rd., Old K.	C 5	4
French St. G40	M18	52
French St., Dalm.	D 6	4
French St., Renf.	J 7	31
Freuchie St. G34	K25	40
Friar Av., Bish.	D19	11
Friars Court Rd., Chr.	E25	14
Friars Pl. G13	F11	19
Friarscourt Av. G13	E11	7
Friarscourt La. G13	F11	19
Arrowsmith Av.		
Friarton Rd. G43	P15	63
Friendship Way, Renf.	J 8	31
Fruin Pl. G22	H17	22
Fruin Rd. G15	E 9	6
Fruin St. G22	H17	22
Fulbar Av., Renf.	H 8	17
Fulbar Ct., Renf.	H 8	17
Fulbar Av.		
Fulbar La., Renf.	H 8	17
Fulbar Rd. G51	K11	33
Fulbar Rd., Pais.	M 3	45
Fulbar St., Renf.	H 8	17
Fullarton Av. G32	N22	54
Fullarton Rd. G32	O21	54
Fullerton St., Pais	K 5	30
Fullerton Ter., Pais.	K 6	30
Fulmar Ct., Bish.	F18	22
Fulmar Pl., John.	OO8	43
Fulton Cres., Kilb.	MO7	42
Fulton St. G13	F11	19
Fulwood Av. G13	F 9	18
Fulwood Av., Linw.	L 1	28
Fulwood Pl. G13	F 9	18
Fynloch Pl., Clyde	B 6	4
Fyvie Av. G43	P13	62
Gadie Av., Renf.	J 9	32
Gadie St. G33	K20	37
Gadloch Av., Lenz.	E23	13
Gadloch Gdns., Lenz.	D23	13
Gadloch St. G22	G17	22
Gadloch Vw. G66	E23	13
Gadsburn Ct. G21	G20	23
Wallacewell Quadrant		
Gadshill St. G21	J18	36
Gailes Pk., Both.	R27	69
Gailes St. G40	M19	53
Gairbraid Av. G20	G14	20
Gairbraid Ct. G20	G14	20
Gairbraid Pl. G20	G14	20
Gairbraid Ter., Bail.	L28	41
Gairn St. G11	J13	34
Castlebank St.		
Gala Av., Renf.	J 9	32
Gala St. G33	J21	38
Galbraith Av. G51	K12	33
Burghead Dr.		
Galbraith Dr. G51	K11	33
Galbraith St. G51	K11	33
Moss Rd.		
Galdenoch St. G33	J22	38
Gallacher Av., Pais.	N 4	45
Gallan Av. G23	E15	9
Galloway Dr. G73	Q19	65
Galloway St. G21	G18	22
Gallowflat St. G73	O19	53
Gallowgate G1	L17	36
Gallowhill Av., Lenz.	C23	13
Gallowhill Gro., Lenz.	C23	13
Gallowhill Rd., Lenz.	C23	13
Gallowhill Rd., Pais.	L 6	30
Galston St. G53	P 9	60
Gamrie Dr. G53	O10	48
Gamrie Gdns. G53	O10	48
Gamrie Rd. G53	O10	48

Gannochy Dr., Bish. E20 11
Gantock Cres. G33 K22 38
Gardenside Av. G32 O22 54
Gardenside Av., Udd. P27 69
Gardenside Cres. G32 O22 54
Gardenside Pl. G32 O22 54
Gardenside St., Udd. P27 69
Gardner La., Bail. M26 56
  Church St.
Gardyne St. G34 J25 40
Garfield St. G31 L19 37
Garforth Rd., Bail. M24 55
Gargrave Av., Bail. M24 55
Garion Dr. G13 G10 18
Garion Dr. G13 G10 18
  Talbot Dr.
Garlieston Rd. G33 L24 39
Garmouth Ct. G51 K12 33
  Garmouth St.
Garmouth Gdns. G51 K12 33
Garmouth St. G51 K12 33
Garnet La. G3 J16 35
  Garnet St.
Garnet St. G3 J16 35
Garnethill St. G3 J16 35
Garngaber Av., Lenz. C23 13
Garngaber Ct. G66 C24 13
  Woodleigh Rd.
Garnie Av., Renf. F 5 16
Garnie Cres., Renf. E 5 4
Garnie La., Renf. E 5 4
Garnie Oval, Renf. E 5 4
Garnie Pl., Renf. E 5 4
Garnieland Rd., Renf. E 5 4
Garnkirk La. G33 G24 25
Garnkirk St. G21 J18 36
Garnock St. G21 J18 36
Garrell Way, Cumb. C 2 70
Garrioch Cres. G20 G14 20
Garrioch Dr. G20 G14 20
Garrioch Gate G20 G14 20
Garrioch Quad. G20 G14 20
Garrioch Rd. G20 H14 20
Garriochmill Rd. G20 H15 21
  Raeberry St.
Garriochmill Way G20 H15 21
  Woodside Rd.
Garrowhill Dr., Bail. M24 55
Garry Av., Bear. E13 8
Garry Dr., Pais. N 4 45
Garry St. G44 O16 51
Garscadden G13 F10 18
Garscadden Rd. G15 E10 6
Garscadden Vw., Clyde. D 8 5
  Kirkoswald Dr.
Garscube Rd. G20 H16 21
Gartcarron Hill, Cumb. B 1 70
  Dunbrach Rd.
Gartconnel Dr., Bear. C12 7
Gartconnel Gdns., C12 7
  Bear.
Gartconnel Rd., Bear. C12 7
Gartcosh Rd., K28 41
  Bail. & Gart.
Gartcraig Rd. G33 K21 38
Gartferry Av., Chr. E27 15
Gartferry Rd., Chr. E27 15
Gartferry St. G21 H19 23
Garth St. G1 K17 36
Garthamlock Rd. G33 J24 39
Garthland Dr. G31 K19 37
Garthland La., Pais. L 6 30
Gartliston Ter., Bail. L28 41
Gartloch Cotts., Chr. G25 26
Gartloch Cotts., Gart. H27 27
Gartloch Rd. G33 J21 38
Gartly St. G44 Q15 63
  Clarkston Rd.
Gartmore Gdns., Udd. O27 57
Gartmore La., Chr. E28 15
Gartmore Rd., Pais. M 8 47
Gartmore Ter. G72 Q21 66
Gartness St. G31 K19 37
Gartocher Rd. G32 L23 39
Gartochmill Rd. G20 H15 21
Gartons Rd. G21 H20 23
Gartshore Rd., C27 15
  Drumbreck
Garturk St. G42 N16 51

Garvald Ct. G40 M19 53
  Baltic St.
Garvald St. G40 M19 53
Garve Av. G44 Q16 63
Garvel Cres. G33 L24 39
Garvel Rd. G33 L24 39
Garvock Dr. G43 P13 62
Gas St., John. M 1 44
Gask Pl. G13 F 9 18
Gatehouse St. G32 L22 38
Gateside Av. G72 P23 67
Gateside Cres., Barr. R 7 59
Gateside Pl., Kilb. M07 42
Gateside Rd., Barr. R 7 59
Gateside St. G31 L19 37
Gauldry Av. G52 M11 49
Gauze St., Pais. L 6 30
Gavins Rd., Clyde. C 7 5
Gavinton St. G44 Q15 63
Gear Ter. G40 N19 53
Geary St. G23 E14 8
  Torrin Rd,
Geddes Rd. G21 F20 23
Gelston St. G32 M22 54
General Terminus Quay L15 35
  G51
Generals Gate, Udd. P27 69
  Cobbleriggs Way
Gentle Row, Clyde. C 6 4
George Av., Clyde. D 8 5
  Robert Burns Av.
George Cres., Clyde. D 8 5
George Gray St. G73 O20 53
George Mann Ter. G73 P19 65
George Pl., Pais. M 6 46
George Reith Av. G12 G12 19
George Sq. G2 K17 36
George St. G1 K17 36
George St., Bail. M25 56
George St., Barr. Q 7 59
George St., John. M09 43
George St., Pais. M 5 46
Gertrude Pl., Barr. R 7 59
Gibb St. G21 J18 36
  Royston Rd.
Gibson Cres., John. N09 43
Gibson Rd., Renf. J 7 31
Gibson St. G12 J15 35
Gibson St. G40 L18 36
Giffnock Park Av., Giff. Q14 62
Gifford Dr. G52 L10 32
Gilbert St. G3 K14 34
Gilbertfield Pl. G33 J22 38
Gilbertfield Rd. G72 Q23 67
Gilbertfield St. G33 J22 38
Gilfillan Way, Pais. O 3 45
  Ashton Way
Gilhill St. G20 F14 20
Gilia St. G72 P21 66
Gillies La., Bail. M26 56
  Bredisholm Rd.
Gills Ct. G31 L19 37
Gilmerton Rd., Linw. L 1 28
Gilmerton St. G32 M22 54
Gilmour Av., Clyde. C 7 5
Gilmour Cres. G73 O18 52
Gilmour Pl. G5 M17 52
Gilmour St., Clyde. D 8 5
Gilmour St., Pais. L 6 30
Girthon St. G32 M23 55
Girvan St. G33 J20 37
Gladney Av. G13 F 9 18
Gladsmuir Rd. G52 L10 32
Gladstone Av., Barr. R 7 59
Gladstone St. G4 J16 35
Gladstone St., Dalm. E 6 4
Glaive Rd. G13 E11 7
Glamis Av., John. N 1 44
Glamis Gdns., Bish. D19 11
Glamis Pl. G31 M20 53
  Glamis Rd.
Glamis Rd. G31 M20 53
Glanderston Av., Barr. R 9 60
Glanderston Dr. G13 F10 18
Glaselune St. G34 K26 40
  Lochdochart Rd.
Glasgow Bridge B21 12
Glasgow Rd. G72 P21 66
Glasgow Rd. G72 & E.K. R21 66
Glasgow Rd. G73 N18 52

Glasgow Rd., Bail. M24 55
Glasgow Rd., Barr. Q 8 59
Glasgow Rd., Blan. R26 68
Glasgow Rd., Clyde. C 7 5
Glasgow Rd., Clyde. F 7 17
Glasgow Rd., Cumb. B 3 71
Glasgow Rd., Cumb. D 1 70
Glasgow Rd., Pais. L 7 31
Glasgow Rd., Renf. H 9 18
Glasgow Rd., Udd. O26 56
Glasgow St. G12 H15 21
Glassel Rd. G34 J26 40
Glasserton Pl. G43 P15 63
Glasserton Rd. G43 P15 63
Glassford St. G1 K17 36
Glebe Av. G71 R28 69
  Green St.
Glebe Ct. G4 K17 36
Glebe Hollow G71 R28 69
  Glebe Wynd
Glebe Pl. G72 P22 66
Glebe Pl. G73 O18 52
Glebe St. G4 J17 36
Glebe St., Renf. H 8 17
Glebe Wynd G71 R28 69
Glebe, The, Both. R28 69
Gleddoch Rd. G52 L 9 32
Glen Affric Av. G53 Q11 61
Glen Affric Dr. G53 Q11 61
Glen Affric Pl. G53 Q11 61
Glen Alby Pl. G53 Q11 61
Glen Av. G32 L22 38
Glen Av., Chr. E27 15
Glen Clunie Av. G53 Q11 61
Glen Clunie Dr. G53 Q11 61
Glen Clunie Pl. G53 Q11 61
Glen Cona Dr. G53 P11 61
Glen Cres. G13 F 9 18
Glen Esk Dr. G53 Q11 61
Glen Gdns., John. M 2 44
Glen La., Pais. L 6 30
Glen Livet Pl. G53 Q11 61
Glen Loy Pl. G53 Q11 61
Glen Mallie Dr. G53 Q11 61
Glen Markie Dr. G53 Q11 61
Glen Moriston Rd., Q11 61
  Thorn. G53
Glen Nevis Pl. G73 R20 65
Glen Ogle St. G32 M23 55
Glen Orchy Dr. G53 Q11 61
Glen Orchy Pl. G53 Q11 61
Glen Park Av., Thorn. R12 61
Glen Rd. G32 K22 38
Glen Sax Dr., Renf. J 9 32
Glen Sq. G33 H22 24
Glen St. G72 Q23 67
Glen St., Barr. O 8 59
Glen St., Pais. L 6 30
Glen Vw., Cumb. B 4 71
Glenacre Cres., Udd. O27 57
Glenacre Dr. G45 Q17 64
Glenacre Quad. G45 Q17 64
Glenacre Rd., Cumb. D 2 70
Glenacre St. G45 Q17 64
Glenacre Ter. G45 Q17 64
Glenallan Way, Pais. O 3 45
Glenalmond Rd. G73 Q20 65
Glenalmond St. G32 M22 54
Glenapp Av., Pais. N 7 47
Glenapp Rd., Pais. N 7 47
Glenapp St. G41 M15 51
Glenarklet Dr., Pais. N 7 47
Glenartney Row, Chr. E26 14
Glenashdale Way, Pais. N 7 47
  Glenbrittle Dr.
Glenavon Av. G73 Q20 65
Glenavon Rd. G20 F14 20
  Thornton St.
Glenavon Ter. G11 J13 34
  Crow Rd.
Glenbank Av., Lenz. D23 13
Glenbank Dr., Thorn. R12 61
Glenbank Rd., Lenz. D23 13
Glenbarr St. G21 J18 36
Glenbervie Pl. G23 E14 8
Glenbrittle Dr., Pais. N 7 47
Glenbrittle Way, Pais. N 6 46
Glenbuck Av. G33 G21 24
Glenbuck Dr. G33 G21 24
Glenburn Av. G73 P20 65

Glenburn Av., Bail. L26 40
Glenburn Av., Chr. E27 15
Glenburn Cres., Pais. O 5 46
Glenburn Gdns., Bish. E18 10
Glenburn Rd., Bear. C11 7
Glenburn Rd., Giff. R13 62
Glenburn Rd., Pais. O 4 45
Glenburn St. G20 F15 21
Glenburnie Pl. G34 K25 40
Glencairn Dr. G41 N14 50
Glencairn Dr. G73 O18 52
Glencairn Dr., Chr. E27 15
Glencairn Gdns. G41 N15 51
Glencairn Dr.
Glencairn Rd., Cumb. C 4 71
Glencairn Rd., Pais. K 7 31
Glencally Av., Pais. N 7 47
Glencart Gro., John. N08 43
Milliken Park Rd.
Glenclora Dr., Pais. N 7 47
Glencloy St. G20 F14 20
Glencoe Pl. G13 F12 19
Glencoe Rd. G73 Q20 65
Glencoe St. G13 F12 19
Glencorse Rd., Pais. N 5 46
Glencorse St. G32 K21 38
Glencroft Av., Udd. O27 57
Glencroft Rd. G44 P17 64
Glencryan Rd., Cumb. D 3 71
Glendale Cres., Bish. F20 23
Glendale Dr., Bish. F20 23
Glendale Pl. G31 L19 37
Glendale St.
Glendale Pl. G64 F20 23
Glendale St. G31 L19 37
Glendaruel Av., Bear. D13 8
Glendaruel Rd. G73 R21 66
Glendee Gdns., Renf. J 8 31
Glendee Rd., Renf. J 8 31
Glendenning Rd. G13 E12 7
Glendevon Pl., Dalm. D 6 4
Glendevon Sq. G33 J22 38
Glendore St. G14 J12 33
Glendower Way O 3 45
Spencer Dr.
Glenduffhill Rd., Bail. L24 39
Gleneagles Av., Cumb. A 3 71
Muirfield Rd.
Gleneagles Cotts. G14 H11 19
Dumbarton Rd.
Gleneagles Dr., Bish. D19 11
Gleneagles Gdns., Bish. D19 11
Gleneagles La. N. G14 H11 19
Dunglass Av.
Gleneagles Pk., Both. R27 69
Gleneagles Ter. G14 H11 19
Dumbarton Rd.
Glenelg Quad. G34 J26 40
Glenetive Pl. G73 R21 66
Glenfarg Cres., Bear. D13 8
Glenfarg Rd. G73 Q19 65
Glenfarg St. G20 J16 35
Glenfield Cres., Pais. P 5 58
Glenfield Rd., Pais. P 5 58
Glenfinnan Dr. G20 G14 20
Glenfinnan Dr., Bear. D14 8
Glenfinnan Pl. G20 G14 20
Glenfinnan Rd. G20 G14 20
Glenfruin Dr., Pais. N 7 47
Glengarry Dr. G52 L10 33
Wedderlea Dr.
Glengavel Cres. G33 G21 24
Glengyre St. G34 J26 40
Glenhead Cres. G22 G17 22
Glenhead Rd., Dalm. C 7 5
Glenhead Rd., Lenz. D23 13
Glenhead St. G22 G17 22
Glenholme, Pais. N 4 45
Glenhove Rd., Cumb. C 3 71
Gleniffer Av. G13 G10 18
Gleniffer Cres., John. N 2 44
Gleniffer Dr., Barr. P 7 59
Gleniffer Rd., Pais. O 4 45
Gleniffer Rd., Renf. J 7 31
Gleniffer Vw., Clyde. D 8 5
Kirkoswald Dr.
Glenisa Av., Chr. D28 15
Glenisla St. G31 M20 53
Glenkirk Dr. G15 E10 6
Glenlee Cres. G52 M 9 48

Glenlora Dr. G53 O10 48
Glenlora Ter. G53 O10 48
Glenluce Dr. G32 M23 55
Glenlui Av. G73 P19 65
Glenlyon Pl. G73 Q20 65
Glenmalloch Pl., John. M 2 44
Glenmanor Av., Chr. E27 15
Glenmore Av. G42 O18 52
Glenmuir Dr. G53 P10 60
Glenpark Rd. G31 L19 37
Glenpark St. G31 L19 37
Glenpark Ter. G72 O21 54
Glenpatrick Bldgs., N 2 44
John.
Glenpatrick Rd., John. N 2 44
Glenraith Rd. G33 H22 24
Glenraith Sq. G33 H22 24
Glenraith Wk. G33 H23 25
Glenshee St. G31 M20 53
Glenshiel Av., Pais. N 7 47
Glenside Av. G53 N10 48
Glenside Dr. G73 P20 65
Glenspean Pl. G43 P14 62
Glenspean St.
Glenspean St. G43 P14 62
Glentanar Pl. G22 F16 21
Glentarbert Rd. G73 Q20 65
Glenturret St. G32 M22 54
Glentyan Av., Kilb. M07 42
Glentyan Dr. G53 P10 60
Glentyan Ter. G53 O10 48
Glenview Cres., Chr. D28 15
Glenview Pl., Blan. R26 68
Glenville Av., Giff. Q13 62
Glenwood Ct., Kirk. C22 12
Glenwood Dr., Thorn. R12 61
Glenwood Gdns., Kirk. C22 12
Glenwood Pl., Kirk. C22 12
Glenwood Rd., Kirk. C22 12
Gloucester Av. G73 P20 65
Gloucester St. G5 L16 35
Gockston Rd., Pais. K 5 30
Gogar Pl. G33 K21 38
Gogar St. G33 K21 38
Goldberry Av. G14 G10 18
Goldie Rd., Udd. Q28 69
Golf Ct. G44 R15 63
Golf Dr. G15 E 9 6
Golf Dr., Pais. M 8 47
Golf Rd. G73 Q19 65
Golf Vw., Bear. C10 6
Golf Vw., Dalm. D 6 4
Golfhill Dr. G31 K19 37
Golfhill La. G31 K19 37
Whitehill St.
Golfhill Ter. G31 K18 36
Firpark St.
Golspie St. G51 K13 34
Goosedubbs G1 L17 36
Stockwell St.
Gopher Av., Udd. O28 57
Myrtle Rd.
Gorbals Cross G5 L17 36
Gorbals La. G5 L16 35
Oxford St.
Gorbals St. G5 L16 35
Gordon Av. G44 R15 63
Gordon Av., Bail. L24 39
Gordon Dr. G44 Q15 63
Gordon La. G1 K16 35
Gordon St.
Gordon Rd. G44 R15 63
Gordon St. G1 K16 35
Gordon St., Pais. M 6 46
Gordon Ter., Blan. R26 68
Gorebridge St. G32 K21 38
Gorget Av. G13 E11 7
Gorget Pl. G13 E11 7
Gorget Quad. G15 E10 6
Gorget Av.
Gorse Dr., Barr. Q 7 59
Gorse Pl., Udd. O28 57
Myrtle Rd.
Gorsewood, Bish. E18 10
Gorstan Pl. G20 G14 20
Wyndford Rd.
Gorstan St. G23 F14 20
Gosford La. G13 G 9 18
Dumbarton Rd.
Goudie St., Pais. K 5 30

Gough St. G33 K20 37
Gourlay Path G21 H17 22
Endrick St.
Gourlay St. G21 H17 22
Gourlay St. G21 H18 22
Millarbank St.
Gourock St. G5 M16 51
Govan Cross G51 K13 34
Govan Rd. G51 K12 33
Govanhill St. G42 N16 51
Gowanbank Gdns., N09 43
John.
Floors St.
Gowanbrae, Lenz. C23 13
Gallowhill Rd.
Gowanlea Av. G15 E10 6
Gowanlea Dr., Giff. Q14 62
Gowanlea Ter., Udd. O28 57
Gower La. G51 L14 34
Gower St.
Gower St. G43 M14 50
Gower Ter. G41 L14 34
Goyle Av. G15 D11 7
Grace Av., Bail. L27 41
Grace St. G3 K15 35
Graffham Av., Giff. Q14 62
Grafton Pl. G4 K17 36
Graham Av. G72 P23 67
Graham Av., Clyde. D 7 5
Graham Sq. G31 L18 36
Graham St., Barr. Q 7 59
Graham St., John. N09 43
Graham Ter., Bish. F19 23
Grahamston Cres., Pais. O 8 47
Grahamston Ct., Pais. O 8 47
Grahamston Pl., Pais. O 8 47
Grahamston Rd.
Grahamston Rd., Barr. P 7 59
Graighead Av. G33 H20 23
Grainger Rd., Bish. E20 11
Grampian Av., Pais. O 5 46
Grampian Cres. G32 M22 54
Grampian Pl. G32 M22 54
Grampian St. G32 M22 54
Grampian Way, Barr. R 8 59
Gran St., Clyde. F 9 18
Granby La. G12 H14 20
Great George St.
Granby Pl. G12 H14 20
Great George St.
Grandtully Dr. G12 G14 20
Grange Gdns. G71 R28 69
Blairston Av.
Grange Rd. G42 O16 51
Grange Rd., Bear. C12 7
Grangeneuk Gdnd., C 1 70
Cumb.
Grant St. G3 J15 35
Grantlea Gro. G32 M23 55
Grantlea Ter. G32 M23 55
Grantley Gdns. G41 O14 50
Grantley St. G41 O14 50
Granton St. G5 N18 52
Granville St. G3 K15 35
Granville St., Clyde. D 7 5
Gray Dr., Bear. D12 7
Gray St. G3 J14 34
Great Dovehill G1 L17 36
Great George La. G12 H14 20
Great George St.
Great George St. G12 H14 20
Great Hamilton St., Pais. N 6 46
Great Kelvin La. G12 H15 21
Glasgow St.
Great Western Rd. G12 H14 20
Great Western Ter. G12 H14 20
Great Western Terrace H14 20
La. G12
Westbourne Gdns. W.
Green Av., Lenz. B23 13
Green Farm Rd., Linw. L 1 28
Green Lodge Ter. G40 M18 52
Greenhead St.
Green Pk., Both. R28 69
Green St.
Green Rd. G73 O19 53
Green Rd., Pais. M 4 45
Green St. G40 L18 36
Green St., Both. R28 69
Green St., Clyde. D 7 5

Name	Ref		Name	Ref		Name	Ref
Green, The, G40	L18 36		Grosvenor La. G12	H14 20		Hampden Way, Renf.	J 8 31
Greenan Av. G42	O18 52		*Byers Rd.*			*Lewis Av.*	
Greenbank Dr., Pais.	O 5 46		Grosvenor Mansions	H14 20		Hangingshaw Pl. G42	O17 52
Greenbank Rd., Cumb.	C 1 70		G12			Haning, The, Renf.	J 8 31
Greenbank St. G43	P13 62		*Observatory Rd.*			Hanover St. G1	K17 36
Harriet St.			Grosvenor Ter. G12	H14 20		Hanson St. G31	K18 36
Greenbank St. G73	O19 53		Grove Pk., Lenz.	D23 13		Hapland Av. G53	N11 49
Greendyke St. G1	L17 36		Grove, The, Giff.	S13 62		Hapland Rd. G53	N11 49
Greenend Av., John.	N08 43		Grove, The, Kilb.	M07 42		Harbour La., Pais.	L 6 30
Greenend Pl. G32	K23 39		Groveburn Av., Thorn.	Q13 62		Harbour Rd., Pais.	K 6 30
Greenfaulds Cres.,	D 3 71		Grovepark Pl. G20	H16 21		Harburn Pl. G23	E15 9
Cumb.			Grovepark St. G20	H16 21		Harbury Pl. G14	G 9 18
Greenfaulds Rd., Cumb.	D 2 70		Groves, The, Bish.	F20 23		Harcourt Dr. G31	K19 37
Greenfield Av. G32	K22 38		*Woodhill Rd.*			Hardgate Dr. G51	K11 33
Greenfield Pl. G32	L22 38		Grudie St. G34	K25 40		Hardgate Gdns. G51	K11 33
Budhill Av.			Gryffe Av., Renf.	H 7 17		Hardgate Pl. G51	K11 33
Greenfield Rd. G32	L23 39		Gryffe Cres., Pais.	N 3 45		Hardgate Rd. G51	K11 33
Greenfield St. G51	K12 33		Gryffe St. G44	P16 63		Hardie Av. G73	O20 53
Greengairs Av. G51	K11 33		Guildford St. G33	J23 39		Hardridge Av. G52	N11 49
Greenhaugh St. G51	K13 34		Gullane Cres., Cumb.	A 2 70		*Hardridge Rd.*	
Greenhead Rd., Bear.	D12 7		Gullane St. G11	J13 34		Hardridge Pl. G52	N12 49
Greenhead Rd., Renf.	F 5 16		*Purdon St.*			Hardridge Rd. G52	N11 49
Greenhead St. G40	M18 52		Guthrie St. G20	G14 20		Harefield Dr. G14	G10 18
Greenhill Av., Gart.	F27 27					Harelaw Av. G44	Q15 63
Greenhill Av., Giff.	R13 62		Hagg Cres., John.	M09 43		Harelaw Av., Barr.	R 8 59
Greenhill Cres., John.	N 2 44		Hagg Pl., John.	M09 43		Harelaw Cres., Pais.	O 5 46
Greenhill Cres., Linw.	L 2 28		Hagg Rd., John.	N09 43		Harhill St. G51	K12 33
Greenhill Ct. G73	O19 53		Haggs Rd. G41	N14 50		Harland Cotts. G14	J11 33
Greenhill Dr., Linw.	L 2 28		Haggs Wood Av. G41	N14 50		*South St.*	
Greenhill Rd. G73	O19 53		Haghill Rd. G31	K20 37		Harland St. G14	H11 19
Greenhill Rd., Pais.	L 5 30		Haig Dr., Bail.	M24 55		Harlaw Gdns. G64	E20 11
Greenhill St. G73	O19 53		Haig St. G21	H19 23		Harley St. G51	L14 34
Greenhill, Bish.	E19 11		Hailes Av. G32	L23 39		Harmetray St. G22	G17 22
Greenholm Av., Udd.	O27 57		Haining Rd., Renf.	H 8 17		Harmony Pl. G51	K13 34
Greenholme St. G40	P16 63		Hairmyres St. G42	N16 51		Harmony Row G51	K13 34
Holmlea Rd.			*Govanhill St.*			Harmony Sq. G51	K13 34
Greenknowe Rd. G43	P13 62		Hairst St., Renf.	H 8 17		Harmsworth St. G11	J12 33
Greenlaw Av., Pais.	L 7 31		Halbeath Av. G15	D 9 6		Harport St. G46	Q12 61
Greenlaw Dr., Pais.	L 7 31		Halbert St. G41	N15 51		Harriet St. G73	O19 53
Greenlaw Rd. G14	G 9 18		Haldane La. G14	H11 19		Harrington Rd. G20	G15 21
Greenlaw Ter., Pais.	L 7 31		*Haldane St.*			*Maryhill Rd.*	
Greenlaw Av.			Haldane St. G14	H11 19		Harris Rd. G23	E15 9
Greenlea Rd., Chr.	F25 26		Halgreen Av. G15	D 9 6		Harrison Dr. G51	L13 34
Greenlea St. G13	G12 19		Halifax Way, Renf.	J 8 31		Harrow Ct. G15	D 9 6
Greenlees Gdns. G72	Q21 66		*Britannia Way*			*Linkwood Dr.*	
Greenlees Pk. G72	Q22 66		Hall St., Clyde.	E 7 5		Harrow Pl. G15	D 9 6
Greenlees Rd. G72	P22 66		Hallbrae St. G33	J21 38		Hart St. G31	L21 38
Greenloan Av. G51	K11 33		Halley Dr. G13	F 9 18		Hart St., Linw.	L 1 28
Greenmount G22	F16 21		Halley Pl. G13	G 9 18		Hartfield Ter., Pais.	N 7 47
Greenock Av. G44	P16 63		Halley Sq. G13	F 9 18		Hartlaw Cres. G52	L10 32
Greenock Rd., Pais.	K 5 30		Halley St. G13	F 9 18		Hartree Av. G13	F 9 18
Greenock Rd., Renf.	G 5 16		Hallhill Cres. G33	L24 39		Hartstone Pl. G53	O10 48
Greenrig St. G33	H20 23		Hallhill Rd. G32	L22 38		Hartstone Rd. G53	O10 48
Greenrig St., Udd.	P27 69		Hallhill Rd., John.	O08 43		Hartstone Ter. G53	O10 48
Greenrigg Rd., Cumb.	C 3 71		Hallidale Cres., Renf.	J 9 32		Harvey St. G4	J17 36
Greenshields Rd., Bail.	L25 40		Hallrule Dr. G52	L11 33		Harvie St. G51	L14 34
Greenside Cres. G33	H21 24		Hallside Av. G72	P24 67		Harwood St. G32	K21 38
Greenside St. G33	H21 24		Hallside Cres. G72	P24 67		Hastie St. G3	J14 34
Greentree Dr., Bail.	M24 55		Hallside Dr. G72	P24 67		*Old Dumbarton Rd.*	
Greenview St. G43	O14 50		Hallside Rd. G72	Q24 67		Hatfield Dr. G12	G12 19
Greenways Av., Pais.	N 4 45		Hallside St. G5	M17 52		Hathaway Dr., Giff.	R13 62
Greenways Ct., John.	N 4 45		Hallydown Dr. G13	G11 19		Hathaway La. G20	G15 21
Greenwell Pl. G51	K13 34		Halton Gdns., Bail.	M24 55		*Avenuepark St.*	
Greenwell St. G51	K13 34		Hamilton Av. G41	M13 50		Hathaway St. G20	G15 21
Govan Rd.			Hamilton Cres. G72	Q23 67		Hathersage Av., Bail.	L25 40
Greenwood Av. G72	P24 67		Hamilton Cres., Bear.	B12 7		Hathersage Dr., Bail.	L25 40
Greenwood Av., Chr.	E27 15		Hamilton Cres., Renf.	G 8 17		Hathersage Gdns., Bail.	L25 40
Greenwood Dr., Bear.	D13 8		Hamilton Dr. G12	H15 21		Hatters Row G40	M18 52
Greenwood Quad.,	E 8 5		Hamilton Dr. G72	P22 66		*Dalmarnock Rd.*	
Clyde.			Hamilton Dr., Both.	R28 69		Hatton Dr. G52	M10 48
Greer Quad., Clyde.	D 7 5		Hamilton Dr., Giff.	R14 62		Hatton Gdns. G52	M10 48
Grenville Dr. G72	Q21 66		Hamilton Park Av.	H15 21		Haugh Rd. G3	K14 34
Greran Dr., Renf.	H 7 17		G12			Haughburn Pl. G53	O10 48
Gretna St. G40	M19 53		Hamilton Rd. G32	N24 55		Haughburn Rd. G53	O10 48
Greyfriars St. G32	K21 38		Hamilton Rd. G72 &	P22 66		Haughburn Ter. G53	O11 49
Greystone Av. G73	P20 65		Blan.			Havelock La. G11	J14 34
Greywood St. G13	F12 19		Hamilton Rd. G73	O19 53		*Downhill St.*	
Grier Path G31	L20 37		Hamilton Rd., Both.	R28 69		Havelock St. G11	J14 34
Grierson La. G33	K20 37		Hamilton St. G42	N17 52		Hawick Av. G78	N 4 45
Lomak St.			Hamilton St., Clyde.	F 8 17		Hawick St. G13	F 9 18
Grierson St. G33	K20 37		Hamilton St., Pais.	L 6 30		Hawkhead Av., Pais.	N 7 47
Grieve Rd., Cumb.	B 3 71		Hamilton Ter., Clyde.	F 8 17		Hawkhead Rd., Pais.	M 7 47
Griqua Ter. G71	R28 69		Hamilton Vw., Udd.	O28 57		Hawthorn Av., Bish.	F19 23
Grogary Rd. G15	D10 6		Hamiltonhill Rd. G22	H16 21		Hawthorn Av., Lenz.	C23 13
Springside Pl.			Hampden Dr. G42	O16 51		Hawthorn Av., Renf.	F 6 16
Grosvenor Cres. G12	H14 20		*Cathcart Rd.*			Hawthorn Cres., Renf.	E 5 4
Observatory Rd.			Hampden La. G42	O16 51		Hawthorn Cres., Renf.	F 5 16
Grosvenor Cres. La.	H14 20		*Cathcart Rd.*			Hawthorn Dr., Barr.	S 8 59
G12			Hampden Ter. G42	O16 51		Hawthorn Quad. G22	G17 22
Byers Rd.			*Cathcart Rd.*			Hawthorn Rd., Renf.	F 6 16

Name	Grid	No.
Hawthorn St. G22	G17	22
Hawthorn St., Clyde.	D 7	5
Hawthorn Wk. G72	P20	65
Hawthorn Wk., Bish.	F20	23
Letham Dr.		
Hawthornden Gdns.	E15	9
G23		
Hawthorne Av., Bear.	B13	8
Hawthorne Av., John.	N 1	44
Hawthorne Ter., Udd.	O28	57
Douglas St.		
Hay Dr., John.	M 1	44
Hayburn Cres. G11	H13	20
Hayburn Ct. G11	J13	34
Hayburn La. G12	H13	20
Queensborough Gdns.		
Hayburn St. G11	J13	34
Hayfield St. G5	M17	52
Hayhill Cotts., Gart.	G28	27
Hayle Gdns., Chr.	D27	15
Haylynn St. G14	J12	33
Haymarket St. G32	K21	38
Haystack Pl., Lenz.	D23	13
Hayston Cres. G22	G16	21
Hayston St. G22	G16	21
Haywood St. G22	G16	21
Hazel Av. G44	Q15	63
Clarkston Rd.		
Hazel Av., John.	N 1	44
Hazel Av., Lenz.	C23	13
Hazel Dene, Bish.	E19	11
Hazel Gro., Lenz.	C23	13
Hazel Rd., Cumb.	B 4	71
Hazel Ter., Udd.	O28	57
Douglas St.		
Hazelden Gdns. G44	Q15	63
Hazellea Dr., Giff.	Q14	62
Hazelwood Av. G78	O 3	45
Hazelwood Dr., Blan.	S26	68
Hazelwood Gdns. G73	Q20	65
Hazelwood Rd. G41	M14	50
Hazlitt St. G20	G16	21
Heath Av., Bish.	F19	23
Heath Av., Lenz.	D23	13
Heathcliffe Av., Blan.	R26	68
Heathcot Av. G15	E 9	6
Heathcot Pl. G15	E 9	6
Heathcot Av.		
Heather Av., Barr.	P 7	59
Heather Dr., Lenz.	D22	12
Heather Gdns., Lenz.	D22	12
Heather Pl., John.	N 1	44
Heather Pl., Lenz.	C22	12
Heather St. G41	L15	35
Scotland St.		
Heatherbrae, Bish.	E18	10
Heatheryknowe Rd.,	K27	41
Bail.		
Heathfield Av., Chr.	E27	15
Heathfield St. G33	K23	39
Heathfield Ter. G21	G18	22
Broomfield Rd.		
Heathside Rd., Giff.	Q14	62
Heathwood Dr., Thorn.	Q13	62
Hecla Av. G15	D 9	6
Hecla Pl. G15	D 9	6
Hector Rd. G41	O14	50
Heggie Ter. G14	H11	19
Dumbarton Rd.		
Helen St. G52	L12	33
Helenburgh Dr. G13	G11	19
Helenslea G72	Q23	67
Helenvale Ct. G31	L20	37
Helenvale St.		
Helenvale St. G31	M20	53
Helmsdale Av., Blan.	Q26	68
Helmsdale Ct. G72	P23	67
Hemlock St. G13	F12	19
Henderland Rd., Bear.	E12	7
Henderson Av. G72	P23	67
Henderson St. G20	H15	21
Henderson St., Clyde.	F 9	18
Henderson St., Pais.	L 5	30
Henrietta St. G14	H11	19
Henry St., Barr.	Q 7	59
Hepburn Rd. G52	K10	32
Herald Av. G13	E11	7
Herald Way, Renf.	J 8	31
Viscount Av.		
Herbert St. G20	H15	21
Herbertson St. G5	L16	35
Eglinton St.		
Hercules Way, Renf.	J 8	31
Friendship Way		
Herichell St. G13	G12	19
Foulis La.		
Heriot Av., Pais.	O 3	45
Heriot Cres., Bish.	D19	11
Heriot Rd., Lenz.	D23	13
Herma St. G23	F15	21
Hermiston Av. G32	L23	39
Hermiston Pl. G32	L23	39
Hermiston Rd. G32	K22	38
Hermitage Av. G13	G11	19
Heron Ct., Clyde.	C 7	5
Heron Pl., John.	O08	43
Heron St. G40	M18	52
Heron Way, Renf.	J 8	31
Britannia Way		
Herries Rd. G41	N14	50
Herriet St. G41	M15	51
Herschell St. G13	G12	19
Foulis La.		
Hertford Av. G12	G13	20
Hexham Gdns. G41	N14	50
Heys St., Barr.	R 8	59
Hickman St. G42	N16	51
Hickory St. G42	G18	22
High Barholm, Kilb.	M07	42
High Calside, Pais.	M 5	46
High Craighall Rd. G4	J16	35
High Parksail, Renf.	F 5	16
High Rd., Pais.	M 5	46
High St. G1	L17	36
High St. G73	O19	53
High St., John.	M09	43
High St., Pais.	M 5	46
High St., Renf.	H 8	17
Highburgh Dr. G73	P19	65
Highburgh Rd. G12	J14	34
Highburgh Ter. G12	J14	34
Highburgh Rd.		
Highcraig Av., John.	N08	43
Highcroft Av. G44	P17	64
Highfield Av., Pais.	O 5	46
Highfield Cres., Pais.	O 5	46
Highfield Dr. G12	G13	20
Highfield Dr. G73	Q20	65
Highfield Pl. G12	G13	20
Highkirk Vw., John.	N09	43
Highland La. G51	K14	34
Hilary Av. G73	P20	65
Hilary Dr., Bail.	L24	39
Hilda Cres. G33	H21	24
Hill Path G52	L10	32
Hill Pl. G52	L10	32
Hill St. G3	J16	35
Hillcrest Av. G32	O22	54
Hillcrest Av. G44	Q15	63
Hillcrest Av., Clyde.	B 7	5
Hillcrest Av., Cumb.	C 2	70
Hillcrest Av., Pais.	P 5	58
Hillcrest Ct., Cumb.	C 2	70
Hillcrest Rd. G32	O23	55
Hillcrest Rd., Bear.	D12	7
Hillcrest Rd., Udd.	O28	57
Hillcrest Ter., Both.	Q28	69
Churchill Cres.		
Hillcrest, Chr.	F26	26
Hillcroft Ter., Bish.	F18	22
Hillend Cres., Clyde.	B 6	4
Hillend Rd. G22	F16	21
Hillend Rd. G73	P19	65
Hillfoot Av. G73	O19	53
Hillfoot Av., Bear.	C12	7
Hillfoot Dr., Bear.	C12	7
Hillfoot Gdns., Udd.	O27	57
Hillfoot St. G31	K19	37
Hillfoot Ter., Bear.	C13	8
Milngavie Rd.		
Hillhead Av. G73	Q19	65
Hillhead Av., Chr.	E27	15
Hillhead Gdns. G12	J14	34
Hillhead St.		
Hillhead Pl. G12	J15	35
Bank St.		
Hillhead St. G12	J14	34
Hillhouse St. G21	H19	23
Hillington Gdns. G52	M11	49
Hillington Ind. Est. G52	K 9	32
Hillington Pk. Cres. G52	L11	33
Hillington Quad. G52	L10	32
Hillington Rd. G52	J 9	32
Hillington Rd. S., Renf.	L10	32
Hillington Ter. G52	L10	32
Hillkirk Pl. G21	H18	22
Hillkirk St. G21	H18	22
Hillkirk Street La. G21	H18	22
Hillkirk St.		
Hillneuk Av., Bear.	C12	7
Hillneuk Dr., Bear.	C13	8
Hillpark Av., Pais.	N 5	46
Hillpark Dr. G43	P14	62
Hillsborough Rd., Bail.	L24	39
Hillsborough Sq. G12	J14	34
Hillhead St.		
Hillsborough Ter. G12	H15	21
Bower St.		
Hillside Av., Bear.	C12	7
Hillside Ct., Thorn.	Q12	61
Hillside Dr., Barr.	Q 7	59
Hillside Dr., Bear.	C13	8
Hillside Dr., Bish.	E19	11
Hillside Gardens La. G11	H13	20
North Gardner St.		
Hillside Gdns. G11	H13	20
Turnberry Rd.		
Hillside Gro., Barr.	Q 7	59
Hillside Quad. G43	P13	62
Hillside Rd. G43	P13	62
Hillside Rd., Barr.	Q 7	59
Hillside Rd., Pais.	N 7	47
Hillswick Cres. G22	F16	21
Hilltop Rd., Chr.	E27	15
Eastwood Rd.		
Hillview Cres., Udd.	O27	57
Hillview Dr., Blan.	R26	68
Hillview Rd., John.	N 2	44
Hillview St. G32	L21	38
Hilton Gardens La. G13	F12	19
Fulton St.		
Hilton Gdns. G13	F12	19
Hilton Pk., Bish.	D18	10
Hilton Rd., Bish.	D18	10
Hilton Ter. G13	F12	19
Hilton Ter. G72	Q21	66
Hilton Ter., Bish.	D18	10
Hinshaw St. G20	H16	21
Hinshelwood Dr. G51	L13	34
Hinshelwood Pl. G51	L13	34
Edmiston Dr.		
Hirsel Pl., Bush.	R28	69
Lomond Dr.		
Hobart Cres., Dalm.	C 5	4
Hobart St. G22	H16	21
Hobden St. G21	H19	23
Hoddam Av. G45	Q19	65
Hoddam Ter. G45	Q19	65
Ardencraig Rd.		
Hoey St. G51	K14	34
Hogan Ct., Clyde.	C 6	4
Dalgleish Av.		
Hogarth Av. G32	K20	37
Hogarth Cres. G32	K20	37
Hogarth Dr. G32	K20	37
Hogarth Gdns. G32	K20	37
Hogg Av., John.	N09	43
Hogganfield St. G33	J20	37
Holburn Av., Pais.	L 4	29
Hole Brae, Cumb.	B 3	71
Holeburn Rd. G43	P14	62
Holehouse Dr. G13	G10	18
Holland St. G2	K16	35
Hollinwell Rd. G23	F15	21
Hollowglen Rd. G32	L22	38
Hollows Av., Pais.	O 3	45
Hollows Cres., Pais.	O 3	45
Holly Pl., John.	O 1	44
Holly St., Clyde.	D 7	5
Hollybank Pl. G72	Q22	66
Hollybank St. G21	J19	37
Hollybrook St. G42	N16	51
Hollybush Av., Pais.	O 4	45
Hollybush Rd. G52	L 9	32
Hollymount, Bear.	E12	7
Holm Av., Pais.	N 6	46
Holm Av., Udd.	O27	57
Holm Pl., Linw.	K 1	28
Holm St. G2	K16	35

Name	Grid	Page
Holmbank Av. G41	O14	50
Holmbrae Av., Udd.	O27	57
Holmbrae Rd., Udd.	O27	57
Holmbyre Rd. G45	R17	64
Holmbyre Ter. G45	R17	64
Holmes Av., Renf.	J 8	31
Holmfauldhead Dr.	K12	33
G51		
Holmhead Cres. G44	P16	63
Holmhead Pl. G44	P16	63
Holmhead Rd. G44	P16	63
Holmhill Av. G72	Q22	66
Holmhills Dr. G72	Q21	66
Holmhills Gdns. G72	Q21	66
Holmhills Gro. G72	Q21	66
Holmhills Pl. G72	Q21	66
Holmhills Rd. G72	Q21	66
Holmhills Ter. G72	Q21	66
Holmlea Rd. G44	O16	51
Holms Pl., Gart.	F27	27
Holmswood Av., Blan.	R26	68
Holmwood Av., Udd.	O27	57
Holmwood Gdns., Udd.	P27	69
Holyrood Cres. G20	J15	35
Holyrood Quad. G20	J15	35
Holywell St. G31	L19	37
Homeston Av., Udd.	Q28	69
Honeybog Rd. G52	L 9	32
Hood St., Clyde.	E 8	5
Hope St. G2	K16	35
Hopefield Av. G12	G14	20
Hopehill Pl. G20	H16	21
Hopehill Rd		
Hopehill Rd. G20	H16	21
Hopeman Av. G46	Q12	61
Hopeman Dr. G46	Q12	61
Hopeman Rd. G46	Q12	61
Hopeman St. G46	Q12	61
Hopetoun Pl. G23	E15	9
Hornal Rd., Udd.	Q28	69
Hornbeam Dr., Dalm.	D 7	5
Hornbeam Rd., Udd.	O28	57
Myrtle Rd.		
Horndean Cres. G33	J23	39
Horndean Ct., Bish.	D19	11
Horne St. G22	G18	22
Hawthorn St.		
Hornshill Rd. G33	F24	25
Hornshill St. G21	H19	23
Horsburgh St. G33	J23	39
Horse Shoe La., Bear.	D12	7
Horse Shoe Rd., Bear.	C12	7
Horslethill Rd. G12	H14	20
Hospital St. G5	M16	51
Hotspur St. G20	H15	21
Houldsworth La. G3	K15	35
Finnieston St.		
Houldsworth St. G3	K15	35
Househillmuir Cres. G53	O11	49
Househillmuir La. G53	O11	49
Househillmuir Pl. G53	O11	49
Househillmuir Rd. G53	P10	60
Househillwood Cres.	O10	48
G53		
Househillwood Rd. G53	P10	60
Housel Av. G13	F10	18
Houston Pl. G5	L15	35
Houston Pl., John.	N 2	44
Houston Rd., Loanhead	H 1	28
Houston Sq., John.	M09	43
Houston St. G5	L15	35
Houston St., Renf.	H 8	17
Howard St. G1	L16	35
Howard St., Pais.	M 7	47
Howat St. G51	K13	34
Howden Dr., Linw.	L 1	28
Howe St., Pais.	M 3	45
Howford Rd. G52	M10	48
Howgate Av. G15	D 9	6
Howieshill Av. G72	P22	66
Howieshill Rd. G72	Q22	66
Howth Dr. G13	F12	19
Howth Ter. G13	F12	19
Howwood St. G41	L15	35
Hoylake Pk., Both.	R27	69
Hoylake Pl. G23	E15	9
Hozier Cres., Udd.	O27	57
Hozier St. G40	M18	52
Hubbard Dr. G11	J12	33
Hugh Murray Gro. G72	P23	67
Hughenden Dr. G12	H13	20
Hughenden Gdns. G12	H13	20
Hughenden La. G12	H13	20
Hughenden Rd. G12	H13	20
Hughenden Ter. G12	H13	20
Hughenden Rd.		
Hugo St. G20	G15	21
Hume Dr., Both.	Q28	69
Hume Dr., Udd.	O27	57
Hume Rd., Cumb.	B 3	71
Hume St., Clyde.	E 7	5
Hunter Pl. G78	N07	42
Hunter Rd. G33	N20	53
Hunter St. G4	L18	36
Hunter St., Pais.	L 6	30
Hunterfield Dr. G72	P21	66
Hunterhill Av., Pais.	M 6	46
Hunterhill Rd.		
Hunterhill Rd., Pais.	M 6	46
Huntersfield Rd., John.	N08	43
Huntershill Rd., Bish.	F18	22
Huntershill St. G21	G18	22
Huntershill Way, Bish.	F18	22
Crowhill Rd.		
Huntingdon Sq. G21	J18	36
Huntingdon Rd.		
Huntington Rd. G21	J18	36
Huntingtower Rd., Bail.	M25	56
Huntley Dr., Bear.	B12	7
Tweedsmuir Dr.		
Huntley Rd. G52	K 9	32
Huntly Av., Giff.	R14	62
Huntly Dr. G72	Q22	66
Huntly Gdns. G12	H14	20
Huntly Path, Chr.	E28	15
Burnbrae Av.		
Huntly Rd. G12	H14	20
Huntly Ter., Pais.	N 7	47
Hurlet Rd., Pais.& G53	N 8	47
Hurley Hawkin, Bish.	F20	23
Hurlford Av. G13	F 9	18
Hutcheson Rd., Thorn.	R13	62
Hutcheson St. G1	K17	36
Hutchinson Ct. G2	K16	35
Hope St.		
Hutchinson Pl. G72	Q24	67
Hutchison Ct., Giff.	Q13	62
Berryhill Rd.		
Hutchison Dr., Bear.	E13	8
Hutton Dr. G51	K12	33
Huxley St. G20	G15	21
Hydepark Pl. G21	G18	22
Springburn Rd.		
Hydepark St. G3	K15	35
Hyndal Av. G53	N11	49
Hyndford St. G51	K13	34
Hyndland Av. G11	J13	34
Hyndland Rd. G12	H13	20
Hyndland St. G11	J14	34
Hyndlee Dr. G52	L11	33
Hyslop Pl., Clyde.	D 7	5
Albert Rd.		
Iain Dr., Bear.	C11	7
Iain Rd., Bear.	C11	7
Ibrox St. G51	L14	34
Ibrox Ter. G51	L13	34
Ibrox Terrace La. G51	L13	34
Ibroxholm La. G51	L14	34
Paisley Rd. W.		
Ibroxholm Oval G51	L13	34
Ibroxholm Pl. G51	L14	34
Ilay Av., Bear.	F12	19
Ilay Ct., Bear.	F13	20
Ilay Rd., Bear.	F13	20
Inchbrae Rd. G52	M11	49
Inchfad Dr. G15	D 9	6
Inchholm St. G11	J12	33
Inchinnan Rd., Pais.	K 6	30
Inchinnan Rd., Renf.	H 7	17
Inchkeith Pl. G32	K22	38
Inchlee St. G14	J12	33
Inchmurrin Dr. G73	R20	65
Inchmurrin Gdns. G73	R20	65
Inchmurrin Pl. G73	R20	65
Inchoch St. G33	J24	39
Inchrory Pl. G15	D 9	6
Incle St., Pais.	L 6	30
India Dr., Renf.	G 5	16
India St. G2	K16	35
India St. G73	O19	53
Inga St. G20	F15	21
Ingerbreck Av. G73	Q20	65
Ingleby Dr. G31	K19	37
Inglefield St. G42	N16	51
Ingleneuk Av. G33	G22	24
Inglestone Av., Thorn.	R13	62
Inglis St. G31	L19	37
Ingram St. G1	K17	36
Inishail Rd. G33	J23	39
Inkerman Rd. G52	L 9	32
Innerwick Dr. G52	L10	32
Inver Rd. G33	K24	39
Inverary Dr., Bish.	D19	11
Invercanny Dr. G15	D 9	6
Invercanny Pl. G15	D10	6
Inverclyde Gdns. G11	H12	19
Broomhill Dr.		
Inverclyde Gdns. G73	Q21	66
Inveresk Cres. G32	L22	38
Inveresk St. G32	L22	38
Inverewe Av. G46	Q11	61
Inverewe Dr. G46	R11	61
Inverewe Gdns. G46	R11	61
Inverewe Pl. G46	Q11	61
Invergarry Av. G46	R11	61
Invergarry Ct. G46	R11	61
Invergarry Dr. G46	R11	61
Invergarry Gdns. G46	R11	61
Invergarry Gro. G46	R11	61
Invergarry Pl. G46	R11	61
Invergarry Quad. G46	R12	61
Invergarry Vw. G46	R12	61
Inverglas Av., Renf.	J 9	32
Morriston Cres.		
Invergordon Av. G43	O15	51
Invergyle Dr. G52	L10	32
Inverkar Dr., Pais.	N 4	45
Inverkip St. G5	L17	36
Inverlair Av. G43	P15	63
Inverleith St. G32	L20	37
Inverlochy St. G33	J23	39
Inverness St. G51	L11	33
Inveroran Dr., Bear.	D13	8
Invershin Dr. G20	G14	20
Invershiel Rd. G23	E14	8
Wyndford Rd.		
Inverurie St. G21	H17	22
Inzievar Ter. G32	N22	54
Iona Ct. G51	K13	34
Iona Dr., Pais.	O 5	46
Iona La., Chr.	E28	15
Heathfield Av.		
Iona Rd. G73	Q21	66
Iona Rd., Renf.	J 8	31
Iona St. G51	K13	34
Irongray St. G31	K20	37
Irvine Dr., Linw.	L 1	28
Irvine St. G40	M19	53
Irving Av., Clyde.	C 7	5
Stewart Dr.		
Irving Quad., Clyde.	C 7	5
Stewart Dr.		
Iser La. G41	O15	51
Island Rd., Cumb.	D 1	70
Islay Av. G73	Q21	66
Islay Cres., Pais.	O 5	46
Ivanhoe Rd. G13	F11	19
Ivanhoe Rd., Cumb.	D 2	70
Ivanhoe Rd., Pais.	N 3	45
Ivanhoe Way, Pais.	N 3	45
Ivanhoe Rd.		
Ivybank Ave. G72	Q23	67
Jacks Rd., Udd.	P28	69
Jagger Gdns., Bail.	M24	55
Jamaica St. G1	L16	35
James Dunlop Gdns.,	F19	23
Bish.		
Graham Ter.		
James Gray St. G41	O15	51
James Morrison St. G1	L17	36
St. Andrews Sq.		
James Nisbet St. G21	K18	36
James St. G40	M18	52
James Watt La. G2	K16	35
James Watt St.		
James Watt St. G2	K16	35
Jamieson Ct. G42	N16	51
Jamieson St., Clyde.	B 7	5

Name	Ref	No.
Jamieson Path G42	N16	51
Jamieson St.		
Jamieson St. G42	N16	51
Janebank Av. G72	Q23	67
Janefield Av., John.	N 9	43
Janefield St. G31	L19	37
Janes Brae, Cumb.	D 2	70
Janetta St., Clyde.	D 7	5
Jardine St. G20	H15	21
Jardine Ter., Gart.	G27	27
Jasgray St. G42	N15	51
Jean Armour Dr., Clyde.	D 8	5
Jedburgh Av. G73	O19	53
Jedburgh Dr., Pais.	N 4	45
Jedburgh Gdns. G20	H15	21
Jedworth Av. G15	D10	6
Jellicoe St. Dalm.	D 6	4
Jennys Well Rd., Pais.	N 7	47
Jerviston Rd. G33	J23	39
Jessie St. G42	N17	52
Jessiman Sq., Renf.	J 7	31
John Brown Pl., Chr.	F26	26
John Knox La. G4	K18	36
Drygate		
John Knox St. G4	K18	36
John Knox St., Clyde.	F 8	17
John Lang St., John.	M 1	44
John St. G1	K17	36
John St., Barr.	Q 7	59
John St., Pais.	M 5	46
Johnshaven St. G43	O14	50
Bengal St.		
Johnston Rd., Gart.	G28	27
Johnston St., Pais.	M 6	46
Gordon St.		
Johnstone Av. G52	L10	32
Johnstone Av., Clyde.	F 8	17
Johnstone Cotts., Kirk.	B21	12
Johnstone Dr. G72	P22	66
Johnstone Dr. G73	O19	53
Joppa St. G33	K21	38
Jordan St. G14	J11	33
Jordanhill Cres. G13	G11	19
Jordanhill Dr. G13	G11	19
Jordanhill La. G13	G12	19
Austen Rd.		
Jordanvale Av. G14	J11	33
Jowitt Av., Clyde.	E 8	5
Joycelyn Sq. G1	L17	36
Jubilee Bank, Lenz.	D23	13
Heriot Rd.		
Jubilee Path, Bear.	D12	7
Jubilee Ter., John.	N08	43
Julian Av. G12	H14	20
Julian La. G12	H14	20
Julian Av.		
Juniper Ct., Lenz.	C22	12
Juniper Pl. G32	M24	55
Juniper Pl., John.	O 1	44
Juniper Ter. G32	M24	55
Jura Av., Renf.	J 8	31
Jura Ct. G52	L12	33
Jura Dr., Blan.	Q26	68
Jura Rd., Pais.	O 5	46
Jura St. G52	L12	33
Kaim Dr. G53	P11	61
Kames St. G5	M16	51
Karol Path G4	J16	35
St. Peters St.		
Katewell Av. G15	D 9	6
Katrine Av., Bish.	E19	11
Katrine Dr., Pais.	N 3	45
Kay St. G21	H18	22
Kaystone Rd. G15	E10	6
Keal Av. G15	F10	18
Keal Cres. G15	F10	18
Keal Dr. G15	F10	18
Keal Pl. G15	F10	18
Kearn Av. G15	E10	6
Kearn Pl. G15	E10	6
Keats Pk., Udd.	Q28	69
Keir Dr., Bish.	E18	10
Keir St. G41	M15	51
Keirhill Rd, Cumb.	C 1	70
Woodburn Rd.		
Keirs Wk. G72	P22	66
Keith Av., Giff.	Q14	62
Keith Ct. G11	J14	34
Keith St.		
Keith St. G11	J14	34
Kelbourne St. G20	H15	21
Kelburn St., Barr.	R 7	59
Kelburne Dr., Pais.	L 7	31
Kelburne Gdns., Bail.	M25	56
Kelburne Gdns., Pais.	L 7	31
Kelburne Oval, Pais.	L 7	31
Kelhead Av. G52	L 9	32
Kelhead Dr. G52	L 9	32
Kelhead Path G52	L10	32
Kelhead Pl. G52	L 9	32
Kellas St. G51	L13	34
Kells Pl. G15	D 9	6
Kelso Av. G73	O19	53
Kelso Av., Pais.	N 4	45
Kelso St. G13	G 9	18
Kelton St. G32	M22	54
Kelty Pl. G5	L16	35
Bedford St.		
Kelty St. G5	M16	51
Eglinton St.		
Kelvin Av. G52	J 9	32
Kelvin Cres., Bear.	E12	7
Kelvin Ct. G12	G12	19
Kelvin Dr. G20	H14	20
Kelvin Dr., Barr.	R 8	59
Kelvin Dr., Bish.	E19	11
Kelvin Dr., Chr.	E27	15
Kelvin Rd., Cumb.	D 3	71
Kelvin Rd., Udd.	O27	57
Kelvin Way G3	J14	34
Kelvin Way, Udd.	Q28	69
Bracken Ter.		
Kelvindale Bldgs. G12	G14	20
Kelvindale Rd.		
Kelvindale Cotts. G12	G14	20
Kelvindale Rd.		
Kelvindale Glen G12	G14	20
Kelvindale Rd.		
Kelvindale Pl. G20	G14	20
Kelvindale Rd. G12	G14	20
Kelvingrove St. G3	K15	35
Kelvingrove Ter. G3	K15	35
Kelvingrove St.		
Kelvinhaugh Pl. G3	K14	34
Kelvinhaugh St.		
Kelvinhaugh St. G3	K14	34
Kelvinside Av. G20	H15	21
Queen Margaret Dr.		
Kelvinside Dr. G20	H15	21
Kelvinside Gdns. E. G20	H15	21
Kelvinside Gdns. G20	H15	21
Kelvinside Ter. S. G20	H15	21
Kelvinside Ter. W. G20	H15	21
Kemp Av., Renf.	J 7	31
Kemp St. G21	H18	22
Kempock St. G31	M20	53
Kempsthorn Cres. G53	N10	48
Kempsthorn Path G53	N10	48
Kempsthorn Rd. G53	N10	48
Kendal Av., Giff.	Q14	62
Kendal Dr. G12	G13	20
Kendal Ter. G12	G13	20
Kendoon Av. G15	D 9	6
Kenilworth Av. G41	O14	50
Kenilworth Cres., Bear.	C11	7
Kenilworth Way, Pais.	O 3	45
Kenmar Gdns., Udd.	O26	56
Kenmore Gdns., Bear.	C13	8
Kenmore Rd., Cumb.	C 3	71
Kenmore St. G32	L22	38
Kenmuir Av. G32	M24	55
Kenmuir Rd. G32	O23	55
Kenmuirhill Rd. G32	N23	55
Kenmure Av., Bish.	E18	10
Kenmure Cres., Bish.	E18	10
Kenmure Dr., Bish.	E18	10
Kenmure Gdns., Bish.	E18	10
Kenmure Row G22	E16	9
Kenmure St. G41	M15	51
Kenmure Way G73	O19	65
Kennedar Dr. G51	K12	33
Kennedy Ct., Giff.	Q14	62
Braidholm Cres.		
Kennedy St. G4	K17	36
Kennet St. G21	J19	37
Kennishead Av. G46	P12	61
Kennishead Pl. G46	P12	61
Kennishead Rd. G46	P12	61
Kennishead Rd. G53	Q11	61
Kennisholm Av. G46	P12	61
Kennisholm Pl. G46	P12	61
Kennoway Dr. G11	J12	33
Kennoway La. G11	J12	33
Thornwood Dr.		
Kennyhill Sq. G31	K19	37
Kensington Dr., Giff.	R14	62
Kensington Gate G12	H14	20
Kensington Rd.		
Kensington Rd. G12	H14	20
Kent Dr. G73	P20	65
Kent Rd. G3	K15	35
Kent St. G40	L18	36
Kentallen Rd. G33	L24	39
Kentigern Ter., Bish.	F19	23
Keppel Dr. G44	O18	52
Keppoch St. G21	H17	22
Keppochhill Rd. G22	H17	22
Kerfield Pl. G15	D 9	6
Kerr St. G40	L18	36
Kerr St., Barr.	R 7	59
Kerr St., Blan.	S27	69
Kerr St., Pais.	L 5	30
Kerrera Pl. G33	L23	39
Kerrera Rd. G33	L23	39
Kerry Pl. G15	D 9	6
Kerrycroy Av. G42	O17	52
Kerrycroy Pl. G42	O17	52
Kerrycroy Av.		
Kerrycroy St. G42	O17	52
Kerrydale St. G40	M19	53
Kerrylamont Av. G42	O18	52
Kersland La. G12	H14	20
Kersland St.		
Kersland St. G12	H14	20
Kessington Dr., Bear.	D13	8
Kessington Rd., Bear.	D13	8
Kestral Ct., Clyde.	C 7	5
Kestrel Pl., John.	O08	43
Kestrel Rd. G13	G11	19
Kew Gdns. G12	H14	20
Ruthven St.		
Kew Gdns., Udd.	O28	57
Kew La. G12	H14	20
Saltoun St.		
Kew Ter. G12	H14	20
Keyden St. G41	L15	35
Kibbleston Rd., Kilb.	M07	42
Kidston St. G5	M17	52
Kierhill Rd., Cumb.	C 1	70
Kilbarchan Rd., John.	N08	43
Kilbarchan St. G5	L16	35
Bedford St.		
Kilbeg Ter. G46	Q11	61
Kilberry St. G21	J19	37
Kilbowie Ct., Clyde.	D 7	5
Crown Av.		
Kilbowie Rd., Clyde.	C 7	5
Kilbowie Rd., Cumb.	C 3	71
Kilbrennan Rd., Linw.	L 1	28
Kilbride St. G5	N17	52
Kilbride Vw., Udd.	O28	57
Hamilton Vw.		
Kilburn Gro., Blan.	R26	68
Kilburn Pl. G13	G10	18
Kilchattan Dr. G44	O17	52
Kilchoan Rd. G33	J23	39
Kilcloy Av. G15	D10	6
Kildale Way G73	O18	52
Kildary Av. G44	P16	63
Kildary Rd. G44	P16	63
Kildermorie Rd. G34	K25	40
Kildonan Dr. G11	J13	34
Kildonan Ter. G51	L13	34
Copland Rd.		
Kildrostan St. G41	N15	51
Terregles Av.		
Kildrum Rd., Cumb.	B 3	71
Kilearn Rd., Pais.	K 7	31
Kilfinan St. G22	F16	21
Kilkerran Dr. G33	G21	24
Killarn Way, Pais.	K 7	31
Killearn Dr., Pais.	M 9	48
Killearn St. G22	H16	21
Killermont Av., Bear.	E13	8
Killermont Ct., Bear.	D13	8
Killermont Meadows, Both.	R27	69

Killermont Rd., Bear.	D13	8
Killermont St. G1	K17	36
Killermont Vw. G20	E13	8
Killiegrew Rd. G41	N14	50
Killin Dr., Linw.	L 1	28
Killin St. G32	M22	54
Killoch Av., Pais.	L 4	29
Killoch Dr. G13	F10	18
Killoch Dr., Barr.	R 8	59
Killoch Rd., Pais.	L 4	29
Kilmailing Rd. G44	P16	63
Kilmair Pl. G20	G14	20
Wyndford Rd.		
Kilmaluag Ter. G46	Q11	61
Kilmany Dr. G32	L21	38
Kilmardinny Av., Bear.	C12	7
Kilmardinny Cres., Bear.	C12	7
Kilmardinny Dr., Bear.	C12	7
Kilmardinny Gate, Bear.	C12	7
Kilmardinny Av.		
Kilmardinny Gro., Bear.	C12	7
Kilmarnock Rd. G43	P14	62
Kilmartin Pl., Thorn.	Q12	61
Kilmaurs Dr., Giff.	Q15	63
Kilmaurs St. G51	L12	33
Kilmorie Dr. G73	O18	52
Kilmory Av., Udd.	O28	57
Spindlehow Rd.		
Kilmuir Cres. G46	Q11	61
Kilmuir Dr. G46	Q12	61
Kilmuir Rd. G46	Q12	61
Kilmuir Rd., Udd.	N27	57
Kilmun La. G20	F14	20
Kilmun St.		
Kilmun Pl. G20	F14	20
Kilmun St.		
Kilmun St. G20	F14	20
Kilnside Rd., Pais.	L 6	30
Kiloran St. G46	Q12	61
Kilpatrick Av., Pais.	N 4	45
Kilpatrick Cres., Pais.	N 5	46
Kiltearn Rd. G33	K24	39
Kilvaxter Dr. G46	Q12	61
Kilwynet Way, Pais.	K 7	31
Kimberley St., Dalm.	C 5	4
Kinalty Rd. G44	P16	63
Kinarvie Cres. G53	O 9	48
Kinarvie Gdns. G53	O 9	48
Kinarvie Rd.		
Kinarvie Pl. G53	O 9	48
Kinarvie Rd. G53	O 9	48
Kinarvie Ter. G53	O 9	48
Kinbuck St. G22	H17	22
Kincardine Cres., Bish.	F19	23
Graham Ter.		
Kincardine Pl., Bish.	F19	23
Kincardine Pl., Bish.	F20	23
Kincardine Sq. G33	J23	39
Kincath Av. G73	Q20	65
Kinclaven Av. G15	D10	6
Kincraig St. G51	L11	33
Kinellan Rd., Bear.	E12	7
Kinellar Dr. G14	G10	18
Kinfauns Dr. G15	D 9	6
Kinfauns Ter. G51	L13	34
Copland Rd.		
King Edward Rd. G13	G12	19
King George V Bridge G5	L16	35
King St. G1	L17	36
King St. G73	O19	53
King St., Clyde.	F 8	17
King St., Pais.	L 5	30
Kingarth St. G42	N16	51
Kinghorn Dr. G44	O17	52
Kinglas Rd., Bear.	E11	7
Kings Cres. G72	P22	66
Kings Cres., John.	M 2	44
Kings Cross G31	K18	36
Kings Dr. G40	M18	52
Kings Dr., Cumb.	A 2	70
Kings Inch Rd., Renf.	G 8	17
Kings La. W., Renf.	H 8	17
Bell St.		
Kings Park Av. G44	P17	64
Kings Park Rd. G44	O16	51
Kings Pl. G22	F16	21
Kings Rd., John.	N 1	44
Kingsacre Rd. G44	O17	52
Kingsbarns Dr. G44	O16	51
Kingsborough Gate G12	H13	20
Prince Albert Rd.		
Kingsborough Gdns. G12	H13	20
Kingsborough Ter. G12	H13	20
Hyndland Rd.		
Kingsbrae Dr. G44	O17	52
Kingsbridge Cres. G44	P17	64
Kingsbridge Dr. G44	P17	64
Kingsburgh Dr., Pais.	L 7	31
Kingsburn Dr. G73	P19	65
Kingsburn Gro. G73	P19	65
Kingscliffe Av. G44	P17	64
Kingscourt Av. G44	P17	64
Kingsdale Av. G44	O17	52
Kingsdyke Av. G44	O17	52
Kingsford Av. G44	Q15	63
Kingshall Cotts., Gart.	H28	27
Kingsheath Av. G73	P18	64
Kingshill Dr. G44	P17	64
Kingshouse Av. G44	P17	64
Kingshurst Av. G44	O17	52
Kingsknowe Dr. G73	P18	64
Kingsland Cres. G52	L10	32
Kingsland Dr. G52	L10	32
Kingsley Av. G42	N16	51
Kingsley Ct., Udd.	O28	57
Kingslynn Dr. G44	P17	64
Kingslynn La. G44	P17	64
Kingslynn Dr.		
Kingsmuir Dr. G73	P18	64
Kingston Bri. G3	L15	34
Kingston Pl., Dalm.	D 5	4
Kingston St. G5	L16	35
Kingsway Ct. G14	G10	18
Kingsway G14	G10	18
Kingswood Dr. G44	P17	64
Kingussie Dr. G44	P17	64
Kiniver Dr. G15	E10	6
Kinloch Av. G72	Q22	66
Kinloch Av., Linw.	L 1	28
Pentland Dr.		
Kinloch Rd., Renf.	J 7	31
Kinloch St. G40	M20	53
Kinmount Av. G44	O16	51
Kinmount La. G44	O16	51
Kinmount Av.		
Kinnaird Cres., Bear.	D13	8
Kinnaird Dr., Linw.	L 1	28
Kinnaird Pl. G64	F19	23
Kinnear Rd. G40	M19	53
Kinnell Av. G52	M11	49
Kinnell Cres. G52	M11	49
Kinnell Pl. G52	N12	49
Mosspark Dr.		
Kinnell Sq. G52	M11	49
Kinning St. G5	L15	35
Kinnoul Pl. G12	H13	20
Crown Rd.		
Kinpurnie Rd., Pais.	L 8	31
Kinross Av. G52	M10	48
Kinsail Dr. G52	L 9	32
Kinstone Av. G14	G10	18
Kintessack Pl., Bish.	E20	11
Kintillo Dr. G13	G10	18
Kintore Rd. G43	P15	63
Kintra St. G51	L13	34
Kintyre Av., Linw.	L 1	28
Kintyre St. G21	J19	37
Kippen St. G22	G17	22
Kippford St. G32	M23	55
Kirk La. G43	O14	50
Riverbank St.		
Kirk Pl., Udd.	P27	69
Kirk Rd., Bear.	C12	7
Kirkaig Av., Renf.	J 9	32
Kirkbean Av. G73	Q19	65
Kirkburn Av. G72	Q22	66
Kirkcaldy Rd. G41	N14	58
Kirkconnel Av. G13	G 9	18
Kirkconnel Dr. G73	P18	64
Kirkdale Dr. G52	M12	49
Kirkfield Rd., Udd.	Q28	69
Kirkford Rd., Chr.	E27	15
Bridgeburn Dr.		
Kirkhill Av. G72	Q22	66
Kirkhill Dr. G20	G14	20
Kirkhill Gdns. G72	Q22	66
Kirkhill Gro. G72	Q22	66
Kirkhill Pl. G20	G14	20
Kirkhill Rd., Gart.	G27	27
Kirkhill Rd., Udd.	O27	57
Kirkhill Ter. G72	Q22	66
Kirkhope Dr. G15	E10	6
Kirkinner Rd. G32	M23	55
Kirkintilloch Rd., Bish.	F18	22
Kirkintilloch Rd., Lenz.	C23	13
Kirkland St. G20	H15	21
Kirklandneuk Rd., Renf.	H 7	17
Kirklands Cres., Udd.	Q28	69
Kirklea Av., Pais.	L 4	29
Kirklee Circus G12	H14	20
Kirklee Gardens La. G12	G14	20
Bellshaugh Rd.		
Kirklee Gdns. G12	G14	20
Bellshaugh Rd.		
Kirklee Pl. G12	H14	20
Kirklee Quad. G12	H14	20
Kirklee Quad. La. G12	H14	20
Kirklee Quad.		
Kirklee Rd. G12	H14	20
Kirklee Ter. G12	H14	20
Kirklee Terrace La. G12	H14	20
Kirklee Ter.		
Kirkliston St. G32	L21	38
Kirkmuir Av., Renf.	J 7	31
Kirkmuir Dr. G73	Q19	65
Kirknewton St. G32	L22	38
Kirkoswald Dr., Clyde.	D 8	5
Kirkoswald Rd. G43	P14	62
Kirkpatrick St. G40	L19	37
Kirkriggs Av. G73	P19	65
Kirkriggs Gdns. G73	P19	65
Kirkriggs Way, Ruth.	P19	65
Kirkstall Gdns., Bish.	D19	11
Kirkstonside, Barr.	R 7	59
Kirkton Av. G13	G10	18
Kirkton Cres. G13	G10	18
Kirkton Rd. G72	P22	66
Kirkview Gdns., Udd.	O27	57
Glencroft Av.		
Kirkville Pl. G15	E10	6
Kirkwall Av., Blan.	Q26	68
Kirkwall, Cumb.	A 3	71
Kirkwell Rd. G44	P16	63
Kirkwood Av., Clyde.	E 8	5
Kirkwood Quad., Clyde.	E 8	5
Kirkwood Av.		
Kirkwood Rd., Udd.	N27	57
Newlands Rd.		
Kirkwood St. G51	L14	34
Kirkwood St. G73	O19	53
Kirn St. G20	F14	20
Kilmun St.		
Kirriemuir Av. G52	M11	49
Kirriemuir Gdns., Bish.	E20	11
Kirriemuir Rd., Bish.	E20	11
Kirtle Dr., Renf.	J 9	32
Kirton Av., Barr.	R 7	59
Kishorn Pl. G32	J23	39
Knapdale St. G22	F16	21
Knightsbridge Rd. G13	G11	19
Knightscliffe Av. G13	F11	19
Knightswood Cross G13	F11	19
Knightswood Rd. G13	E11	7
Knightswood Ter., Blan.	R27	69
Knock Way, Pais.	K 7	31
Knockburnie Rd., Udd.	Q28	69
Knockhall St. G33	J23	39
Knockhill Dr. G44	O16	51
Knockhill La. G44	O16	51
Mount Annan Dr.		
Knockhill Rd., Renf.	J 7	31
Knockside Av., Pais.	O 5	46
Knowe Rd., Chr.	F26	26
Knowe Rd., Pais.	K 7	31
Knowe Ter. G22	F16	21
Hillend Rd.		
Knowehead Dr., Udd.	P27	69
Knowehead Gdns. G41	M15	51
Knowehead Ter.		
Knowehead Gdns., Udd.	P27	69
Knowehead Ter. G41	M15	51
Knowetap St. G20	F15	21
Knox St., Pais.	M 4	45
Kyle Dr., Giff.	Q14	62
Kyle Rd., Cumb.	B 3	71
Kyle Sq. G73	P19	65
Kyle St. G4	J17	36

Lochy Gdns., Bish. E19 11
Lockhart Av. G72 P23 67
Lockhart Dr. G72 P23 67
Lockhart St. G21 J19 37
Locksley Av. G13 F11 19
Locksley Rd., Pais. N 3 45
Logan Dr., Cumb. B 1 70
Logan Dr., Pais. L 5 30
Logan St. G5 N17 52
Logan Tower G72 Q24 67
Claude Av.
Loganswell Dr. G46 R11 61
Loganswell Gdns. G46 R12 61
Loganswell Pl. G46 R12 61
Loganswell Rd. G46 R12 61
Logie St. G51 K13 34
Lomax St. G33 K20 37
Lomond Av., Renf. J 7 31
Lomond Cres., Pais. O 5 46
Lomond Ct., Barr. R 8 59
Lomond Dr., Barr. Q 7 59
Lomond Dr., Udd. Q28 69
Lomond Gdns., John. N 2 44
Lomond Pl. G33 H23 25
Lomond Rd., Bear. E12 7
Lomond Rd., Bish. D18 10
Lomond Rd., Lenz. C23 13
Lomond Rd., Udd. N27 57
Lomond St. G22 G16 21
Lomond Vw., Clyde. D 7 5
Granville St.
London Arcade G1 L17 36
London Rd.
London La. G1 L17 36
London Rd.
London Rd. G1 L17 36
London St., Renf. G 8 17
Long Row, Bail. L26 40
Longay Pl. G22 F17 22
Longay St. G22 F17 22
Longcroft Dr., Renf. H 8 17
Longdale Rd., Chr. E27 15
Longden St., Clyde. F 8 17
Longford St. G33 K20 37
Longlee, Bail. M25 56
Longmeadow, John. N08 43
Longstone Rd. G33 K22 38
Longwill Ter., Cumb. B 3 71
Lonmay Rd. G33 K23 39
Lonsdale Av., Giff. Q14 62
Loom St. G40 L18 36
Stevenson St.
Loom Wk., Kilb. M07 42
Shuttle St.
Lora Dr. G52 M12 49
Loretto Pl. G33 K21 38
Loretto St. G33 K21 38
Lorne Av., Chr. F26 26
Lorne Cres., Bish. E20 11
Lorne Dr., Linw. L 1 28
Lorne Pl. G42 O16 51
Cathcart Rd.
Lorne Rd. G52 K 9 32
Lorne St. G51 L14 34
Lorne Ter. G72 Q21 66
Lorraine Gdns. G12 H14 20
Kensington Rd.
Lorraine Rd. G12 H14 20
Loskin Dr. G22 F16 21
Lossie Cres., Renf. J 9 32
Lossie St. G33 J20 37
Lothian Cres., Pais. N 5 46
Lothian Dr., Clark. R14 62
Lothian Gdns. G20 H15 21
Lothian St. G52 K 9 32
Loudon Gdns. M 1 44
Loudon Rd. G33 G22 24
Loudon Ter. G12 H14 20
Observatory Rd.
Lounsdale Cres., Pais. N 4 45
Lounsdale Dr., Pais. N 4 45
Lounsdale Pl. G14 H10 18
Lounsdale Rd., Pais. N 4 45
Lourdes Av. G52 M11 49
Lovat Pl. G73 Q20 65
Lovat St. G4 J17 36
Love St., Pais. L 6 30
Low Barholm, Kilb. N07 42
Low Cres., Clyde. F 9 18
Low Parksail, Renf. F 5 16
Low Rd., Pais. M 5 46
Lower Bourtree Dr. G73 Q20 65
Lower English Bldgs. G42 M16 51
Lower Millgate, Udd. O27 57
Lowndes La., Pais. L 6 30
New Sneddon St.
Lowndes St., Barr. R 8 59
Lowther Ter. G12 H14 20
Loyne Dr., Renf. J 9 32
Morriston Cres.
Luath St. G51 K13 34
Lubas Av. G42 O17 52
Lubas Pl. G42 O17 52
Lubnaig Rd. G43 P15 63
Luckingsford Av., Renf. F 5 16
Luckingsford Dr., Renf. F 5 16
Luckingsford Rd., Renf. F 5 16
Lucy Brae, Udd. O27 57
Ludovic Sq., John. M09 43
Luffness Gdns. G32 N22 54
Lugar Dr. G52 M12 49
Lugar Pl. G44 P18 64
Luggiebank Pl., Bail. M28 57
Luing Rd. G52 L12 33
Lumloch St. G21 H19 23
Lumsden La. G3 K14 34
Lumsden St.
Lumsden St. G3 K14 34
Lunan Dr., Bish. F20 23
Lunan Pl. G51 K12 33
Luncarty Pl. G32 M22 54
Luncarty St. G32 M22 54
Lunderston Dr. G53 O10 48
Lundie Gdns., Bish. F20 23
Lundie St. G32 M21 54
Lunn Brae, John. N09 43
Luss Rd. G51 K12 33
Lusset Vw., Clyde. D 7 5
Radnor St.
Lusshill Ter., Udd. N25 56
Lyall Pl. G21 H17 22
Keppochhill Rd.
Lyall St. G21 H17 22
Lybster Cres. G73 Q20 65
Lye Brae, Cumb. C 3 71
Lyle Ter., Pais. N 6 46
Lymburn St. G3 K14 34
Lyndale Pl. G20 F14 20
Lyndale Rd. G20 F14 20
Lyndhurst Gdns. G20 H15 21
Lyne Croft, Bish. D19 11
Lyne Dr. G23 E15 9
Lynedoch Cres. G3 J15 35
Lynedoch Pl. G3 J15 35
Lynedoch St. G3 J15 35
Lynedoch Ter. G3 J15 35
Lynn Gdns. G12 H14 20
Great George St.
Lynn Wk., Udd. P28 69
Flax Rd.
Lynnhurst, Udd. O27 57
Lynton Av., Giff. R13 62
Lyon Cross Av., Barr. R 8 59
Lyon Rd., Pais. N 3 45
Lyoncross Cres., Barr. Q 8 59
Lyoncross Rd. G53 N10 48
Lytham Dr. G23 E15 9
Lytham Meadows, Both. R27 69

Macbeth Pl. G31 M20 53
Macbeth St.
Macbeth St. G31 M20 53
Macdougal St. G43 O14 50
Macdowall St., John. M09 43
Macdowall St., Pais. L 5 30
Macduff Pl. G31 M20 53
Macduff St. G31 M20 53
Mace Rd. G13 E11 7
Macfarlane Rd., Bear. E12 7
Machrie Dr. G45 Q18 64
Machrie Rd. G45 Q18 64
Machrie St. G45 Q18 64
Mackean St., Pais. L 5 30
Mackeith St. G40 M18 52
Mackenchnie St. G51 K13 34
Mackenzie Dr. John. O07 42
Mackie St. G4 H17 22
Borron St.
Mackiesmill Rd., John. O 2 44
Mackinlay St. G5 M16 51
Maclay Av., Kilb. N07 42
Maclean St. G41 L15 35
Maclean St. G51 L14 34
Maclean St., Clyde. F 9 18
Wood Quadrant
Maclehose Rd., Cumb. B 4 71
Maclellan St. G41 L14 34
Madison Av. G44 P16 63
Madison La. G44 P16 63
Carmunnock Rd.
Madras Pl. G40 M18 52
Madras St.
Madras St. G40 M18 52
Mafeking St. G51 L13 34
Magdalen Way, Pais. O 2 44
Magnus Cres. G44 Q16 63
Mahon Ct., Chr. E27 15
Maida St. G43 O13 50
Maidland Rd. G53 O11 49
Mailerbeg Gdns., Chr. D27 15
Mailing Av., Bish. E19 11
Main Rd., John. M 2 44
Main Rd., Pais. M 5 46
Main St. G40 M18 52
Main St. G72 P22 66
Main St. G73 O19 53
Main St., Bail. M25 56
Main St., Barr. R 7 59
Main St., Both. R28 69
Main St., Chr. E26 14
Main St., Cumb. A 3 71
Main St., Thorn. Q12 61
Main St., Udd. P27 69
Mainhead Ter., Cumb. A 3 71
Roadside
Mainhill Av., Bail. L26 40
Mainhill Pl., Bail. L26 40
Mainhill Rd., Bail. L27 41
Mains Av., Giff. R13 62
Mains Dr., Renf. E 5 4
Mains Hill, Renf. E 5 4
Mains Holm, Renf. E 5 4
Mains River, Renf. E 5 4
Mains Wood, Renf. E 5 4
Mainscroft, Renf. E 5 4
Mair St. G51 L15 35
Maitland Pl., Renf. J 7 31
Maitland St. G4 J16 35
Malcolm St. G31 L20 37
Malin Pl. G33 K21 38
Mallaig Path G51 K11 33
Mallaig Pl. G51 K11 33
Mallaig Rd. G51 K11 33
Mallard Rd., Clyde. C 7 5
Malloch Cres., John. N 1 44
Malloch St. G20 G15 21
Malta St., Clyde. F 8 17
Maltbarns St. G20 H16 21
Malvern Ct. G31 L19 37
Malvern Way, Pais. K 5 30
Mambeg Dr. G51 K12 33
Mamore Pl. G43 P14 62
Mamore St. G43 P14 62
Manchester Dr. G12 G13 20
Manitoba Pl. G31 L19 37
Janefield St.
Mannering Ct. G41 O14 50
Pollokshaws Rd.
Mannering Rd. G31 O14 50
Mannering Rd., Pais. O 3 45
Mannofield, Bear. D11 7
Chesters Rd.
Manor Rd. G14 H12 19
Manor Rd. G15 E 9 6
Manor Rd., Gart. G27 27
Manor Rd., Pais. N 3 45
Manor Way G73 Q19 65
Manse Av., Bear. C12 7
Manse Brae G44 P16 63
Manse Ct., Barr. Q 8 59
Manse Rd. G32 M23 55
Manse Rd., Bail. L27 41
Manse Rd., Bear. C12 7
Manse St., Renf. H 8 17
Mansefield Av. G72 Q22 66
Mansefield Dr., Udd. P28 69
Mansefield St. G11 J14 34
Mansel St. G21 G18 22
Mansewood Rd. G43 P13 62

Mansfield Rd. G52   K 9 32
Mansion Ct. G72   P22 66
Mansion St. G22   G17 22
Mansion St. G72   P22 66
Mansionhouse Av. G32   O23 55
Mansionhouse Dr. G32   L23 39
Mansionhouse Gdns.   O15 51
G41
Mansionhouse Rd.
Mansionhouse Rd. G32   M24 55
Mansionhouse Rd. G42   O15 51
Mansionhouse Rd., Pais.   L 7 31
Maple Ct., Barr.   S 8 59
Oakbank Dr.
Maple Dr., Dalm.   C 6 4
Maple Dr., John.   O 1 44
Maple Dr., Lenz.   C22 12
Maple Rd. G41   M13 50
Mar Gdns. G73   Q20 65
March La. G41   N15 51
Nithsdale Dr.
March St. G41   N15 51
Marchfield Av., Pais.   K 5 30
Marchfield, Bish.   D18 10
Marchfield, Bish.   D18 10
Westlands
Marchglen Pl. G51   K11 33
Mallaig Rd.
Marchmont Gdns., Bish.   D18 10
Marchmont Ter. G12   H14 20
Observatory Rd.
Maree Dr. G52   M12 49
Maree Gdns., Bish.   E19 11
Maree Rd., Pais.   N 4 45
Marfield St. G32   L21 38
Margaret St. G41   K17 36
Martha St.
Margarette Bldgs. G44   P16 63
Clarkston Rd.
Marguerite Av., Lenz.   C23 13
Marguerite Dr., Lenz.   C23 13
Marguerite Gdns., Lenz.   C23 13
Marguerite Gdns., Udd.   Q28 69
Marguerite Gro., Lenz.   C23 13
Mariscat Rd. G41   N15 51
Marjory Dr., Pais.   K 7 31
Marjory Rd., Renf.   J 7 31
Market Rd., Lenz.   B25 14
Market St. G40   L18 36
Markinch St. G5   L16 35
West St.
Marlborough Av. G11   H12 19
Marlinford Rd., Renf.   H10 18
Marlow St. G41   M15 51
Marlow Ter. G41   L15 35
Seaward St.
Marmion Pl., Cumb.   D 2 70
Marmion Rd., Cumb.   D 2 70
Marmion Rd., Pais.   O 3 45
Marmion St. G20   H15 21
Marne St. G31   K19 37
Marnock Ter., Pais.   N 7 47
Marnock Way, Chr.   E27 15
Braeside Av.
Marr St. G51   K13 34
Marshalls La., Pais.   M 6 46
Mart St. G1   L17 36
Martha St. G1   K17 36
Martin Cres., Bail.   L26 40
Martin St. G40   M18 52
Martlet Dr., John.   O08 43
Martyr St. G4   K18 36
Martyrs Pl. G64   F19 23
Marwick St. G31   K19 37
Marwood Av., Chr. &   C25 14
Waterside
Mary St. G4   J16 35
Mary St., John.   M 1 44
Mary St., Pais.   N 6 46
Maryhill Rd.,   E13 8
Bear.& G20
Maryland Dr. G52   L12 33
Maryland Gdns. G52   L12 33
Marys La., Pais.   H 8 17
Maryston Pl. G33   J20 37
Maryston St. G33   J20 37
Maryview Gdns., Udd.   N26 56
Edinburgh Rd.
Maryville Av., Giff.   R14 62
Maryville Vw., Udd.   N26 56

Marywood Sq. G41   N15 51
Masonfield Av., Cumb.   C 1 70
Masterton St. G21   H17 22
Mathieson La. G5   M17 52
Mathieson St.
Mathieson Rd. G73   N20 53
Mathieson St. G5   M17 52
Mathieson St., Pais.   L 7 31
Matilda Rd. G41   M15 51
Mauchline St. G5   M16 51
Maukinfauld Ct. G31   M21 54
Maukinfauld Rd. G32   M21 54
Mauldslie St. G40   M19 53
Maule Dr. G11   J13 34
Mause Av., Both.   R28 69
Mavis Bank, Bish.   F18 22
Mavisbank Rd. G51   K13 34
Govan Rd.
Mavisbank Ter., Pais.   M 6 46
Maxton Av., Barr.   Q 7 59
Maxton Gro., Barr.   Q 7 59
Maxton Ter. G72   Q21 66
Maxwell Av. G41   M15 51
Maxwell Av., Bail.   M25 56
Maxwell Av., Bear.   E12 7
Maxwell Dr. G41   M14 50
Maxwell Dr., Bail.   L25 40
Maxwell Gdns. G41   M14 50
Maxwell Gro. G41   M14 50
Maxwell Oval G41   M15 51
Maxwell Pl. G41   M16 51
Maxwell Rd. G41   M15 51
Maxwell Sq. G41   M15 51
Maxwell St. G18   L17 36
Maxwell St., Bail.   M25 56
Maxwell St., Dalm.   D 6 4
Maxwell St., Pais.   L 6 30
Maxwellton Rd. G78   M 4 45
Maxwellton St., Pais.   M 5 46
Maxwelton Rd. G33   J20 37
May Rd., Pais.   O 6 46
May Ter. G42   O16 51
Prospecthill Rd.
May Ter., Giff.   Q14 62
Maybank La. G42   N16 51
Victoria Rd.
Maybank St. G42   N16 51
Mayberry Cres. G32   L23 39
Mayberry Gdns. G32   L23 39
Maybole St. G53   P 9 60
Mayfield St. G20   G15 21
McAlpine St. G2   L16 35
McArthur St. G43   O14 50
Pleasance St.
McArthur St., Clyde.   G 8 17
McAslin Ct. G4   K17 36
McAslin St. G4   K18 36
McCallum Av. G73   O19 53
McClue Av., Renf.   H 7 17
McClue Rd., Renf.   H 7 17
McCracken Av., Renf.   J 7 31
McCreery St., Clyde.   F 8 17
McCulloch St. G41   M15 51
McDonald Av., John.   N09 43
McDonald Cres., Clyde.   F 8 17
McEwan St. G31   L20 37
McFarlane St. G4   L18 36
McFarlane St., Pais.   K 5 30
McGhee St., Clyde.   D 7 5
McGown St., Pais.   L 5 30
McGregor Av., Renf.   J 7 31
Porterfield Rd.
McGregor Rd., Cumb.   C 2 70
McGregor St. G51   L12 33
McGregor St., Clyde.   F 8 17
McIntosh Ct. G31   K18 36
McIntosh St.
McIntosh St. G31   K18 36
McIntyre Pl., Pais.   N 5 46
McIntyre St. G72   K15 35
McIntyre Ter. G72   P22 66
McIver St. G72   P23 67
McKay Cres., John.   N 1 44
McKenzie Av., Clyde.   D 7 5
McKenzie St., Pais.   L 5 30
McKerrel St., Pais.   L 7 31
McLaren Av., Renf.   J 8 31
Newmains Rd.
McLaurin Cres., John.   N08 43
McLean Pl., Pais.   K 5 30

McLean Sq. G51   L14 34
McLean St., Clyde.   F 9 18
Wood Quad.
McLennan St. G42   O16 51
McNair St. G32   L22 38
McNeil St. G5   M17 52
McNeill Av., Clyde.   E 9 6
McPhail St. G40   M18 52
McPhater St. G4   J16 35
Dunblane St.
McPherson Dr., Udd.   Q28 69
Wordsworth Way
McPherson St. G1   L17 36
High St.
McTaggart Rd., Cumb.   D 2 70
Meadow La., Renf.   G 8 17
Meadow Rd. G11   J13 34
Meadow Vw., Cumb.   B 4 71
Meadowbank La., Udd.   P27 69
Meadowburn Av. G66   C24 13
Meadowburn, Bish.   D19 11
Meadowhead Av., Chr.   E27 15
Meadowpark St. G31   K19 37
Meadowside Av., John.   N 2 44
Meadowside St. G11   J13 34
Meadowside St., Renf.   G 8 17
Meadowwell St. G32   L22 38
Meadside Av. G78   M07 42
Meadside Rd., Kilb.   M07 42
Mears Way, Bish.   E20 11
Medlar Rd., Cumb.   C 4 71
Medwin St. G72   P24 67
Mill Rd.
Medwyn St. G14   H11 19
Meek Pl. G72   P22 66
Meetinghouse La., Pais.   L 6 30
Moss St.
Megan Gate G40   M18 52
Megan St.
Megan St. G40   M18 52
Meikle Av., Renf.   J 8 31
Meikle Rd. G53   O11 49
Meiklerig Cres. G53   N11 49
Meikleriggs Dr., Pais.   N 4 45
Meiklewood Rd. G51   L11 33
Melbourne Av., Dalm.   C 5 4
Melbourne Ct., Giff.   Q14 62
Melbourne St. G31   L18 36
Meldon Pl. G51   K12 33
Meldrum Gdns. G41   N14 50
Meldrum St., Clyde.   F 9 18
Melford Av., Giff.   R14 62
Melford Way, Pais.   K 7 31
Knock Way
Melfort Av., Clyde.   D 7 5
Melfort Av., G41   M13 50
Melfort Gdns., John.   N08 43
Milliken Park Rd.
Mellerstain Dr. G14   G 9 18
Melness Pl. G51   K11 33
Mallaig Rd.
Melrose Av. G73   O19 53
Melrose Av., Bail.   L27 41
Melrose Av., Linw.   L 1 28
Melrose Av., Pais.   N 4 45
Melrose Gdns. G20   H15 21
Melrose Gdns., Udd.   N27 57
Lincoln Av.
Melrose Pl., Blan.   R26 68
Melrose St. G4   J16 35
Queens Cres.
Melvaig Pl. G20   G14 20
Melvick Pl. G51   K11 33
Mallaig Rd.
Melville St. G1   K17 36
Brunswick St.
Melville Gdns., Bish.   E19 11
Melville St. G41   M15 51
Memel St. G21   G18 22
Memus Av. G52   M11 49
Mennock Dr., Bish.   D19 11
Mennock Rd. G44   P16 63
Menteith Av., Bish.   E19 11
Menteith Dr. G73   R20 65
Menteith Pl. G73   R20 65
Menzies Dr. G21   G19 23
Menzies Pl. G21   G19 23
Menzies Rd. G21   G19 23
Merchant La. G1   L17 36
Clyde St.

Merchants Clo., Pais. M07 42
Church St.
Merchiston Av., Linw. L 1 28
Merchiston St. G32 K21 38
Merkland Ct. G11 J13 34
Vine St.
Merkland St. G11 J13 34
Merksworth Way, Pais. K 5 30
Mosslands Rd.
Merlewood Av. G71 Q28 69
Merlin Way, Pais. K 7 31
Merrick Gdns. G51 L13 34
Merrick Ter., Udd. O28 57
Merrick Way G73 Q19 65
Merryburn Av., Giff. P14 62
Merrycrest Av., Giff. Q14 62
Merrycroft Av., Giff. Q14 62
Merryland Pl. G51 K14 34
Merryland St. G51 K13 34
Merrylee Cres., Giff. P14 62
Merrylee Park Av., Giff. Q14 62
Merrylee Park La., Giff. Q14 62
Merrylee Park Ms., Q14 62
Giff.
Merrylee Rd. G43 P14 62
Merryton Av. G15 D10 6
Merryton Av., Giff. Q14 62
Merryton Pl. G15 D10 6
Merryvale Av., Giff. Q14 62
Merryvale Pl., Giff. P14 62
Merton Dr. G52 L10 32
Meryon Gdns. G32 N23 55
Meryon Rd. G32 N23 55
Methil St. G14 H11 19
Methuen Rd., Renf. J 7 31
Methven Av., Bear. C13 8
Methven St. G31 M20 53
Methven St., Dalm. D 6 4
Metropole La. G1 L16 35
Howard St.
Michillen Rd., C14 8
Bear.& G23
Mid Cotts, Gart. H26 26
Midcroft Av. G44 P17 64
Midcroft, Bish. D18 10
Middle Hard St., Clyde. B 8 5
Middlemuir Av., Lenz. C23 13
Middlemuir Rd., Lenz. C23 13
Middlerigg Rd., Cumb. C 1 70
Middlesex St. G41 L15 35
Middleton Cres., Pais. L 5 30
Middleton Rd., Linw. K 2 28
Middleton St. G51 L14 34
Midland St. G1 L16 35
Midlem Dr. G52 L11 33
Midlem Oval G52 L11 33
Midlock St. G51 L14 34
Midlothian Dr. G41 N14 50
Midton Cotts., Chr. E28 15
Midton St. G21 H18 22
Midwharf St. G4 J17 36
Migvie Pl. G20 G14 20
Wyndford Rd.
Milan St. G41 M16 51
Milford St. G33 K22 38
Mill Cres. G40 M18 52
Mill Ct. G73 O19 53
Mill Pl., Linw. L 1 28
Mill Rd. G72 Q23 67
Mill Rd., Barr. Q 7 59
Mill Rd., Both. R28 69
Mill Rd., Clyde. F 8 17
Mill River, Lenz. D23 13
Mill Road Gdns. G40 L18 36
Mill St. G40 M18 52
Mill St. G73 O19 53
Mill St., Pais. M 6 46
Mill Vennel, Renf. H 9 18
High St.
Mill Way, Lenz. C25 14
Millands Av., Blan. R26 68
Millar St., Pais. L 6 30
Millar Ter. G73 N19 53
Millarbank St. G21 H18 22
Millarston Av., Pais. M 4 45
Millarston Dr., Pais. M 4 45
Millbeg Cres. G33 L24 39
Millbeg Pl. G33 L24 39
Millbrae Cres. G13 F 8 17
Millbrae Cres. G42 O15 51

Millbrae Ct. G42 O15 51
Millbrae Rd.
Millbrae Rd. G42 O15 51
Millbrix Av. G14 G10 18
Millburn Av. G73 P19 65
Millburn Av., Clyde. F 9 18
Millburn Av., Renf. H 9 18
Millburn Dr., Renf. H 8 17
Millburn Rd., Renf. H 8 17
Millburn St. G21 J19 37
Millburn Way, Renf. H 9 18
Millcroft Rd. G73 N18 52
Millcroft Rd., Cumb. C 3 71
Miller St. G1 K17 36
Miller St., Bail. M25 56
Miller St., Clyde. E 7 5
Miller St., John. M 1 44
Millerfield Pl. G40 M19 53
Millerfield Rd. G40 M19 53
Millers Pl., Lenz. D23 13
Millersneuk Av., Lenz. D23 13
Millersneuk Cres. G33 G22 24
Millersneuk Dr., Lenz. D23 13
Millerston St. G31 L19 37
Millford Dr., Linw. L 1 28
Millgate Av., Udd. O27 57
Millgate, Udd. O27 57
Millholm Rd. G44 Q16 63
Millhouse Cres. G20 F14 20
Millhouse Dr. G20 F14 20
Milliken Dr., Kilb. N08 43
Milliken Park Rd., Kilb. N08 42
Millpond Dr. G40 L18 36
Millport Av. G44 O17 52
Millroad Dr. G40 L18 36
Millroad St. G40 L18 36
Millwood St. G41 O15 51
Milnbank St. G31 K19 37
Milncroft Rd. G33 J22 38
Milner Rd. G13 G12 19
Milngavie Rd., Bear. D12 7
Milnpark Gdns. G41 L15 35
Milnpark St. G41 L15 35
Milovaig St. G23 E14 8
Milrig Rd. G73 O18 52
Milton Av. G72 P21 66
Milton Douglas Rd., C 7 5
Clyde.
Milton Dr., Bish. F18 22
Milton Gdns., Udd. O27 57
Milton Mains Rd., Dalm. C 7 5
Milton St. G4 J17 35
Milverton Av., Bear. C11 7
Milverton Rd., Giff. R13 62
Minard Rd. G41 N15 51
Minard Way, Udd. O28 57
Newton Dr.
Minerva St. G3 K15 35
Minerva Way G3 K15 35
Mingarry La. G20 H14 20
Clouston St.
Mingary St. G20 H15 21
Mingulay Cres. G22 F17 22
Mingulay Pl. G22 F18 22
Mingulay St. G22 F17 22
Minmoir Rd. G53 O 9 48
Minstrel Rd. G13 E11 7
Minto Av. G73 Q20 65
Minto Cres. G52 L12 33
Minto St. G52 L12 33
Mireton St. G22 G16 21
Mirrlees Dr. G12 H14 20
Mirrlees La. G12 H14 20
Redlands Rd.
Mitchell Av. G72 P24 67
Mitchell Av., Renf. J 7 31
Mitchell Dr. G73 P19 65
Mitchell La. G1 K16 35
Buchanan St.
Mitchell Rd., Cumb. C 3 71
Mitchell St. G1 K16 35
Mitchell St., Coat. M28 57
Mitchellhill Rd. G42 R18 64
Mitchison Rd., Cumb. B 3 71
Mitre Ct. G14 H11 19
Mitre Rd.
Mitre La. G14 H12 19
Mitre La. W. G14 H12 19
Mitre La.
Mitre Rd. G14 H12 19

Moat Av. G13 F11 19
Mochrum Rd. G43 P15 63
Moffat Pl., Blan. R26 68
Moffat St. G5 M17 52
Mogarth Av., Pais. O 4 45
Amochrie Rd.
Moidart Av., Renf. H 7 17
Moidart Cres. G52 L12 33
Moidart Rd.
Moidart Ct., Barr. P 8 59
Moidart Pl. G52 L12 33
Moidart Rd.
Moidart Rd. G52 L12 33
Moir La. G1 L17 36
Moir St.
Moir St. G1 L17 36
Molendinar St. G1 L17 36
Mollinsburn St. G21 H18 22
Monach Rd. G33 K23 39
Monachie Gdns. E20 11
Muirhead Way
Moncrieff Av., Lenz. C23 13
Moncrieff Gdns., Lenz. C23 13
Moncrieff Pl. G4 J16 35
North Woodside Rd.
Moncrieff St. G4 J16 35
Balnain St.
Moncur St. G40 L18 36
Moness Dr. G52 M12 49
Monifieth Av. G52 M11 49
Monikie Gdns., Bish. E20 11
Muirhead Way
Monkcastle Dr. G73 P22 66
Monkland Av., Lenz. C23 13
Monkland View Cres., L28 41
Bail.
Monkland Vw, Udd. N28 57
Lincoln Av.
Monksbridge Av. G13 E11 7
Monkscroft Av. G11 H13 20
Monkscroft Ct. G11 J13 34
Monkscroft Gdns. G11 H13 20
Monkscroft Av.
Monkton Dr. G15 E10 6
Monmouth Av. G12 G13 20
Monreith Av., Bear. E11 7
Monreith Rd. E. G44 P16 63
Monreith Rd. G43 P14 62
Monroe Dr., Udd. N27 57
Monroe Pl., Udd. N27 57
Montague La. G12 H13 20
Montague St. G4 J15 35
Montague Ter. G12 H13 20
Hyndland Rd.
Montclair Pl., Linw. L 1 28
Monteith Dr., Clark. S15 63
Monteith Gdns., Clark. S15 63
Monteith Pl. G40 L18 36
Monteith Pl., Blan. R27 69
Monteith Row G40 L18 36
Monteith Row La. G40 L18 36
Monteith Pl.
Montford Av. G44 O17 52
Montgomerie Gdns. G14 H11 19
Lennox Av.
Montgomery Av., Pais. K 7 31
Montgomery Dr., Giff. R14 62
Montgomery Dr., Kilb. M07 42
Meadside Av.
Montgomery La. G42 O16 51
Somerville Dr.
Montgomery Rd., Pais. K 7 31
Montgomery St. G42 M18 52
London Rd.
Montgomery St. G72 P24 67
Mill Rd.
Montrave St. G52 M11 49
Montrave St. G73 N19 53
Montreal Ho., Dalm. C 5 4
Perth Cres.
Montron Dr. G15 E10 6
Moraine Av.
Montrose Av. G32 N22 54
Montrose Av. G52 K 9 32
Montrose Dr., Bear. B12 7
Montrose Gdns., Blan. R26 68
Montrose Pl., Linw. L 1 28
Montrose Rd., Pais. O 3 45
Montrose St. G4 K17 36
Montrose St., Clyde. E 7 5

Name	Grid	Page
Montrose Ter., Bish.	F20	23
Monymusk Gdns., Bish.	E20	11
Monymusk Pl. G15	C 9	6
Moodies Ct. G2	K16	35
Argyle St.		
Moodiesburn St. G33	J20	37
Moorburn Av., Giff.	Q13	62
Moore Dr., Bear.	D12	7
Moore St. G31	L19	37
Gallowgate		
Moorehouse Av. G13	G 9	18
Moorehouse Av., Pais.	N 4	45
Moorfoot Av. G46	Q13	62
Moorfoot Av., Pais.	N 5	46
Moorfoot St. G32	L21	38
Moorfoot, Bish.	E20	11
Moorhouse Av. G13	G 9	18
Moorhouse St., Barr.	R 8	59
Moorpark Av. G52	L 9	32
Moorpark Av., Chr.	F26	26
Moorpark Dr. G52	L10	32
Moorpark Pl. G52	L 9	32
Moorpark Sq., Renf.	J 7	31
Morag Av., Blan.	R26	68
Moraine Av. G15	E10	6
Moraine Circus G15	E10	6
Moraine Dr. G15	E10	6
Moraine Pl. G15	E10	6
Moraine Dr.		
Morar Cres., Bish.	E18	10
Morar Ct., Cumb.	DO	70
Morar Dr. G73	Q19	65
Morar Dr., Bear.	D13	8
Morar Dr., Cumb.	DO	70
Morar Dr., Linw.	L 1	28
Morar Dr., Pais.	N 4	45
Morar Pl., Renf.	H 7	17
Morar Rd. G52	L12	33
Morar Ter., Udd.	O28	57
Moravia Av., Both.	Q28	69
Moray Gate, Both.	Q27	69
Moray Gdns., Udd.	O27	57
Moray Pl. G41	N15	51
Moray Pl., Bish.	E20	11
Moray Pl., Linw.	L 1	28
Mordaunt St. G40	M19	53
Moredun Cres. G32	K23	39
Moredun Dr., Pais.	N 4	45
Moredun Rd., Pais.	N 4	45
Moredun St. G32	K23	39
Morefield Rd. G51	K11	33
Morgan Ms. G42	M16	51
Morion Rd. G13	F11	19
Morley St. G42	O16	51
Morna Pl. G41	J12	33
Victoria Park Dr. S.		
Morningside St. G33	K20	37
Morrin Path G21	H18	22
Crichton St.		
Morrin Sq. G4	K18	36
Collins St.		
Morrin St. G21	H18	22
Morris Pl. G40	L18	36
Morrison Quad., Clyde.	E 9	6
Morrison St. G5	L16	35
Morrison St., Clyde.	C 6	4
Morrisons Ct. G2	K16	35
Argyle St.		
Morriston Cres., Renf.	J 9	32
Morriston St. G72	P22	66
Mortimer St. G20	H15	21
Hotspur St.		
Morton Gdns. G41	N14	50
Morven Av., Bish.	E20	11
Morven Av., Blan.	R26	68
Morven Av., Pais.	O 5	46
Morven Dr., Linw.	L 1	28
Morven Gdns., Udd.	O27	57
Morven Rd. G72	Q21	66
Morven Rd., Bear.	C12	7
Morven St. G52	L12	33
Mosesfield St. G21	G18	22
Mosesfield St. G21	G18	22
Balgray Hill Rd.		
Moss Av., Linw.	L 1	28
Moss Dr., Barr.	P 7	59
Moss Heights Av. G52	L11	33
Moss Knowe, Cumb.	C 4	71
Moss Rd. G51	K11	33
Moss Rd., Chr.	F26	26
Moss Rd., Cumb.	B 4	71
Moss Rd., Lenz.	C23	13
Moss Sq. G33	J22	38
Moss St., Pais.	L 6	30
Moss-side Rd. G41	N15	51
Mossbank Dr. G33	H21	24
Mosscastle Rd. G33	J23	39
Mossend La. G33	K23	39
Mossend Rd., Pais.	K 5	30
Mosslands Rd.		
Mossend St. G33	K23	39
Mossgiel Av. G73	P19	65
Mossgiel Dr., Clyde.	D 8	5
Mossgiel Gdns., Udd.	O27	57
Mossgiel Pl. G73	P19	65
Mossgiel Rd. G43	P14	62
Mossgiel Rd., Cumb.	C 3	71
Mossgiel Ter., Blan.	R26	68
Mosshead Rd., Bear.	B13	8
Mossland Rd. G52	K 9	32
Mosslands Pl. G52	J 9	32
Mosslands Rd., Pais.	K 5	30
Mossneuk Dr., Pais.	O 5	46
Mosspark Av. G52	M12	49
Mosspark Boulevard	M12	49
G52		
Mosspark Dr. G52	M11	49
Mosspark La. G52	N12	49
Mosspark Dr.		
Mosspark Oval G52	M12	49
Mosspark Sq. G52	M12	49
Mossvale Cres. G33	J23	39
Mossvale La., Pais.	L 5	30
Mossvale Path G33	H23	25
Mossvale Rd. G33	J24	39
Mossvale Sq. G33	J23	39
Mossvale St., Pais.	K 5	30
Mossvale Ter., Chr.	D28	15
Mossvale Way G33	J23	39
Mossvale Wk. G33	J23	39
Mossview Cotts., Chr.	G26	26
Mossview Quad. G52	L11	33
Mossview Rd. G33	G24	25
Mote Hill Rd., Pais.	L 7	31
Moulin Circus G52	M10	48
Moulin Pl. G52	M10	48
Moulin Rd. G52	M10	48
Moulin Ter. G52	M10	48
Mount Annan Dr. G44	O16	51
Mount Harriet Av. G33	G24	25
Mount Harriet Dr. G33	G23	25
Mount St. G20	H15	21
Mount Stuart St. G41	O15	51
Mount Vernon Av. G32	M24	55
Mountainblue St. G31	L19	37
Mountblow Ho., Dalm.	C 5	4
Melbourne Av.		
Mountblow Rd., Dalm.	C 6	4
Mountgarrie Path G51	K11	33
Mountgarrie Rd.		
Mountgarrie Rd. G51	K11	33
Mowbray Av., Gart.	G27	27
Mowcraigs Ct., Clyde.	F 8	17
Yokerburn Ter.		
Moy St. G11	J14	34
Church St.		
Moyne Rd. G53	N10	48
Muckcroft Rd., Chr.	D25	14
Muir Park Ter. G64	F18	22
Muir St. G21	H18	22
Muir St., Bish.	E19	11
Muir St., Renf.	H 8	17
Muir Ter., Pais.	K 7	31
Muirbank Av. G73	O18	52
Muirbank Gdns. G73	O18	52
Muirbrae Rd. G73	Q19	65
Muirbrae Way G73	Q19	65
Muirburn Av. G44	Q15	63
Muirdrum Av. G52	M11	49
Muirdykes Av. G52	L10	32
Muirdykes Cres., Pais.	L 4	29
Muirdykes Rd. G52	L10	32
Muirdykes Rd., Pais.	L 4	29
Muiredge Ct., Udd.	P27	69
Watson St.		
Muiredge Ter., Bail.	M25	56
Muirend Av. G44	Q15	63
Muirend Rd. G44	Q15	63
Muirfield Cres. G23	E15	9
Muirfield Rd., Cumb.	A 3	71
Muirhead Ct., Bail.	M26	56
Muirhead Dr., Linw.	L 1	28
Muirhead Gdns., Bail.	M26	56
Muirhead Rd., Udd. &	M25	56
Bail.		
Muirhead St. G11	J13	34
Purdon St.		
Muirhead Way, Bish.	E20	11
Muirhill Av., G44	Q15	63
Muirhill Cres., G13	F10	18
Muirhouse St. G41	N15	51
Pollokshaws Rd.		
Muirkirk Dr. G13	F12	19
Muirpark Av., Renf.	J 8	31
Muirpark Dr., Bish.	F19	23
Muirpark St. G11	J13	34
Muirpark Ter., Bish.	F18	22
Crowhill Rd.		
Muirshiel Av. G53	P11	61
Muirshiel Cres. G53	P11	61
Muirside Av. G32	M24	55
Muirside Rd., Bail.	M25	56
Muirside St., Bail.	M25	56
Muirskeith Cres. G43	P15	63
Muirskeith Pl. G43	P15	63
Muirskeith Rd. G43	P15	63
Muirton Dr., Bish.	D18	10
Muirton Gdns., Bish.	D18	10
Muiryfauld Dr. G31	M21	54
Mulben Cres. G53	O 9	48
Mulben Pl. G53	O 9	48
Mulben Ter. G53	O 9	48
Mulberry Rd. G43	P14	62
Mull Av., Pais.	O 6	46
Mull Av., Renf.	J 8	31
Mull St. G21	J19	37
Mullardoch St. G23	E14	8
Rothes Dr.		
Mungo Pl., Udd.	N28	57
Lincoln Av.		
Munlochy Rd. G51	K11	33
Munro St., Clyde.	C 6	4
Gentle Row		
Munro La. G13	G12	19
Munro Pl. G13	G12	19
Munro Pl., Udd.	N28	57
Kirkwood Rd.		
Munro Rd. G13	G12	19
Munro Vw., Udd.	N28	57
Kirkwood Rd.		
Murano St. G20	H15	21
Murdoch St. G21	G18	22
Lenzie St.		
Muriel St., Barr.	Q 8	59
Murray Pl., Barr.	Q 8	59
Murray Rd., Both.	Q28	69
Murray St., Pais.	L 5	30
Murray St., Renf.	H 8	17
Murrayfield Dr., Bear.	E12	7
Murrayfield St. G32	K21	38
Murrayfield, Bish.	D19	11
Ashfield		
Murrin Av., Bish.	E20	11
Murroes Rd. G51	K11	33
Muslin St. G40	M18	52
Mybster Pl. G51	K11	33
Mybster Rd. G51	K11	33
Myers Cres., Udd.	P28	69
Myres Rd. G53	O11	49
Myreside Pl. G32	L20	37
Myreside St. G32	L20	37
Myrie Gdns., Bish.	E19	11
Myroch Pl. G34	J26	40
Myrtle Av., Lenz.	C23	13
Myrtle Hill La. G42	O17	52
Myrtle Hill Vw. G42	O17	52
Myrtle Pk. G42	N17	52
Myrtle Pl. G42	O17	52
Myrtle Rd., Dalm.	D 5	4
Myrtle Rd., Udd.	O28	57
Myrtle Sq., Bish.	F19	23
Myrtle St., Blan.	R26	68
Myrtle Wk. G72	P21	66
Naburn St. G5	M17	52
Nairn Av., Blan.	R26	68
Nairn Gdns., Bear.	D11	7
Nairn Pl., Dalm.	D 6	4
Dumbarton Rd.		

Name	Ref	
Northpark Ter. G12	H15	21
Hamilton Dr.		
Northumberland St.	H15	21
G20		
Norval St. G11	J13	34
Norwich Dr. G12	G13	20
Norwood Dr., Giff.	R13	62
Norwood Ter. G12	J15	35
Southpark Rd.		
Norwood Ter., Udd.	O28	57
Norwood, Bear.	D12	7
Nottingham Av. G12	G13	20
Nottingham La. G12	G13	20
Northampton Dr.		
Novar Dr. G12	H13	20
Novar Gdns., Bish.	E18	10
Numrow Ct., Clyde.	C 6	4
Nuneaton St. G40	M19	53
Nurseries Rd., Bail.	L24	39
Nursery La. G41	N15	51
Nursery St. G41	N15	51
Pollokshaws Rd.		
Nursery Street La. G41	N15	51
Nithsdale Dr.		
Nutberry Ct. G42	N16	51
Oak Cres., Bail.	M25	56
Oak Dr. G72	Q23	67
Oak Dr., Lenz.	C22	12
Oak Pl., Bish.	E19	11
Oak Rd., Dalm.	C 6	4
Oak Rd., Pais.	N 7	47
Oakbank Dr., Barr.	S 8	59
Oakbank La. G20	H16	21
Oakbank Ter. G20	H16	21
Oakdene Av., Udd.	O28	57
Oakfield Av. G12	J15	35
Oakfield Ter. G12	J15	35
Oakfield Av.		
Oakhill Av., Bail.	M24	55
Oakley Dr. G44	Q15	63
Oakley Ter. G31	K18	36
Oaks, The, John.	N08	43
Oakshaw School Brae,	L 5	30
Pais.		
Oakshaw St., Pais.	L 5	30
Oakshawhead, Pais.	L 5	30
Oakwood Av., Pais.	N 4	45
Oatfield St. G21	H19	23
Oban Ct. G22	H15	21
Oban Dr. G20	H15	21
Observatory La. G12	H14	20
Observatory Rd.		
Observatory Rd. G12	H14	20
Ochil Dr., Barr.	R 8	59
Ochil Dr., Pais.	O 6	46
Ochil Pl. G32	M22	54
Ochil Rd., Bish.	E20	11
Ochil Rd., Renf.	J 7	31
Ochil St. G32	M22	54
Ochiltree Av. G13	F12	19
Ogilvie Pl. G31	M21	54
Ogilvie St. G31	M20	53
Old Bothwell Rd., Both.	R28	69
Old Castle Rd. G44	P16	63
Old Dalmarnock Rd.	M18	52
G40		
Old Dalnottar Rd.,	C 5	4
Old K.		
Old Dumbarton Rd. G3	J14	34
Old Edinburgh Rd., Udd.	N27	57
Old Gartcosh Rd., Gart.	G27	27
Old Glasgow Rd., Udd.	O26	56
Old Govan Rd., Renf.	H 9	18
Old Greenock Rd., Renf.	F 5	16
Old Manse Rd. G32	L23	39
Old Mill Rd. G72	P23	67
Old Mill Rd., Both.	R28	69
Old Mill Rd., Clyde.	C 7	5
Old Mill Rd., Udd.	P27	69
Old Rd., John.	M 2	44
Old Renfrew Rd., Renf.	J10	32
Old Roundknowe Rd.,	N26	56
Udd.		
Old Rutherglen Rd. G5	M17	52
Old Shettleston Rd. G32	L21	38
Old Sneddon St., Pais.	L 6	30
Old St., Clyde.	C 6	4
Old Wood Rd., Bail.	M25	56
Old Wynd G1	L17	36

Name	Ref	
Oldhall Rd., Pais.	L 8	31
Olifard Av., Udd.	Q28	69
Oliphant Cres., Pais.	O 3	45
Olive St. G33	H20	23
Olrig Ter. G41	M15	51
Shields Rd.		
Olympia St. G40	L18	36
Onslow Dr. G31	K19	37
Onslow Rd., Clyde.	E 8	5
Onslow Sq. G31	K19	37
Onslow Dr.		
Oran Gate G20	H15	21
Oran Gdns. G20	G15	21
Oran Pl. G20	G15	21
Oran St. G20	G15	21
Oransay Cres., Bear.	D13	8
Orcades Dr. G44	Q16	63
Orchard Av. G17	R28	69
Orchard Ct. G32	O22	54
Orchard Ct., Thorn.	Q13	62
Orchard Dr. G73	O18	52
Orchard Dr., Giff.	Q13	62
Orchard Gro., Giff.	Q13	62
Orchard Park Av.,	Q13	62
Thorn. & Giff.		
Orchard Pk., Giff.	Q14	62
Orchard Pl., Lenz.	B24	13
Orchard Sq., Pais.	M 6	46
Orchard St., Pais.	M 6	46
Orchard St., Renf.	H 8	17
Orchardfield, Lenz.	D23	13
Orchy Cres., Bear.	E11	7
Orchy Cres., Pais.	N 3	45
Orchy Ct., Clyde.	C 8	5
Orchy Dr., Clark.	R15	63
Orchy Gdns., Clark.	R15	63
Orchy St. G44	P16	63
Oregon Pl. G5	M17	52
Orkney Pl. G51	K13	34
Orkney St.		
Orkney St. G51	K13	34
Orleans Av. G14	H12	19
Orleans La. G14	H12	19
Ormiston Av. G14	H11	19
Ormiston La. G14	H11	19
Ormiston Av.		
Ormiston La. S. G14	H11	19
Ormiston Av.		
Ormonde Av. G44	Q15	63
Ormonde Cres. G44	Q15	63
Ormonde Ct. G44	Q15	63
Ormonde Dr. G44	Q15	63
Ornsay St. G22	F17	22
Orr Pl. G40	L18	36
Orr Sq., Pais.	L 6	30
Orr St. G40	L18	36
Orr St., Pais.	L 6	30
Orr St., Pais.	M 6	46
Orton St. G51	L13	34
Orwell St. G21	H18	22
Osborn Ter. G51	L13	34
Copland Rd.		
Osborne St. G1	L17	36
Osborne St., Clyde.	D 7	5
Osborne Vill. G44	P16	63
Holmhead Rd.		
Osprey Dr., Udd.	O28	57
Ossian Av., Pais.	L 9	32
Auchmannoch Av.		
Ossian Rd. G43	P15	63
Oswald La. G1	L16	35
Oswald St.		
Oswald St. G1	L16	35
Otago La. G12	J15	35
Otago St.		
Otago La. N. G12	J15	35
Otago St.		
Otago St. G12	J15	35
Ottawa Cres., Dalm.	D 5	4
Otter La. G11	J13	34
Castlebank St.		
Otterburn Dr., Giff.	R14	62
Otterswick Pl. G33	J23	39
Oval, The, Clark.	R15	63
Overbrae Pl. G15	C 9	6
Overdale Av. G42	O15	51
Overdale Gdns. G42	O15	51
Overdale St. G42	O15	51
Overdale Vills. G42	O15	51
Overdale St.		

Name	Ref	
Overlea Av. G73	P20	65
Overnewton Pl. G3	K14	34
Kelvinhaugh St.		
Overnewton Sq. G3	K14	34
Overnewton St. G3	J14	34
Overton Cres., John.	M 1	44
Overton Rd. G72	Q23	67
Overton Rd., John.	N 1	44
Overton St. G72	Q23	67
Overtoun Ct., Dalm.	D 6	4
Dunswin Av.		
Overtoun Dr. G73	O19	53
Overtoun Dr., Dalm.	D 6	4
Overtoun Rd.,	D 6	4
Dalm. & Clyde.		
Overtown Av. G53	P10	60
Overtown St. G31	L19	37
Overwood Dr. G44	P17	64
Oxford Dr., Linw.	L 1	28
Oxford La. G5	L16	35
Oxford Rd., Renf.	H 8	17
Oxford St. G5	L16	35
Oxgang Pl., Lenz.	B24	13
Oxton Dr. G52	L10	32
Paisley Ct., Barr.	Q 7	59
Paisley Rd.		
Paisley Rd. G5	L15	35
Paisley Rd. W. G5	M10	48
Paisley Rd., Barr.	Q 7	59
Paisley Rd., Renf.	J 7	31
Palace St. G31	M20	53
Paladin Av. G13	F11	19
Palermo St. G21	H18	22
Palmer Av. G13	E11	7
Palmerston Pl. G3	K14	34
Kelvinhaugh St.		
Palmerston Pl., John.	O08	43
Pandora Way, Udd.	O28	57
Hillcrest Rd.		
Panmure St. G20	H16	21
Park Av. G3	J15	35
Park Av., Bar.	R 7	59
Park Av., Bish.	D19	11
Park Av., John.	N 2	44
Park Av., Pais.	N 5	46
Park Bank, Renf.	E 4	4
Park Brae, Renf.	F 5	16
Park Dr.		
Park Burn Av., Lenz.	B23	13
Park Circus C3	J15	35
Park Circus La. G3	J15	35
Lynedoch Pl.		
Park Circus Pl. G3	J15	35
Park Cres., Bear.	C10	6
Park Cres., Bish.	D19	11
Park Cres., Renf.	F 5	16
Park Ct., Bish.	D19	11
Park Ct., Dalm.	D 6	4
Little Holm		
Park Ct., Giff.	Q13	62
Belmont Dr.		
Park Ct., Giff.	R13	62
Park Dr. G3	J15	35
Park Dr. G73	O19	53
Park Dr., Renf.	F 5	16
Park Gardens La. G3	J15	35
Clifton St.		
Park Gate G3	J15	35
Park Gdns. G3	J15	35
Park Gdns., Kilb.	M07	42
Park Gro., Renf.	F 5	16
Park La. G40	L18	36
Park La., Blan.	S26	69
Park La., Pais.	L 6	30
Netherhill Rd.		
Park Pl. G20	F14	20
Fingal St.		
Park Quad. G3	J15	35
Park Rd. G4	J15	35
Park Rd., Bail.	L27	41
Park Rd., Bish.	E19	11
Park Rd., Chr.	F26	26
Park Rd., Dalm.	D 6	4
Park Rd., Giff.	R14	62
Park Rd., John.	N09	43
Park Rd., Pais.	N 5	46
Park Rd., Renf.	F 5	16
Park Ridge, Renf.	F 5	16
Park Dr.		

Park St. S. G3 — J15 35
Park Ter. G3 — J15 35
Park Ter. G42 — N15 51
Queens Dr.
Park Ter., Giff. — R14 62
Park Top, Renf. — F 5 16
Park Way, Cumb. — B 3 71
Park Winding, Renf. — F 5 16
Park Wood, Renf. — E 4 4
Parkburn Av., Lenz. — C23 13
Parker St. G14 — J12 33
Parkglade, Renf. — F 4 16
Parkgrove Av., Giff. — Q14 62
Parkgrove Ct., Giff. — Q14 62
Parkgrove Ter. G3 — J15 35
Parkgrove Ter. La. G3 — K15 35
Derby St.
Parkhall Rd., Dalm. — D 6 4
Parkhall Ter., Dalm. — C 6 4
Parkhead Cross G31 — L20 37
Parkhill Dr. G73 — O19 53
Parkhill Rd. G43 — O14 50
Parkholm La. G5 — L15 35
Paisley Rd.
Parkhouse La. G4 — K18 36
Parkhouse Path G53 — Q10 60
Parkhouse Rd. G53 — Q 9 60
Parklands Rd. G44 — Q15 63
Parklea, Bish. — D18 10
Midcroft
Parkmoor, Renf. — F 4 16
Parkneuk Rd. G43 — Q14 62
Parksail Dr., Renf. — F 5 16
Parksail, Renf. — F 5 16
Parkview Av., Lenz. — C23 13
Parkview Ct., Lenz. — B23 13
Parkview Dr. G33 — G24 25
Parkview G78 — M07 42
Parkview, Pais. — N 5 46
Parliament Rd. G21 — K18 36
Parnie St. G1 — L17 36
Parson St. G4 — K18 36
Partick Bridge St. G11 — J14 34
Partickhill Av. G11 — H13 20
Partickhill Ct. G11 — H13 20
Partickhill Av.
Partickhill Rd. G11 — H13 20
Paterson St. G5 — L16 35
Pathead Gdns. G33 — G21 24
Patna St. G40 — M19 53
Paton St. G31 — K19 37
Patrick St., Pais. — M 6 46
Patterton Dr., Barr. — R 8 59
Pattison St., Dalm. — D 6 4
Payne St. G4 — J17 36
Peacock Dr., Pais. — M 3 45
Pearce St. G51 — K13 34
Pearson Dr., Renf. — J 8 31
Pearson Pl., Linw. — L 1 28
Peat Pl. G53 — P10 60
Peat Rd. G53 — P10 60
Peathill Av., Chr. — F25 26
Peathill St. G21 — H17 22
Peebles Dr. G73 — P20 65
Peel Glen Rd., Bear. & G15 — C10 6
Peel La. G11 — J13 34
Burgh Hall St.
Peel Pl., Both. — Q28 69
Peel St. G11 — J13 34
Peel Vw., Clyde. — D 8 5
Kirkoswald Dr.
Peirshill St. G32 — K21 38
Pembroke St. G3 — K15 35
Pencaitland Dr. G32 — M22 54
Falside Rd.
Pencaitland Gro. G32 — M22 54
Falside Rd.
Pencaitland Pl. G23 — E15 9
Pendeen Cres. G33 — L24 39
Pendeen Pl. G33 — L24 39
Pendeen Rd. G33 — L24 39
Pendicle Cres., Bear. — D11 7
Pendicle Rd., Bear. — D11 7
Penicuik St. G32 — L20 37
Penilee Rd., Pais. — L 9 32
Penilee Ter. G52 — K 9 32
Peninver Dr. G73 — K12 33
Penman Av. G73 — O18 52
Pennan Pl. G14 — G10 18

Penneld Rd. G52 — L 9 32
Penrith Av., Giff. — R14 62
Penrith Dr. G12 — G13 20
Penryn Gdns. G32 — M23 55
Penston Rd. G33 — K23 39
Pentland Cres., Pais. — O 5 46
Pentland Ct., Barr. — R 7 59
Pentland Dr., Barr. — R 8 59
Pentland Dr., Bish. — E20 11
Pentland Dr., Linw. — L 1 28
Pentland Dr., Renf. — K 7 31
Pentland Pl. G40 — M18 52
Pentland Pl., Bear. — B10 6
Pentland Rd. G43 — P14 62
Pentland Rd., Chr. — F26 26
Penzance Way, Chr. — D27 15
Peockland Gdns. — M 1 44
Peockland Pl., John. — M 1 44
Percy Dr., Giff. — R14 62
Percy Rd., Renf. — K 7 31
Percy St. G51 — L14 34
Perran Gdns., Chr. — E27 15
Perth Cres., Dalm. — C 5 4
Peters Ct. G20 — F14 20
Maryhill Rd.
Petershill Ct. G21 — H19 23
Petershill Dr. G21 — H19 23
Petershill Pl. G21 — H19 23
Petershill Rd. G21 — H18 22
Petition Pl., Udd. — P28 69
Pettigrew St. G32 — L22 38
Peveril Av. G41 — N14 50
Peveril Av. G73 — P20 65
Pharonhill St. G31 — L21 38
Quarrybrae St.
Phoenix Park Ter. G4 — J16 35
Corn St.
Phoenix Pl., John. — M 2 44
Phoenix Rd. G4 — J16 35
Great Western Rd.
Piccadilly St. G3 — K15 35
Pikeman Av. G13 — G11 19
Pikeman Rd. G13 — G11 19
Pilmuir Av. G44 — Q15 63
Pilrig St. G32 — K21 38
Pilton Rd. G15 — D10 6
Pine Cres., John. — N 1 44
Pine Gro., Udd. — O28 57
Douglas Cres.
Pine Pl. G5 — M17 52
Pine Pl., Cumb. — B 5 71
Pine Pl., Cumb. — B 5 71
Pine Rd., Dalm. — D 5 4
Pine St., Pais. — N 7 47
Pinelands, Bish. — D19 11
Pinewood Av., Lenz. — C22 12
Pinewood Ct., Lenz. — C22 12
Pinewood Pl., Kirk. — C22 12
Pinewood Pl., Lenz. — C22 12
Pinkerton Av. G73 — O18 52
Pinkston Dr. G21 — J17 36
Pinkston Rd. G21 — H17 22
Pinmore Path G53 — P 9 60
Pinmore Pl. G53 — P 9 60
Pinmore St. G53 — P 9 60
Pinwherry Pl., Udd. — Q28 69
Hume Dr.
Pirn St. G40 — M18 52
Pitcairn St. G31 — M21 54
Pitcaple Dr. G43 — P13 62
Pitlochry Dr. G52 — M10 48
Pitmedden Rd., Bish. — E20 11
Pitmilly Rd. G15 — D11 7
Pitreavie Pl. G33 — J23 39
Pitt St. G2 — K16 35
Pladda Rd., Renf. — J 8 31
Plane Tree Pl., John. — N 1 44
Planetree Rd., Dalm. — C 7 5
Planetrees Av., Pais. — N 6 46
Carriagehill Dr.
Plant St. G31 — L20 37
Plantation Pl. G51 — L15 35
Govan Rd.
Plantation Sq. G51 — L15 35
Playfair St. G40 — M19 53
Pleaknowe Cres., Chr. — E27 15
Pleamuir Pl., Cumb. — C 1 70
Plean St. G14 — G10 18
Pleasance La. G43 — O14 50
Pleasance St. G43 — O14 50

Plover Pl., John. — O08 43
Pollock Dr., Bish. — E18 10
Pollock Rd., Bear. — D13 8
Pollokshaws Rd. — O13 50
Polmadie Av. G42 — N17 52
Polmadie Rd. G5 — N17 52
Polmadie St. G42 — N17 52
Polnoon Av. G13 — G10 18
Polson Dr., John. — N09 43
Polwarth Gdns. G12 — H13 20
Novar Dr.
Polwarth La. G12 — H13 20
Novar Dr.
Polwarth St. G12 — H13 20
Poplar Av. G11 — H12 19
Poplar Av., John. — N 1 44
Poplar Cotts. G14 — G 9 18
Dumbarton Rd.
Poplar Dr., Dalm. — C 6 4
Poplar Dr., Lenz. — C22 12
Poplar Pl., Blan. — R26 68
Poplar Rd. G41 — L13 34
Urrdale Rd.
Poplin St. G40 — M18 52
Porchester St. G33 — J23 39
Port Dundas Pl. G2 — K17 36
Port Dundas Rd. G4 — J17 36
Port St. G3 — K15 35
Portal Rd. G13 — F11 19
Porterfield Rd., Renf. — J 7 31
Portman Pl. G12 — J15 35
Cowan St.
Portman St. G41 — L15 35
Portmarnock Dr. G23 — F14 20
Portreath Rd., Chr. — D27 15
Portsoy Av. G13 — F 9 18
Portsoy Pl. G13 — F 9 18
Portugal La. G5 — L16 35
Bedford St.
Portugal St. G5 — L16 35
Norfolk St.
Possil Cross G22 — H16 21
Possil Rd. G4 — H16 21
Post La., Renf. — H 8 17
Potassels Rd., Chr. — F26 26
Potter Pl. G32 — M21 54
Potter St. G32 — M21 54
Potterhill Av., Pais. — O 6 46
Potterhill Rd. G53 — N10 48
Powburn Cres., Udd. — O26 56
Powfoot St. G31 — L20 37
Powrie St. G33 — H23 25
Preston Pl. G42 — N16 51
Prestwick St. G53 — P10 60
Priesthill Av. G53 — P11 61
Priesthill Cres. G53 — P11 61
Priesthill Rd. G53 — P10 60
Primrose Ct. G14 — H11 19
Primrose St. G14 — H11 19
Prince Albert Rd. G12 — H13 20
Prince Edward St. G42 — N16 51
Prince of Wales Gdns. G20 — F14 20
Prince of Wales Ter. G12 — H14 20
Byres Rd.
Princes Gate G73 — O19 53
Greenbank St.
Princes Gdns. G12 — H13 20
Princes Pl. G12 — H14 20
Princes Sq. G1 — K17 36
Princes Sq., Barr. — Q 8 59
Princes St. G73 — O19 53
Princes Ter. G12 — H14 20
Princess Cres., Pais. — L 7 31
Priory Av., Pais. — K 7 31
Priory Cotts., Blan. — R26 68
Priory Dr., Udd. — O26 56
Priory Pl. G13 — F11 19
Priory Rd. G13 — F11 19
Prosen St. G32 — M21 54
Prospect Av. G72 — P21 66
Prospect Av., Udd. — O27 57
Prospect Rd. G43 — O14 50
Prospecthill Circus G42 — N17 52
Prospecthill Cres. G42 — O18 52
Prospecthill Dr. G42 — O17 52
Prospecthill Pl. G42 — O18 52
Prospecthill Rd. G42 — O16 51
Prospecthill Sq. G42 — O17 52
Provan Rd. G33 — J20 37

Provand Hall Cres., Bail. M25 56
Provanhill Pl. G21 J18 36
Provanmill Pl. G33 H20 23
Provanmill Rd.
Provanmill Rd. G33 H20 23
Purdon St. G11 J13 34
Pykestone Rd. G33 J23 39

Quadrant Rd. G43 P15 63
Quadrant, The, Clark. S15 63
Quarrelton Rd., John. N09 43
Quarry Av. G72 Q24 67
Quarry Pl. G72 P21 66
Quarry Rd., Barr. Q 7 59
Quarry Rd., Pais. N 6 46
Quarry St., John. M09 43
Quarrybank, John. N08 43
Quarrybrae St. G31 L21 38
Quarryknowe G73 O18 52
Quarryknowe St. G31 L21 38
Quarrywood Av. G21 H20 23
Quarrywood Rd. G21 H20 23
Quay Rd. G73 N19 53
Quay Rd. N. G73 N19 53
Quebec Ho., Dalm. C 5 4
Perth Cres.
Queen Arc. G2 K16 5
Renfrew St.
Queen Elizabeth Av. K 9 32
G52
Queen Elizabeth Sq. G5 M17 52
Queen Margaret Cres. H15 21
G12
Hamilton Dr.
Queen Margaret Ct. G20 H15 21
Queen Margaret Dr. G12 H14 20
Queen Margaret Dr. G20 H15 21
Queen Margaret Rd. G20 H15 21
Queen Mary Av. G42 N16 51
Queen Mary St. G40 M18 52
Queen Sq. G41 N15 51
Queen St. G1 K17 36
Queen St. G73 O19 53
Queen St., Pais. M 5 46
Queen St., Renf. H 8 17
Queen Victoria Dr. G14 H11 19
Queen Victoria Gate G13 G11 19
Queenbank Av., Gart. F27 27
Queens Av. G72 P22 66
Queens Cres. G4 J16 35
Queens Cres., Bail. L27 41
Queens Cross G20 H15 21
Queens Dr. G42 N15 51
Queens Dr., Cumb. A 2 70
Queens Drive La. G42 N16 51
Queens Gdns. G12 H14 20
Victoria Crescent Rd.
Queens Park Av. G42 N16 51
Queens Pl. G12 H14 20
Queens Rd., John. N 2 44
Queensborough Gdns. H13 20
G12
Queensferry St. G5 N18 52
Rosebery St.
Queenshill St. G21 H18 22
Queensland Ct. G52 L11 33
Queensland Dr. G52 L11 33
Queensland Gdns. G52 L11 33
Queensland La. E. G52 L10 32
Kingsland Dr.
Queensland La. W. G52 L11 33
Queensland Dr.
Queenslie Ind. Est. G33 K23 39
Queenslie St. G33 J20 37
Quentin St. G41 N15 51
Quinton Gdns., Bail. L25 40

Raasay Dr., Pais. O 5 46
Raasay Pl. G22 F17 22
Raasay St. G22 F17 22
Rachan St. G34 J26 40
Radnor St. G3 K15 35
Argyle St.
Radnor St., Clyde. D 7 5
Raeberry St. G20 H15 21
Raeswood Dr. G53 O 9 48
Raeswood Gdns. G53 O 9 48
Raeswood Pl. G53 O 9 48
Raeswood Rd. G53 O 9 48

Raglan St. G4 J16 35
Raith Av. G44 Q17 64
Raithburn Av. G45 Q17 64
Raithburn Rd. G45 Q17 64
Ralston Av., Pais. M 9 48
& G52
Ralston Ct. G52 M 9 48
Ralston Dr. G52 M 9 48
Ralston Path G52 M 9 48
Ralston Dr.
Ralston Pl. G52 M 9 48
Ralston Rd., Bear. C12 7
Ralston St., Barr. R 8 59
Ralston St., Pais. M 7 47
Seedhill Rd.
Ram St. G32 L21 38
Rampart Av. G13 F10 18
Ramsay Av., John. N09 43
Ramsay Cres., John. O07 42
Ramsay Pl., John. N09 43
Ramsay St., Dalm. D 6 4
Ranald Gdns. G73 Q20 65
Randolph Av., Clark. R15 63
Randolph Dr., Clark. R15 63
Randolph Gdns., Clark. R15 63
Randolph Rd. G11 H12 19
Randolph Ter. G72 P22 66
Hamilton Rd.
Ranfurley Rd. G52 L 9 32
Rankine Pl., John. M09 43
Rankine St.
Rankine St., John. M09 43
Rankines La., Renf. H 8 17
Manse St.
Rannoch Av., Bish. E19 11
Rannoch Dr., Bear. E13 8
Rannoch Dr., Renf. H 8 17
Rannoch Gdns., Bish. E19 11
Rannoch Pl., Pais. M 7 47
Rannoch Rd., John. N09 43
Rannoch Rd., Udd. N27 57
Rannoch St. G44 P16 63
Ranza Pl. G33 H20 23
Raploch Av. G14 H10 18
Ratford St. G51 K13 34
Rathlin St. G51 K13 34
Ratho Dr. G21 G18 22
Rattray St. G32 M21 54
Ravel Row G31 L20 37
Ravelston Rd., Bear. E12 7
Ravelston St. G32 L20 37
Ravens Ct., Bish. F18 22
Lennox Cres.
Ravenscliffe Dr., Giff. Q13 62
Ravenscraig Av., Pais. N 5 46
Ravenscraig Dr. G53 P10 60
Ravenscraig Ter. G53 P11 61
Ravenshall Rd. G41 O14 50
Ravenstone Rd., Giff. Q14 62
Ravenswood Av. G78 O 3 45
Ravenswood Dr. G41 N14 50
Ravenswood Rd., Bail. L26 40
Rayne Pl. G15 D10 6
Red Rd. G21 H19 23
Red Road Ct. G21 H19 23
Redan St. G40 L18 36
Redcastle Sq. G33 J23 39
Redford St. G33 K20 37
Redgate Pl. G14 H10 18
Redhill Rd., Cumb. B 1 70
Redlands La. G12 H14 20
Kirklee Rd.
Redlands Rd. G12 H14 20
Redlands Ter. G12 H14 20
Redlands Terrace La. H14 20
G12
Julian Av.
Redlawood Pl., G72 P25 68
Redlawood Rd.
Redlawood Rd. G72 P25 68
Redmoss Rd., Clyde. C 6 4
Redmoss St. G22 G16 21
Rednock St. G22 H17 22
Redpath Dr. G52 L10 32
Redwood Pl., Lenz. C22 12
Redwood Rd., Cumb. C 4 71
Reelick Av. G13 F 9 18
Reelick Quad. G13 F 9 18
Regent Moray St. G3 J14 34
Regent Park Sq. G41 N15 51

Regent Park Ter. G41 N15 51
Pollokshaws Rd.
Regent Pl., Dalm. D 6 4
Regent Sq., Lenz. D23 13
Regent St., Dalm. D 6 4
Regent St., Pais. L 7 31
Regents Gate, Both. Q27 69
Regwood St. G41 O14 50
Reid Av., Bear. C13 8
Reid Av., Linw. L 1 28
Reid Pl. G40 M18 52
Muslin St.
Reid St. G40 M18 52
Reid St. G73 O19 53
Reidhouse St. G21 H18 22
Muir St.
Reids Row, Bail. M26 56
Reidvale St. G31 L18 36
Renfield St. G2 K16 35
Renfield St., Renf. H 8 17
Renfrew Ct. G2 K16 35
Renfrew St.
Renfrew La. G2 K16 35
Renfield St.
Renfrew Rd. G51 J10 32
Renfrew Rd., Pais. L 6 30
Renfrew Rd., Renf. J10 32
Renfrew St. G3 J16 35
Rennies Rd., Renf. F 5 16
Renshaw Dr. G52 L10 32
Renshaw Rd., John. N 2 44
Renton St. G4 J17 36
Renwick St. G41 L15 35
Scotland St.
Residdl Rd. G33 G24 25
Reston Dr. G52 L10 32
Revoch Dr. G13 F10 18
Rhannan Rd. G44 P16 63
Rhannan Ter. G44 P16 63
Rhindmuir Av., Bail. L26 40
Rhindmuir Rd., Bail. L26 40
Rhinds St., Coat. M28 57
Rhinsdale Cres., Bail. L26 40
Rhumhor Gdns., John. N08 43
Rhymer St. G21 J18 36
Rhymie Rd. G32 M23 55
Rhynie Dr. G51 L13 34
Riccarton St. G42 N17 52
Riccartsbar Av., Pais. M 5 46
Richard St., Renf. H 8 17
Richmond Ct. G73 O20 53
Richmond Dr. G72 P21 66
Richmond Dr. G73 O20 53
Richmond Dr., Bish. G64 D19 11
Richmond Dr., Linw. K 1 28
Richmond Gdns., Chr. E25 14
Richmond Pl. G73 O20 53
Richmond St. G1 K17 36
Richmond St., Clyde. E 8 5
Riddell St., Clyde. D 8 5
Riddon Av. G13 F 9 18
Riddrie Cres. G33 K21 38
Riddrie Knowes G33 K21 38
Riddrie Ter. G33 H20 23
Provanmill Rd.
Riddrievale Ct. G33 J21 38
Riddrievale St. G33 J21 38
Rigby St. G32 L20 37
Rigg Pl. G33 K24 39
Rigghead Av., Cumb. A 3 71
Riggside Rd. G33 J23 39
Riggside St. G33 J23 39
Riglands Way, Renf. H 8 17
Riglaw Pl. G13 F10 18
Rigmuir Rd. G51 L11 33
Rimsdale St. G40 L19 37
Ringford St. G21 H18 22
Ripon Dr. G12 G13 20
Risk St. G40 L18 36
Risk St., Dalm. D 6 4
Ristol Rd. G13 G11 19
Anniesland Rd.
Ritchie Cres., John. M 2 44
Ritchie Pk., John. M 1 44
Ritchie St. G5 M16 51
River Rd. G32 O22 54
River Rd. Mansion- O15 51
house Rd. G32
Riverbank St. G43 O14 50
Riverford Rd. G43 O14 50

Street	Ref	
Riverford Rd. G73	N20	53
Riversdale Cotts G14	G 9	18
Dumbarton Rd.		
Riversdale La. G14	G 9	18
Dumbarton Rd.		
Riverside Ct. G44	R16	63
Riverside Pk. G44	R16	63
Linnpark Av.		
Riverside Pl. G72	P24	67
Riverside Rd. G43	O15	51
Riverview Av. G5	L16	35
West St.		
Riverview Dr. G5	L16	35
Riverview Gdns. G5	L16	35
Riverview Pl. G5	L16	35
Roaden Av., Pais.	O 3	45
Roaden Rd., Pais.	O 3	45
Roadside, Cumb.	A 3	71
Robb St. G21	H18	22
Robert Burns Av., Clyde.	D 8	5
Robert St. G51	K13	34
Robert Templeton Dr.	P23	67
G72		
Roberton Av. G41	N14	50
Roberts St., Dalm.	D 6	4
Robertson La. G2	K16	35
Robertson St.		
Robertson St. G2	K16	35
Robertson St., Barr.	Q 7	59
Robertson Ter., Bail.	L26	40
Edinburgh Rd.		
Robin Way G32	O23	55
Robroyston Av. G33	H21	24
Robroyston Rd. G33	G21	24
Robslee Cres., Thorn.	Q13	62
Robslee Dr., Giff.	Q13	62
Robslee Rd., Thorn.	R13	62
Robson Gro. G42	N16	51
Rock Dr. G78	N 7	42
Rock St. G4	H16	21
Rockall Dr. G44	Q17	64
Rockbank Pl. G40	L19	37
Broad St.		
Rockbank Pl., Clyde.	C 7	5
Glasgow Rd.		
Rockbank St. G40	L19	37
Rockburn Dr., Clark.	S14	62
Rockcliffe St. G40	M18	52
Rockfield Pl. G21	G20	23
Rockfield Rd. G21	G20	23
Rockmount Av., Barr.	R 8	59
Rockmount Av.,	Q13	62
Thorn.		
Rockwell Av., Pais.	O 5	46
Rodger Dr. G73	P19	65
Rodger Pl., Ruth.	P19	65
Rodil Av. G44	Q17	64
Rodney St. G4	J16	35
Roebank Dr., Barr.	R 8	59
Roebank St. G31	K19	37
Roffey Park Rd., Pais.	L 8	31
Rogart St. G40	L18	36
Rogerfield Rd., Bail.	K26	40
Rokeby Ter. G12	H14	20
Great Western Rd.		
Roman Av. G15	E10	6
Roman Av., Bear.	C12	7
Roman Ct., Bear.	C12	7
Roman Dr., Bear.	C12	7
Roman Gdns., Bear.	C12	7
Roman Rd., Bear.	C12	7
Roman Rd., Clyde.	C 7	5
Romney Av. G44	P17	64
Rona St. G21	J19	37
Rona Ter. G72	Q21	66
Ronaldsay Dr., Bish.	E20	11
Ronaldsay Pl., Cumb.	D 1	70
Ronaldsay St. G22	F17	22
Ronay St. G22	F17	22
Rooksdell Av., Pais.	N 5	46
Rose Cotts. G13	G12	19
Crow Rd.		
Rose Dale, Bish.	F19	23
Rose Knowe G73	N18	52
Rose St. G3	K16	35
Rosebank Av., Blan.	R27	69
Rosebank Dr. G72	Q23	67
Rosebank Ter., Bail.	M27	57
Roseberg Pl., Clyde.	E 7	5
Kilbowie Rd.		

Street	Ref	
Rosebery Pl., Clyde.	E 7	5
Miller St.		
Rosebery St. G5	N18	52
Rosedale Av. G78	O 2	44
Rosedale Dr., Bail.	M25	56
Rosedale Gdns. G20	F14	20
Rosefield Gdns., Udd.	O27	57
Roselea Gdns. G13	F12	19
Roselea Pl., Blan.	R26	68
Rosemont Meadows,	R27	69
Both.		
Rosemount Cres. G21	J19	37
Rosemount St. G21	J18	36
Rosemount Ter. G51	L15	35
Paisley Rd. W.		
Rosemount, Cumb.	A 2	70
Rosevale Rd., Bear.	D12	7
Rosevale St. G11	J13	34
Rosewood Av., Pais.	N 4	45
Rosewood St. G13	F12	19
Roslea Dr. G31	K19	37
Roslyn Dr., Bail.	L27	41
Rosneath St. G51	K13	34
Ross Av., Renf.	J 7	31
Ross Hall Pl., Renf.	H 8	17
Ross St. G40	L17	36
Ross St., Pais.	M 7	47
Rossendale Rd. G43	O14	50
Rosshall Av., Pais.	M 8	47
Rosshill Av. G52	L 9	32
Rosshill Rd. G52	L 9	32
Rossie Cres., Bish.	F20	23
Rosslea Dr., Giff.	R14	62
Rosslyn Av. G73	O19	53
Rosslyn Rd., Bear.	C10	6
Rosslyn Ter. G12	H14	20
Horslethill Rd.		
Rostan Rd. G43	P14	62
Rosyth Rd. G5	N18	52
Rosyth St. G5	N18	52
Rotherwick Dr., Pais.	M 9	48
Rotherwood Av. G13	E11	7
Rotherwood Av., Pais.	O 3	45
Rotherwood La. G13	E11	7
Rotherwood Av.		
Rotherwood Pl. G13	F11	19
Rothes Dr. G23	E14	8
Rothes Pl. G23	E14	8
Rothlinn Av., Lenz.	B24	13
Rottenrow East G4	K17	36
Rottenrow G4	K17	36
Roual Ter., Pais.	L 7	31
Greenlaw Av.		
Rouken Glen Rd.,	R12	61
Thorn.& Giff.		
Roukenburn St. G46	Q12	61
Roundhill Dr., John.	M 3	45
Rowallan Gdns. G11	H13	20
Rowallan La. E. G11	H13	20
Churchill Dr.		
Rowallan La. G11	H13	20
Churchill Dr.		
Rowallan Rd., Thorn.	R12	61
Rowallan Ter. G33	H22	24
Rowan Av., Renf.	H 8	17
Rowan Cres., Lenz.	C23	13
Rowan Dr., Dalm.	D 6	4
Rowan Gate, Pais.	N 6	46
Rowan Gdns. G41	M13	50
Rowan Gdns. G71	Q28	69
Rowan Pl. G72	P22	66
Allison Dr.		
Rowan Pl. G72	P23	67
Caledonian Circuit		
Rowan Pl., Blan.	S26	68
Rowan Rd. G41	M13	50
Rowan Rd., Cumb.	B 4	71
Rowan Rd., Linw.	K 1	28
Rowan St., Pais.	N 6	46
Rowand Av. Giff.	R14	62
Rowandale Av., Bail.	M25	56
Rowanlea Av. G78	O 3	45
Rowanlea Dr., Giff.	Q14	62
Rowanpark Dr., Barr.	P 7	59
Rowans Gdns., Both.	Q28	69
Rowans, The, Bish.	E18	10
Rowantree Av. G73	P19	65
Rowantree Gdns. G73	P19	65
Rowantree Rd., John.	N09	43
Rowchester St. G40	L19	37

Street	Ref	
Rowena Av. G13	E11	7
Roxburgh Dr., Bear.	B12	7
Roxburgh La. G12	H14	20
Saltoun St.		
Roxburgh Rd., Pais.	O 2	44
Roxburgh St. G12	H14	20
Roy St. G21	H17	22
Royal Bank Pl. G1	K17	36
Buchanan St.		
Royal Cres. G3	J15	35
Royal Cres. G42	N16	51
Royal Exchange Bldgs.	K17	36
G1		
Royal Exchange Sq.		
Royal Exchange Ct. G1	K17	36
Queen St.		
Royal Exchange Sq. G1	K17	36
Royal Inch Cres., Renf.	G 8	17
Campbell St.		
Royal Inch Ter., Renf.	G 8	17
Royal Ter. G3	J15	35
Royal Ter. G42	N16	51
Queens Dr.		
Royal Terrace La. G3	J15	35
North Claremont St.		
Royston Hill, G21	J18	36
Royston Rd. G21	J18	36
Royston Sq. G21	J18	36
Rozelle Av. G15	D10	6
Rubislaw Dr., Bear.	D12	7
Ruby St. G40	M19	53
Ruchazie Pl. G33	K21	38
Ruchazie Rd. G32	L21	38
Ruchill Pl. G20	G15	21
Ruchill St. G20	G15	21
Ruel St. G44	O16	51
Rufflees Av., Barr.	Q 8	59
Rugby Av. G13	F10	18
Rullion Pl. G33	K21	38
Rumford St. G40	M18	52
Rupert St. G4	J15	35
Rushyhill St. G21	H19	23
Cockmuir St.		
Ruskin La. G12	H15	21
Great Western Rd.		
Ruskin Pl. G12	H14	20
Ruskin Sq., Bish.	E19	11
Ruskin Ter. G12	H15	21
Ruskin Ter. G73	N19	53
Russel Pl., Linw.	L 1	28
Gilmerton Rd.		
Russell Cres. G81	B 6	4
Russell Cres., Bail.	M26	56
Russell Dr., Bear.	C12	7
Russell Rd., Clyde.	C 6	4
Russell St. G11	J13	34
Vine St.		
Russell St., John.	M 1	44
Russell St., Pais.	K 5	30
Rutaerford Av., Chr. &	C25	14
Waterside		
Chryston Rd.		
Rutherford La. G2	K16	35
Hope St.		
Rutherglen Rd. G5	L17	36
Ruthven Av., Giff.	R14	62
Ruthven La. G12	H14	20
Dowanside St.		
Ruthven Pl., Bish.	F20	23
Ruthven St. G12	H14	20
Rutland Cres. G51	L15	35
Rutland La. G51	L15	35
Govan Rd.		
Rutland Pl. G51	L15	35
Ryan Rd., Bish.	E19	11
Ryan Way G73	Q20	65
Rye Cres. G21	G20	23
Rye Rd. G21	G20	23
Rye Way, Pais.	N 3	45
Ryebank Rd. G21	G20	23
Ryecroft Dr., Bail.	L25	40
Ryedale Pl., G15	D10	6
Ryefield Av., John.	N08	43
Ryefield Pl., John.	N08	43
Ryefield Rd. G21	G19	23
Ryehill Gdns. G21	G20	23
Ryehill Pl. G21	G20	23
Ryehill Rd. G21	G20	23
Ryemount Rd. G21	G20	23
Ryeside Rd. G21	G19	23

Name	Ref	Pg
Rylands Dr. G32	M24	55
Rylands Gdns. G32	M24	55
Rylees Cres. G52	K 9	32
Rylees Pl. G52	L 9	32
Rylees Rd. G52	L 9	32
Ryvra Rd. G13	G11	19
Sackville Av. G13	G12	19
Sackville La. G13	G12	19
Sackville Av.		
Saddell Rd. G15	D10	6
St. Abbs Dr., Pais.	N 4	45
St. Andrews Av., Bish.	E18	10
St. Andrews Av., Both.	R28	69
St. Andrews Cres. G41	M15	51
St. Andrews Cres., Pais.	J 5	30
St. Andrews Cross G41	M16	51
St. Andrews Dr., Pais.	J 6	30
St. Andrews Drive G41	N14	50
St. Andrews La. G1	L17	36
Gallowgate		
St. Andrews Rd. G41	M15	51
St. Andrews Rd., Renf.	J 8	31
St. Andrews Sq. G1	L17	36
St. Andrews St. G1	L17	36
St. Anns Dr., Giff.	R14	62
St. Blanes Dr. G73	P18	64
St. Boswells Cres., Pais.	N 4	45
St. Brides Av., Udd.	O29	57
St. Brides Rd. G43	O14	50
St. Brides Way, Both.	Q28	69
St. Catherines Rd., Giff.	R14	62
St. Clair Av., Giff.	Q14	62
St. Clair St. G20	J15	35
Woodside Rd.		
St. Conval Pl. G43	O13	50
Shawbridge St.		
St. Cyrus Gdns., Bish.	E20	11
St. Cyrus Rd., Bish.	E19	11
St. Enoch Sq. G1	L16	35
St. Enoch Wynd G2	K16	35
Argyle St.		
St. Fillans Rd. G33	G23	25
St. Georges Cross G3	J16	35
St. Georges Pl. G2	J16	35
St. Georges Rd.		
St. Georges Rd. G3	J16	35
St. Germains, Bear.	D12	7
St. Helena Cres., Clyde.	C 8	5
St. Ives Rd., Chr.	D27	15
St. James Av., Pais.	K 4	29
St. James Pl., Pais.	L 6	30
Love St.		
St. James Rd. G4	K17	36
St. James St., Pais.	L 6	30
St. Johns Ct. G41	M15	51
St. Johns Quad. G41	M15	51
St. Johns Rd. G41	M15	51
St. Johns Ter. G12	J15	35
Southpark Av.		
St. Jospehs Pl. G40	L18	36
Abercromby St.		
St. Kenneth Dr. G51	K12	33
St. Kilda Dr. G14	H12	19
St. Leonards Dr., Giff.	Q14	62
St. Margarets Pl. G1	L17	36
Bridgegate		
St. Mark St. G32	L21	38
St. Marnock St. G40	L19	37
St. Marys La. G2	K16	35
West Nile St.		
St. Marys Rd., Bish.	E18	10
St. Mirren St., Pais.	M 6	46
St. Monance St. G21	G18	22
St. Mungo Av. G4	K17	36
St. Mungo Pl. G4	K17	36
St. Mungo St., Bish.	F18	22
St. Mungos Rd. G67	C 2	70
St. Ninian St. G5	L17	36
St. Ninians Cres., Pais.	N 6	46
Rowan St.		
St. Ninians Rd., Pais.	N 6	46
St. Peters La. G2	K16	35
Blythswood St.		
St. Peters St. G4	J16	35
St. Ronans Dr. G41	N14	50
St. Ronans Dr. G73	P20	65
St. Stephens Av. G73	Q20	65
St. Stephens Cres. G73	Q21	66
St. Valleyfield St. G21	H18	22
Ayr St.		
St. Vincent Cres. G3	K14	34
St. Vincent Cres. La. G3	K15	35
Corunna St.		
St. Vincent La. G2	K16	35
Hope St.		
St. Vincent Pl. G1	K17	36
St. Vincent St. G2	K15	35
St. Vincent Ter. G3	K15	35
Salamanca St. G31	L20	37
Salen St. G52	L12	33
Salisbury Pl. G12	H14	20
Great Western Rd.		
Salisbury Pl., Dalm.	C 6	4
Salisbury St. G5	M16	51
Salkeld St. G5	M16	51
Salmona St. G22	H16	21
Saltaire Av., Udd.	P28	69
Salterland Rd. G53	P 9	60
Saltmarket G1	L17	36
Saltmarket Pl. G1	L17	36
King St.		
Saltoun Gdns. G12	H14	20
Roxburgh St.		
Saltoun La. G12	H14	20
Ruthven St.		
Saltoun St. G12	H14	20
Salvia St. G72	P21	66
Sanda St. G20	H15	21
Sandaig Rd. G33	L24	39
Sandbank Av. G20	G14	20
Sandbank Dr. G20	G14	20
Sandbank St. G20	G14	20
Sandbank Ter. G20	F14	20
Sandeman St. G11	J12	33
Sandend Rd. G53	O10	48
Sanderling Rd., John.	O08	43
Sandfield St. G20	G15	21
Maryhill Rd.		
Sandford Gdns., Bail.	L25	56
Scott St.		
Sandgate Av. G32	M23	55
Sandhaven Rd. G53	O10	48
Sandholes, Pais.	M 5	46
Sandholm Pl. G14	G 9	18
Sandholm Ter. G14	G 9	18
Sandiefauld St. G5	M17	52
Sandiefield Rd. G5	M17	52
Sandielands Av., Renf.	F 5	16
Sandilands St. G32	L22	38
Sandmill St. G21	J19	37
Sandra Rd., Bish.	E20	11
Sandringham Dr., John.	O 1	44
Glamis Av.		
Sandringham La. G12	H14	20
Kersland St.		
Sandwood Cres. G52	L10	32
Sandwood Rd.		
Sandwood Path G52	L10	32
Sandwood Rd. G52	L10	32
Sandy La. G11	J13	34
Crawford St.		
Sandy Rd. G11	J13	34
Sandy Rd., Renf.	J 8	31
Sandyford Pl. G3	K15	35
Sauciehall St.		
Sandyford Place La. G3	J15	35
Elderslie St.		
Sandyford Rd., Renf.	K 7	31
Sandyford St. G3	K14	34
Sandyhills Cres. G32	M22	54
Sandyhills Dr. G32	M22	54
Sandyhills Gro. G32	N23	55
Hamilton Rd.		
Sandyhills Pl. G32	M22	54
Sandyhills Rd. G32	M22	54
Sandyknowes Rd., Cumb.	D 3	71
Sanguhar Gdns., Blan.	R25	68
Sanilands St. G32	L22	38
Annick St.		
Sannox Gdns. G31	K19	37
Saracen Gdns. G22	G17	22
Saracen Head La. G1	L17	36
Gallowgate		
Saracen St. G22	H17	22
Sardinia La. G12	H14	20
Great George St.		
Sardinia Ter. G12	H14	20
Cecil St.		
Saucel Lonend, Pais.	M 6	46
Saucel St., Pais.	M 6	46
Saucelhill Ter., Pais.	M 6	46
Sauchenhall Rd., Chr.	C27	15
Sauchiehall St. G3	K15	35
Saughs Av. G33	G21	24
Saughs Dr. G33	G21	24
Saughs Gate G33	G21	24
Saughs Pl. G33	G21	24
Saughs Rd. G33	G21	24
Saughton St. G32	K21	38
Savoy Arcade G40	M18	52
Main St.		
Savoy St. G40	M18	52
Sawfield Pl. G4	J16	35
Garscube Rd.		
Sawmill Rd. G11	J12	33
South St.		
Sawmillfield St. G4	J16	35
Saxon Rd. G13	F11	19
Scadlock Rd., Pais.	L 4	29
Scalpay Pl. G22	F17	22
Scalpay St. G22	F17	22
Scapa St. G23	F15	21
Scapa St. G40	M19	53
Springfield Rd.		
Scaraway Dr. G22	F17	22
Scaraway Pl. G22	F17	22
Scaraway St. G22	F17	22
Scaraway Ter. G22	F17	22
Scarba Dr. G43	P13	62
Scarrell Dr. G45	Q19	65
Scarrell Rd. G45	Q19	65
Scarrell Ter. G45	Q19	65
Schaw Ct., Bear.	C11	7
Schaw Dr., Bear.	C12	7
Schaw Rd., Pais.	L 7	31
Schipka Pass. G1	L17	36
Gallowgate		
School Av. G72	P22	66
School Rd. G33	G24	25
School Rd., Pais.	L 9	32
School Wynd, Pais.	L 6	30
Schoolfield La., Bish.	E19	11
Scioncroft Av. G73	O20	53
Scone St. G21	H17	22
Sconser St. G23	E15	9
Scorton Gdns., Bail.	M24	55
Scotland St. G5	L15	35
Scotland St. W. G5	L14	34
Scotsblair Av., Lenz.	C23	13
Scotsburn Rd. G21	H20	23
Scotstoun Mill Rd. G11	J14	34
Patrick Bridge St.		
Scotstoun Pl. G14	H11	19
Scotstoun St.		
Scotstoun St. G14	H11	19
Scott Av., John.	O09	43
Scott Dr., Bear.	C11	7
Scott Rd. G52	K 9	32
Scott St. G3	J16	35
Scott St., Bail.	M25	56
Scott St., Dalm.	D 6	4
Scotts Rd., Pais.	M 8	47
Sea Path G53	P 9	60
Sea Pl. G53	P 9	60
Seafar Rd., Cumb.	D 2	70
Seafield Dr. G73	Q20	65
Seaforth Cres., Barr.	Q 7	59
Seaforth Rd., Chr.	E28	15
Burnbrae Av.		
Seaforth Rd. G52	K10	32
Seaforth Rd. N. G52	K10	32
Seaforth Rd. S. G52	K10	32
Seaforth Rd., Clyde.	E 7	5
Seagrove St. G32	L20	37
Seamill St. G53	P 9	60
Seamore St. G20	J15	35
Searle Av., Linw.	L 1	28
Killin Dr.		
Seath Rd. G73	N19	53
Seath St. G42	N17	52
Seaward La. G41	L15	35
Seaward St.		
Seaward St. G41	L15	35
Second Av. G33	G22	24
Second Av. G44	P16	63
Second Av., Bear.	D13	8

Second Av., Clyde. D 7 5
Second Av., Lenz. E23 13
Second Av., Renf. J 8 31
Second Av., Udd. N27 57
Second Gdns. G41 M13 50
Second St., Udd. O27 57
Seedhill Rd., Pais. M 6 46
Seggielea La. G13 G11 19
　Helenburgh Dr.
Seggielea Rd. G13 G11 19
Seil Dr. G44 Q17 64
Selborne Pl. G13 G12 19
　Selborne Rd.
Selborne Place La. G13 G12 19
　Selborne Rd.
Selborne Rd. G13 G12 19
Selby Gdns. G32 L24 39
Selkirk Av. G52 M11 49
Selkirk Av., Pais. N 4 45
Selkirk Dr. G73 O20 53
Sella Rd., Bish. E20 11
Selvieland Rd. G52 L 9 32
Semple Pl., Linw. K 1 28
Seres Rd., Clark. S14 62
Sergeantlaw Rd., Pais. P 4 45
Seton Ter. G31 K18 36
Settle Gdns., Bail. M24 55
Seven Sisters, Lenz. C24 13
Seventh Av., Udd. O27 57
Seyton Av., Giff. R14 62
Shaftesbury St., Dalm. E 6 4
Shafton Pl. G13 F12 19
Shafton Rd. G13 F12 19
Shaftsbury St. G3 K15 35
Shakespeare Av., Clyde. D 6 4
Shakespeare St. G20 G15 21
Shamrock Cotts. G13 G12 19
　Crow Rd.
Shamrock St. G4 J16 35
Shandon St. G51 K14 34
　Govan Rd.
Shandwick St. G34 K25 40
Shanks Av., Barr. R 8 59
Shanks Cres., John. N09 43
Shanks St. G20 G15 21
Shannon St. G20 G15 21
Shapinsay St. G22 F17 22
Sharp St. G51 K13 34
Sharrocks St. G51 L14 34
　Clifford St.
Shaw Pl., Linw. L 1 28
Shaw St. G51 K13 34
Shawbridge St. G43 O14 50
Shawfield Dr. G5 N18 52
Shawfield Rd. G5 N18 52
Shawhill Rd. G43 O14 50
Shawholm Cres. G43 O13 50
Shawlands Arcade G41 O15 51
Shawlands Sq. G41 O15 51
Shawmoss Rd. G41 N14 50
Shawpark St. G20 G15 21
Shearer La. G5 L15 35
Shearer Pl. G51 L15 35
Sheepburn Rd., Udd. O27 57
Sheila St. G33 H21 24
Sheldrake Pl., John. O08 43
Shelley Ct. G12 G13 20
　Shelley Rd.
Shelley Dr., Clyde. D 7 5
Shelley Rd. G12 G12 19
Shelly Dr., Udd. Q28 69
Sheppard St. G21 H18 22
　Cowlairs Rd.
Sherbrooke Av. G41 M14 50
Sherbrooke Dr. G41 M14 50
Sherburn Gdns., Bail. M24 55
Sheriff Park Av. G73 O19 53
Sherwood Av., Pais. L 7 31
Sherwood Av., Udd. P28 69
Sherwood Dr. G46 Q13 62
Sherwood Pl. G46 D10 6
Shetland Dr. G44 Q17 64
Shettleston Rd. G31 L20 37
Shettleston Sheddings G31 L21 38
Shiel Ct., Barr. P 7 59
Shiel Rd., Bish. E19 11
Shieldaig Dr. G73 Q19 65
Shieldaig Rd. G22 F16 21
Shieldburn Rd. G51 K11 33

Shieldhall Gdns. G51 K11 33
Shieldhall Rd. G51 K11 33
Shields Rd. G41 L15 35
Shilford Av. G13 F10 18
Shillay St. G22 F18 22
Shilton Dr. G53 P10 60
Shinwell Av., Clyde. E 8 5
Shipbank La. G1 L17 36
　Clyde St.
Shiskine Dr. G20 F14 20
Shore St. G40 N18 52
Shortbridge St. G20 G15 21
　Shanks St.
Shortroods Av., Pais. K 6 30
Shortroods Cres., Pais. K 6 30
Shortroods Rd., Pais. K 5 30
Shotts St. G33 K23 39
Shuna Pl. G20 G15 21
Shuna St. G20 G15 21
Shuttle La. G1 K17 36
　George St.
Shuttle St. G1 K17 36
Shuttle St., Kilb. M07 42
Shuttle St., Pais. M 6 46
Sidelaw Av., Barr. R 8 59
　Ochil Dr.
Sidland Rd. G21 G20 23
Sidlaw Rd., Bear. B10 6
Sielga Pl. G34 K25 40
Siemens Pl. G21 J19 37
Siemens St. G21 J19 37
Sievewright St. G73 N20 53
　Hunter Rd.
Silk St., Pais. L 6 30
Silkin Av., Clyde. E 8 5
Silverburn St. G33 K21 38
Silverdale St. G31 M20 53
Silverfir St. G5 M17 52
Silvergrove St. G40 L18 36
Silverwells Cres., Both. R28 69
Silverwells, Both. R28 69
Simons Cres., Renf. G 8 17
Simpson Ct., Udd. P27 69
Simpson St. G20 H15 21
Simshill Rd. G44 Q16 63
Sinclair Av., Bear. C12 7
Sinclair Dr. G42 O15 51
Sinclair St., Clyde. F 8 17
Singer Rd., D 6 4
　Dalm. & Clyde.
Singer St., Clyde. D 7 5
Sir Michael Pl., Pais. M 5 46
Sixth Av., Renf. J 8 31
Sixth St., Udd. N27 57
Skaethorn Rd. G20 F13 20
Skaterig La. G13 G12 19
Skaterigg Rd. G13 G12 19
　Crow Rd.
Skelbo Path G34 J26 40
　Auchengill Rd.
Skelbo Pl. G34 J26 40
Skene Rd. G51 L13 34
Skerray Quad. G22 F17 22
Skerray St. G22 F17 22
Skerryvore Pl. G33 K22 38
Skerryvore Rd. G33 K22 38
Skibo Dr. G46 Q12 61
Skibo La. G46 Q12 61
Skipness Dr. G51 K12 33
Skirsa Ct. G23 F16 21
Skirsa Pl. G23 F15 21
Skirsa Sq. G23 F15 21
Skirsa St. G23 F15 21
Skirving St. G41 O15 51
Skye Av. G67 J 8 31
Skye Cres., Pais. O 5 46
Skye Ct., Cumb. D 1 70
Skye Dr., Cumb. D 1 70
Skye Gdns., Bear. C10 6
Skye Pl., Cumb. D 1 70
Skye Rd. G73 Q20 65
Skye Rd., Cumb. D 1 70
Skye St. G20 F14 20
　Bantaskin St.
Slakiewood Av., Gart. F27 27
Slatefield St. G31 L19 37
Sleads St. G41 L15 35
Sloy St. G22 H17 22
Smeaton St. G20 G15 21
Smith Cres., Clyde. C 7 5

Smith St. G14 J12 33
Smith Ter. G73 N19 53
Smithhills St., Pais. L 6 30
Smiths La., Pais. L 6 30
Smithy Ends, Cumb. A 3 71
Smithycroft Rd. G33 J21 38
Snaefell Av. G73 Q20 65
Snaefell Cres. G73 P20 65
Society St. G31 L19 37
Soho St. G40 L19 37
Sollas Pl. G13 F 9 18
Solway Pl., Chr. E26 14
Solway Rd., Bish. E20 11
Solway St. G40 N18 52
Somerford Rd., Bear. E12 7
Somerled Av., Renf. J 7 31
Somerset Pl. G3 J15 35
Somerset Place Meuse J15 35
　G3
　Elderslie St.
Somervell St. G72 P21 66
Somerville Dr. G42 O16 51
Somerville St., Clyde. E 7 5
Sorby St. G31 L20 37
Sorn St. G40 M19 53
Souter La., Clyde. D 8 5
South Annandale St. N16 51
　G42
South Av., Clyde. E 7 5
South Av., Pais. O 6 46
South Av., Renf. H 8 17
South Bank St., Clyde. F 8 17
South Brook St., Clyde. D 6 4
South Campbell St., M 6 46
　Pais.
South Carbrain Rd., D 3 71
　Cumb.
South Carmyle Av. O22 54
South Chester St. G32 L22 38
South Cotts. G14 J12 33
　Curle St.
South Croft St., Pais. L 6 30
　Lawn St.
South Crosshill Rd., E19 11
　Bish.
South Deanpark Av., R28 69
　Udd.
South Douglas St., F 8 17
　Clyde.
South Dr., Linw. L 1 28
South Elgin Pl., Clyde. F 8 17
　South Elgin St.
South Elgin St., Clyde. F 8 17
South Erskin Pk., Bear. C11 7
South Exchange Ct. G1 K17 36
　Queen St.
South Frederick St. G1 K17 36
South Frederick St. G1 K17 36
　Ingram St.
South Hill Av. G73 P20 65
South Moraine La. G15 E11 7
　Moraine Av.
South Muirhead Rd., C 3 71
　Cumb.
South Park Dr., Pais. N 6 46
South Portland St. G5 L16 35
South Scott St., Bail. M25 56
South Spiers Wf. G4 J16 35
South St. G14 H10 18
South Vesalius St. G32 L22 38
South Vw., Blan. R26 68
South Vw., Dalm. D 6 4
South Vw., Lenz. E23 13
　Gadloch Av.
South Wardpark Ct., A 4 71
　Cumb.
　Wardpark Rd.
South Wardpark Pl., A 4 71
　Cumb.
South William St., John. N09 43
South Woodside Rd. G4 J15 35
Southampton Dr. G12 G13 20
Southbank St. G31 L20 37
　Sorby St.
Southbar Av. G13 F10 18
Southbrae Dr. G13 G11 19
Southbrae La. G13 G12 19
　Milner Rd.
Southcroft Rd. G73 N18 52
Southcroft St. G51 K13 34

Southdeen Av. G15 D10 6
Southdeen Rd. G15 D10 6
Southend Rd., Clyde. C 7 5
Southern Av. G73 P19 65
Southesk Av., Bish. E18 10
Southesk Gdns., Bish. D18 19
Southfield Av., Pais. O 6 46
Southfield Cres. G53 O11 49
Southfield Rd., Cumb. C 1 70
Southinch Av. G14 G 9 18
Southinch La. G14 G 9 18
Tweedvale Av.
Southlea Av. G46 Q13 62
Southlock St. G21 H18 22
Southmuir Pl. G20 G14 20
Southpark Av. G12 J14 34
Southpark La. G12 H15 21
Glasgow St.
Southpark Ter. G12 J15 35
Southpark Av.
Southview Ct. G64 F18 22
Southview Dr., Bear. C11 7
Southview Pl., Gart. G27 27
Southview Ter. G21 F18 22
Southwold Rd., Pais. L 9 32
Southwood Dr. G44 P17 64
Spateston Rd., John. O08 43
Spean St. G44 O16 51
Speirs Pl., Linw. K 1 28
Speirs Rd., John. M 1 44
Spence St. G20 F14 20
Spencer Dr. G78 O 2 44
Spencer St. G13 F12 19
Spencer St., Clyde. D 7 5
Spey Av., Pais. N 3 45
Spey Dr., Renf. J 9 32
Almond Av.
Spey Pl., John. O08 43
Spey Rd., Bear. E11 7
Spey St. G33 K21 38
Spiers Clo. G14 G 9 18
Spiers Rd., Bear. D13 8
Spiers Ter. G14 G 9 18
Spiersbridge Av., Thorn. Q12 61
Spiersbridge La. G46 Q12 61
Spiersbridge Rd., Thorn. R12 61
Spiersbridge Ter. G46 Q12 61
Spindlehowe Rd., Udd. P27 69
Spingburn Way G21 H18 22
Spinner Gdns., Pais. M 4 45
Spinners La., Clyde. B 7 5
Faifley Rd.
Spinners Row, John. N08 43
Spittal Rd. G73 Q18 64
Spittal Ter. G72 R25 68
Spoutmouth G1 L17 36
Spring La. G5 M17 52
Lawmoor St.
Springbank Rd., Pais. K 5 30
Springbank St. G20 H15 21
Springbank Ter., Pais. K 5 30
Springboig Av. G32 L23 39
Springboig Rd. G32 K23 39
Springburn Rd. G21 G18 22
Springburn Way G21 H18 22
Springfield Av., Bish. F19 23
Springfield Av., Pais. M 8 47
Springfield Av., Udd. P27 69
Springfield Cres., Bish. F19 23
Springfield Ct. G1 K17 36
Springfield Dr., Barr. R 9 60
Springfield Park Rd. G73 P20 65
Springfield Pk., John. N 1 44
Springfield Rd. G40 M19 53
Springfield Rd., Barr. S 8 59
Springfield Rd., Bish. E19 11
Springfield Rd., Cumb. B 3 71
Springfield Sq., Bish. F19 23
Springhill Gdns. G41 N15 51
Springhill Rd., Bail. L24 39
Springhill Rd., Barr. R 7 59
Springkell Av. G41 M14 50
Springkell Dr. G41 M13 50
Springkell Gate G41 N14 50
Springkell Gdns. G41 N14 50
Springside Pl. G15 D10 6
Springvale Ter. G21 H18 22
Hillkirk Pl.
Spruce Av., Blan. S26 68
Spruce Av., John. N 1 44

Spruce Dr., Lenz. C22 12
Spruce Rd., Cumb. B 4 71
Spruce St. G22 G17 22
Spynie Pl., Bish. E20 11
Squire St. G14 J12 33
Staffa Av., Renf. J 8 31
Staffa Dr., Pais. O 6 46
Staffa Rd. G72 Q21 66
Staffa St. G31 K19 37
Staffa Ter. G72 Q21 66
Staffin Dr. G23 E14 8
Staffin St. G23 E15 9
Stag St. G51 K14 34
Stair St. G20 H15 21
Stamford St. G40 L19 37
Stamperland Av., Clark. S15 63
Stamperland Dr., Clark. S15 63
Stamperland Gdns., S15 63
Clark.
Stamperland Hill, Clark. S15 63
Stanalane St. G46 Q12 61
Standburn Rd. G21 F20 23
Stanely Av., Pais. N 4 45
Stanely Cres., Pais. O 4 45
Stanely Ct., Pais. N 4 45
Stanely Dr., Pais. N 5 46
Stanely Rd., Pais. N 5 46
Stanford St., Clyde. E 8 5
Stanhope Dr. G73 P20 65
Stanley Dr., Bish. D19 11
Stanley Pl., Blan. R26 68
Stanley St. G41 L15 35
Stanley Street La. G41 L15 35
Milnpark St.
Stanmore Rd. G42 O16 51
Stark Av., Clyde. C 6 4
Startpoint St. G33 K22 38
Station Rd. G20 F14 20
Station Rd. G33 G22 24
Station Rd. Step. G33 G23 25
Station Rd., Bail. M26 56
Station Rd., Bear. D11 7
Station Rd., Blan. R27 69
Station Rd., Both. R28 69
Station Rd., Chr. G26 26
Station Rd., Giff. Q14 62
Fenwick Rd.
Station Rd., Kilb. N07 42
Station Rd., Pais. M 4 45
Station Rd., Renf. H 8 17
Station Rd., Udd. P27 69
Station Way, Udd. P28 69
Mansefield Dr.
Station Wynd G78 N 7 42
Steel St. G1 L17 36
Steeple St., Kilb. M07 42
Stenton St. G32 K21 38
Stepford Path G33 K25 40
Stepford Rd.
Stepford Pl. G33 K24 39
Stepford Rd. G33 K24 39
Stephen Cres., Bail. L24 39
Stephenson St. G52 K 9 32
Stepps Rd. G33 J23 39
Stepps Rd., Lenz. E24 13
Steppshill Ter. G33 G23 25
Stevbrae, Lenz. C24 13
Stevenson St. G40 L18 36
Stevenson St., Dalm. D 6 4
Stevenson St., Pais. M 6 46
Stewart Av., Renf. J 7 31
Stewart Ct., Barr. Q 8 59
Stewart St.
Stewart Dr., Bail. L28 41
Coatbridge Rd.
Stewart Dr., Clyde. C 7 5
Stewart Rd., Pais. O 6 46
Stewart St. G4 J16 35
Stewart St., Barr. Q 8 59
Stewart St., Dalm. D 6 4
Stewarton Dr. G72 P21 66
Stewarton Rd., Thorn. R12 61
Stewartville St. G11 J13 34
Stirling Av., Bear. E12 7
Stirling Dr. G73 P19 65
Stirling Dr., Bear. C11 7
Stirling Dr., Bish. D18 10
Stirling Dr., John. N08 43
Stirling Dr., Linw. L 1 28
Stirling Fauld Pl. G5 L16 35

Stirling Gdns., Bish. D18 10
Stirling Rd. G4 K17 36
Stirling St., Cumb. B 3 71
Stirling Way, Renf. J 8 31
York Way
Stirrat St. G20 G14 20
Stirrat St., Pais. K 4 29
Stobcross Rd. G3 K15 35
Stobhill Rd. G21 F18 22
Stobs Dr., Barr. P 7 59
Stobs Pl. G34 J26 40
Stock Av., Pais. N 6 46
Stock St., Pais. N 6 46
Stockholm Cres., Pais. M 6 46
Stockiemuir Av., Bear. B11 7
Stockwell Pl. G1 L17 36
Stockwell St. G1 L17 36
Stoddard Sq., John. M 2 44
Glenpatrick Rd.
Stonefield Av. G12 G14 20
Stonefield Av., Pais. N 6 46
Stonefield Cres., Pais. N 6 46
Stonefield Dr., Pais. N 6 46
Stonelaw Dr. G73 O19 53
Stonelaw Rd. G73 O19 53
Stoneside Dr. G43 P13 62
Stoneside Sq. G43 P13 62
Stoney Brae, Pais. L 6 30
Stoneyetts Cotts., Chr. D27 15
Stony Brae, Pais. O 6 46
Stonyhurst St. G22 H16 21
Stonylee Rd., Cumb. C 3 71
Storie St., Pais. M 6 46
Stormyland Way., Barr. R 8 59
Stornoway St. G22 F17 22
Stow Brae, Pais. M 6 46
Stow St., Pais. M 6 46
Strachur St. G22 F16 21
Straiton St. G32 K21 38
Stranka Av., Pais. M 5 46
Stranraer Dr. G15 E11 7
Moraine Av.
Stratford St. G20 G15 21
Strathallan La. G12 J14 34
Highburgh Rd.
Strathallan Ter. G12 J14 34
Caledon St.
Strathallon Pl. G73 Q20 65
Ranald Gdns.
Strathbran St. G31 M20 53
Strathcarron Pl. G20 G14 20
Gelnfinnan Rd.
Strathcarron Rd., Pais. N 7 47
Strathclyde Dr. O19 53
Strathclyde Path, Udd. P27 69
Strathclyde St. G40 N19 53
Strathclyde Vw. G71 R28 69
Strathcona Dr. G13 F12 19
Strathcona Gdns. G13 F13 20
Strathcona Pl. G73 Q20 65
Strathcona St. G13 G12 19
Strathdee Av., Clyde. C 7 5
Strathdee Rd. G44 R15 63
Strathdon Av. G44 R15 63
Strathdon Av., Pais. N 5 46
Strathdon Dr. G44 R15 63
Strathendrick Dr. G44 Q15 63
Strathmore Av., Blan. R26 68
Strathmore Av., Pais. M 8 47
Strathmore Gdns. G12 J15 35
Gibson St.
Strathmore Gdns. G73 Q20 65
Strathmore Rd. G22 F16 21
Strathord Pl., Chr. D28 15
Strathord St. G32 M22 54
Strathtay Av. G44 R15 63
Strathview Gdns., Bear. D11 7
Strathview Gro. G44 R15 63
Strathview Pk. G44 R15 63
Strathy Pl. G20 G14 20
Glenfinnan Rd.
Strathyre Gdns., Bear. C13 8
Strathyre Gdns., Chr. E28 15
Heathfield Av.
Strathyre St. G41 O15 51
Stratton Dr., Giff. R13 62
Strauss Av., Clyde. E 9 6
Stravanan Av. G45 R17 64
Stravanan Rd. G45 R17 64
Stravanan St. G45 R17 64